THE SLATE REGIONS OF
NORTH AND MID WALES
AND THEIR RAILWAYS

Dec. 202

To Ian, Happy Christmas!

Jx.

The Slate Regions of North and Mid Wales and their Railways

Alun John Richards

ISBN: 0-86381-552-9

Cover design: Alan Jones

First published in 1999 by
Gwasg Carreg Gwalch, 12 Iard yr Orsaf, Llanrwst, Wales LL26 0EH
℡ 01492 642031   🖷 01492 641502
📧 books@carreg-gwalch.co.uk   Website: www.carreg-gwalch.co.uk

Warning

All quarries and most rail formations are on private ground, and to visit them permission must be obtained from the owner or occupier, and from the owner or occupier of any private land that must be crossed to reach them. Such permissions are normally readily given provided one's serious interest is made clear, and that one abides by the Country Code.

All quarries are DANGEROUS from rockfalls, unstable tips, decaying buildings, unsafe bridges and unguarded drops or shafts and are often slippery underfoot. This is particularly true underground, and no attempt should be made to venture underground unless properly equipped and with a leader experienced in mine exploration. Even when not going underground one still needs to be correctly kitted, as for hill walking.

Dedication

Dedicated to the late Lewis William Lloyd LL.B., LL.M., Ph.D., F.S.A., F.R.Hist.S., for his friendship, encouragement, advice and example.

SLATE (Geol) A fine grained metamorphic rock with good fissility along cleavage planes. *The Wordsworth Dictionary of Science and Technology.*

The Author
Alun John Richards has spent over a quarter of a century studying the history, archaeology and methods of the Welsh slate industry. Before retirement his work as an engineer also brought him into contact with the active North Wales quarries, where he was responsible for several technical innovations.

He was for many years a Guest Tutor on the Slate Industry at the Snowdonia National Park Study Centre at Plas Tan-y-bwlch, and sometime lecturer at Coleg Harlech Summer Schools.

A native of Swansea he is a past chairman of the South West Wales Industrial Archaeology Society and, besides writing and lecturing on slate quarrying and metal mining, is an active campaigner on behalf of all things Welsh.

By the same author:
A Gazeteer of the Welsh Slate Industry ....ISBN 0-86381-196-5
Slate Quarrying at Corris ....ISBN 0-86381-279-1
Slate Quarrying in Wales ....ISBN 0-86381-319-4
Slate Quarrying in Pembrokeshire ....ISBN 0-86381-484-0
Publisher: Gwasg Carreg Gwalch

My thanks are due to the help and encouragement of, among many others, Peter Crew, Twm Elias, the late Ron Fullegar, Dr David Gwyn, Simon J. Hughes, Gwynfor P. Jones, Griff R. Jones, Robin Jones, Will T. Jones, Dr M.J.T. Lewis, the late Dr Lewis Lloyd, Steffan ab Owain, Dafydd Price, Dr Dafydd Roberts, Edgar Parry Williams, M. Wynne-Williams, Merfyn Williams, Richard M. Williams, Jeremy Wilkinson, as well as my many friends amongst quarrymen past and present.

Also to the landholders and working quarry proprietors and managers who have so generously allowed me access to their properties and records.

And for the assistance of the staffs of the National Library of Wales, the various County Record Offices, the Snowdonia National Park Study Centre and members of Fforwm Tan-y-bwlch.

Plus the continuous support, both with fieldwork and archival research, of my wife Delphine.

Alun John Richards, 1999

Contents

Introduction

For centuries the men of Wales on remote unwelcoming hillsides, have torn rock from the earth, and converted it to product which they carried to market through rugged uncompromising territory. Apart from dominating world output, they also led the world in the technology of their craft. In doing so, they also created proud communities and traditions which survive to this day.

Originally their markets were mainly local but, from the 16th century, Welsh slate found wider acceptance as a tradeable commodity and, by the late 18th century, its production started to become an organised industry.

Expansion gathered pace in the early 19th century and, after the 1831 repeal of the duty on coastwise shipments, built up to the great bonanza of the 1860s and 1870s. This boom abruptly ended with the slump of 1878. Although there was some recovery by the end of the 19th century, the 20th century brought, apart from brief flurries following the two wars, an inexorable decline to near extinction. Happily this trend was reversed in the 1980s and, using modern methods, work continues at about half a dozen sites.

Despite the continuing depredations of time, landscaping and reuse, relics of the industry's days of greatness remain as a record of its achievements, and as monuments to the men who toiled in its service.

A further legacy is the settlement pattern of much of north and mid Wales, moulded by the men and their families migrating into the quarrying districts from other parts of Wales. Some moved into existing villages and towns; others lived in quarry housing, a number of which formed the nuclei of new villages; many created settlements clustered around a chapel, built in defiance of the predominately churchgoing landowners and quarry proprietors. Several, such as Bethesda and Blaenau Ffestiniog, becoming substantial towns.

However, town or village living was not entirely typical. Most labour was drawn from agriculture and, apart from sentimental attachment to the soil, economic necessity meant that quarrymen tended to keep some kind of smallholding; hence the widely spaced cottages and patterns of tiny fields which are characteristic of the quarrying districts. Such dispersal involved long distances to walk to work; some did this daily, others barracked or lodged at the quarry during the week.

Whatever the domicile, there was a fierce sense of regional community centred around a quarry, or a group of quarries. Each had its own individual economic, methodological and social patterns, and had its boundaries substantially defined by the route by which its product went to market. As far as is practicable, the sections of this book follow this regionalisation.

In the regional indexes, sites are 'Starred' according to the interest of the relics surviving at the time of writing:-

****	Very large sites of exceptional interest.
***	Substantial sites of considerable interest.
**	Lesser sites which have features of great interest.
*	Sites which have remains of some interest.
	Additional suffixes.
W	Working quarries.
V	Open to Visitors.
(R)	Quarries which at some time had direct rail connection to a shipping point, canal or a main line railway.

Besides quarries, slate factories within the quarrying districts are included. There were many in places such as Aberystwyth, Bangor, Caernarfon and Porthmadog, unfortunately these, and the great contribution to seafaring, shipbuilding and engineering which these ports made, must be outside the scope of this work.

Alun John Richards 1999

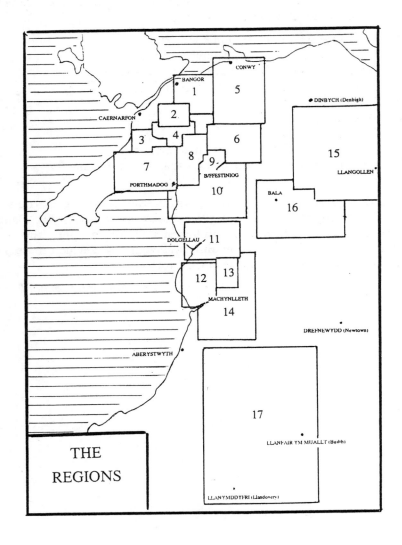

THE
REGIONS

10

The Quarries and their Methods

Most slate quarries started by digging into an outcrop and developing a face which, if successful, might eventually be simultaneously worked on several terraces. The vein sometimes had to be followed downwards into a pit, which required pumping and uphaulage unless adjacent lower ground allowed cuttings, or tunnels.

If following a dipping vein involved removing much overburden, underground working might be necessary. Usually this was done by tunnelling and working upwards along the top of the vein in roofing shafts which were developed into chambers perhaps 70' wide, leaving walls of unworked slate (pillars) 30-40' wide as supports. In any but the smallest quarries this was repeated on several floors, with chambers eventually becoming a continuous void possibly many hundreds of feet in vertical extent, traversed by bridges to maintain communication. Since modern excavators can make short work of overburden little underground extraction is now done.

Originally rock was removed by prising, but gunpowder has been almost universally used since the early 19th century. In recent years some rock has been mechanically extracted by wiresaws, chainsaws, digger-mounted jackhammers etc.

Vast quantities of unusable rock had to be cleared and dumped, and this invariably needed to be weighed, mainly to assess rubblers pay. Good block was then split and trimmed, either as roofing slate or as slab. Traditionally this was entirely done with hammers, chisels etc., augmented from the 17th century by hand saws. This was sometimes done in the open air, but commonly in open-fronted dressing sheds which in a large quarry would be numerous and often in continuous rows.

Although many quarries due to lack of scale or of fortune stuck to historic techniques, others mechanised, some becoming highly complex production units.

The primary mechanisation was sawing, which at first was confined to the production of slab products. Later, block for roofing slate was sawn before splitting (which has never been successfully mechanised). Except where the hard Cambrian rock of Caernarfonshire was worked, trimming was done by dressing machines. Some mills contained 20 or more saws, as many dressers, as well as planers and in some cases lathes and polishers.

The mill power source was invariably water, and the lack of a nearby stream often called for it to be remotely sited. Water was also used for

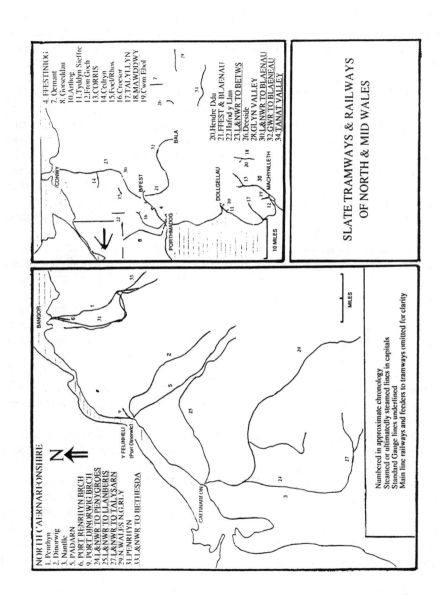

NORTH CAERNARFONSHIRE
1. Penrhyn
2. Dinorwig
3. Nantlle
5. PADARN
6. PORT RENRHYN BRCH
9. PORT DINORWIC BRCH
24. L&NWR TO PENYGROES
25. L&NWR TO LLANBERIS
27. L&NWR TO TALYSARN
29. N.WALES N.G.RLY
31. PENRHYN
33. L&NWR TO BETHESDA

BANGOR

Y FEUNHEU
(Port Dinorwic)

CAE FINARFON

MILES

Numbered in approximate chronology
Steamed or ultimatedly steamed lines in capitals
Standard Gauge lines underlined
Main line railways and feeders to tramways omitted for clarity

4. FFESTINIOG
7. Oernant
8. Gorseddau
10. Arthog
11. Tyddyn Sieffre
12. Fron Goch
13. CORRIS
14. Cedryn
15. Foel/Rhus
16. Croesor
17. TALYLLYN
18. MAWDDWY
19. Cwm Ebol

CONWY

BALA

B.FFEST

PORTHMADOG

DOLGELLAU

MACHYNLLETH

20. Hendre Ddu
21. FFEST & BLAENAU
22. Hafod y Llan
23. L&NWR TO BETWS
26. Deeside
28. GLYN VALLEY
30. L&NWR TO BLAENAU
32. GWR TO BLAENEAU
34. TANAT VALLEY

10 MILES

SLATE TRAMWAYS & RAILWAYS
OF NORTH & MID WALES

12

pumping, haulage and, after powered drills were introduced, for air compression. Where water supply was limited, steam had to be used, later supplemented or supplanted by oil or producer gas. Eventually most large units had electricity, either generated on site or, if available, from public supply. A number survived into the mid 20th century without it.

Any but the smallest unit had a smithy for making and sharpening tools, and most had powder houses with stout walls without windows, a flimsy roof, and generally timber flooring. Similar buildings nearer the working, but with a stout roof, were blast shelters. Most workforce quarries had a *Caban* (Mess-room) which was an important social centre. Underground, part of a worked-out chamber would be partitioned off for the purpose.

Larger quarries also had stables, loco sheds, repair shops, compressor houses, engine houses, power houses and sub-stations. There would be storage sheds of all kinds (including open-fronted ones for holding block awaiting working, kept damp by wet sacking) and the inevitable offices. A few had enamelling kilns, writing slate factories, or other finishing departments.

In addition to any off-site housing, these larger units had on-site houses for maintenance staff and, not too far away but invariably screened by trees, all but the smallest had a manager's house.

The Railways

Internal tramways came into use at the end of the 18th century and, in time, almost every quarry had at least a few yards of line for rubbish tipping. Some became vast networks, many with locomotives. In all quarries, changes in level were dealt with by inclines, the drum-houses of which form the most characteristic monument to slate enterprise.

However it was the development of external rail transport that was absolutely vital to the development of the industry. Most slate reached its market by sea and, although few quarries were far from the coast and there was a legendary abundance of skills to build and to man ships, it was both difficult and expensive to move product to navigable water. Carts could be used where roads existed or could be built; the only and even more costly alternative, being pack animals or, failing that, men's backs. The water within reach was often just a river or creek suitable only for small boats, entailing trans-shipment to sea-going vessels. It could cost more to get a cargo to a port than the sea freight to say, the Baltic.

It was 1801 when the Penrhyn tramway dramatically demonstrated the economies of laying rails to a port. Lines such as the Dinorwig tramway of 1824, the Nantlle of 1828 followed, culminating in the Ffestiniog Railway of 1836. Later there were others; some, such as the Ffestiniog replacing horse/gravity working with steam.

Whatever power was used, these lines besides being central to the 19th century development of the Welsh slate industry, also moulded the pattern of the industry. Areas with rail outlets such as Blaenau Ffestiniog boomed; others, such as Dyffryn Conwy, which were locked into cartage and river boats, waned.

From the mid 19th century the coming of the national railway network to Wales had an even greater effect than the local Narrow Gauge lines.

By direct connection or through short feeder lines, quarries that were remote from the sea, could economically move their product. More importantly, they enabled slate to be competitive with tiles in inland U.K. markets. Furthermore, with ocean going ships becoming larger and increasingly unable to use small harbours, the railways could carry export slate to large ports. When interchanges at Port Penrhyn, Port Dinorwig and Minffordd became available in 1852, 1852 & 1872 respectively, an increasing proportion of slate traffic was carried by rail. Regrettably, this hastened the end of the great partnership between slate and local shipping, a process that was finally ended by the motor lorry.

However, the railways also exposed small quarries serving local needs to the full blast of competition from the big producers, hastening the industry's concentration into fewer and larger units. Besides all this, it must not be forgotten that it was the prosperity created by the Railway Age which fuelled the demand for slate which gave the industry a sling-shot boost, which carried it to its end-of century peak.

Nowadays virtually all movement is by lorry or dumper, but some of the internal tramways do remain in use underground. Of the external narrow gauge lines, the Ffestiniog and the Tal-y-llyn have been preserved as two of the 'Great Little Trains of Wales'; a short length of the Corris has been reopened, and a length of the trackbed of the 4'G Padarn carries the Llanberis Lake Railway. Also there is prospect of the recreation of the Welsh Highland, which absorbed the North Wales Narrow Gauge Railway. As to the rest, all are at least in part readily traceable. Some, such as the Hendre Ddu, are now roads; others, such as some of the Nantlle, form paths. A few such as the Dinorwig are less obvious, but traces of bed and structures do remain.

With the exception of the Blaenau branch along the Conwy and Lledr valleys and the Caernarfon – Dinas section of the Afon Wen line (relaid Narrow Gauge), all of the Standard Gauge lines that were built mainly for slate traffic have closed. However other than where their trackbeds have succumbed to road schemes or as in the case of the G.W.R. Blaenau branch, interrupted by a reservoir, most are easily followed throughout their length, with many bridges and structures extant. The routes of all abandoned lines are described in the relevant regional sections.

Chronology of Railed Slate Transport in North & Mid Wales

1801   Penrhyn Tramway. Horse/gravity, 2'G.(nom) 6m, 3 inclines. Exclusively for Penrhyn quarry freight to Port Penrhyn. **Region 1**

1824   Dinorwig Tramway. Horse/gravity, 2'G.(nom) 7m, 3 inclines. Exclusively for Dinorwig quarry freight to Port Dinorwig. **Region 2**

1828   Nantlle Railway. Horse, 3'6"G. c11m, no inclines. Public railway; mainly freight from Nantlle quarries to Caernarfon. Feeder branch, Carnarvonshire Slate Quarries Railway. **Region 3**

1836   Ffestiniog Railway. Horse/gravity, 2'G.(nom) 14m. 1 Water-wound, 1 gravity incline (to 1842). Public railway for freight from Blaenau quarries to Porthmadog. Principal feeder lines, 1850 **Cwmorthin** horse, 2m 3 inclines & c1863 **Rhiwbach** horse, later part internal combustion, 3½m, 3 inclines, plus direct incline connection to several other quarries. **Region 9**

1843   Padarn Railway. Steam (horse to 1848), 4'G. 7m 1 incline. Dinorwig quarry private, replacement of 1824 line. From 1895 workmen carried. **Region 2**

1852   Port Penrhyn Branch. Steam, Standard Gauge, 1½m. Enabled L&NWR to pick up Penrhyn slate from the port. **Region 1**

1852   Port Dinorwig Branch. Steam, Standard Gauge, 1m. Enabled L&NWR to pick up Dinorwig slate from port. **Region 2**

1856   Oernant Tramway. Horse/gravity, 3'G. 2½m 1 incline. Connected 3 quarries to slate works and canal at Llangollen. **Region 15**

1856   Gorseddau Tramway. Horse/gravity, 3'G. 8m no inclines, 1 reversing loop. Gorseddau product to Porthmadog. **Region 7**

C1858   Arthog. Gravity, 2'G. ½m. almost all incline. Took Arthog slate to a jetty; 1868 re-aligned to a Cambrian Railways siding. **Region 11**

C1858   Tyddyn Sieffre. Horse/gravity, 2'G. 1m. 1 incline. Originally to a wharf, later to Cambrian Railways at Barmouth Junction. **Region 11**

C1859   Fron Goch. Hand pushed, Yards only 2'G. Took Fron Goch product to a jetty. **Region 12**

1859   Corris, Machynlleth & River Dyfi Tramway. Horse, 2'3"G. 12m no inclines. Public line, took output of Corris & Dulas Valley quarries to Derwenlas. Fed by **Upper Corris** 1m & **Ratgoed** 2m tramways, both horse; also quarry branches. **Region 13**

1861   Cedryn Tramway. Horse, 2'G. 5m 4 inclines. Conveyed product of Cedryn quarry to river Conwy, 1865 extended to Cwm Eigiau quarry. **Region 5**

C1862   Foel. Gravity 2'G. 1½m 5/6 inclines. Took Foel & Rhos product to a road loading point, also connected Foel to its lower mill from 1864. **Region 6**

1863   Ffestiniog Railway. Steamed. **Region 9**

1864   Croesor Tramway. Horse, 2'G. 5m, 3 inclines. Public carrier, incline connection to Croesor, Rhosydd and Fron Goch/Pantmawr quarries. **Region 8**

1866   Talyllyn Railway. Steam, 2'3"G. 10m. Built to convey output of Bryneglwys quarry to Tywyn; also acted as public goods and passenger line. **Region 11**

1867   Mawddwy Railway. Steam, Standard Gauge. 7m. Public passenger railway, mainly intended to convey output of Minllyn quarry to the Cambrian Railways at Cemaes. **Region 14**

1868   Nantlle Railway. Superseded Caernarfon-Penygroes by L&NWR Caernarfon-Afon Wen branch over substantially the same route. **Region 3**

C1868   Cwm Ebol. Horse/gravity 3'G (relaid 2'3"G.) 1½m (+branches) no inclines. Connected several quarries with Mawddwy Railway at Aberangell. **Region 14**

1868   Ffestiniog & Blaenau Railway. Steam 2'G. 3m. Public railway; carried Craig Ddu quarry and Llan Ffestiniog quarries output to Blaenau. **Regions 9 & 10**

C1868   Hafod-y-Llan Tramway. Horse/gravity, 1½m 2'G. 2 inclines. Intended to take Hafod y Llan product to an anticipated Beddgelert-Betws-y-coed railway. **Region 8**

1868   Betws-y-coed Branch. L&NWR. 14m, carried slate carted to Betws station. Shipping facility at Deganwy. **Region 6**

1869   Llanberis Branch. L&NWR. 9m, Served quarries south of Llyn Padarn. **Region 2**

1871   Deeside Tramway. Gravity 2'6"G. 3m (part wooden rails) 2 inclines. Connected Deeside quarry to GWR. Later extended to Moel Fferna quarry. **Region 15**

1872   Minffordd Interchange. Gave Ffestiniog Railway access to Cambrian Railways. **Region 9**

1872   **Nantlle Railway.** Superseded Penygroes Tal-y-Sarn by L&NWR sub-branch and Standard Gauge laid to Caernarfon quay. **Region 3**

1873   **Glyn Valley Tramway.** Horse, 2'4¼"G. 6m no inclines, connected Glynceiriog quarries to the Shropshire Union Canal. **Region 15**

1875   **Gorseddau Tramway.** Extended to Prince of Wales quarry and relaid 2'G. loco worked. **Region 7**

1877   **North Wales Narrow Gauge Railway.** Dinas-Rhyd Ddu. Steam 2'G.(nom) 12m (including branch). Public railway. Numerous quarry feeders the most notable being the **Alexandra** 1½m and the **Fron** ¾m, both steam worked. **Region 4**

1879   **Penrhyn Railway.** Steam 2'G. 6½m. Replaced 1801 tramway using slightly different route. Workmen's trains. **Region 1**

1879   **Blaenau Ffestiniog.** Extension of L&NWR Betws branch. 11m. **Region 9**

1879   **Corris Railway.** Steaming of C.M&R.D Tramway 2'3"G. 8¾m, passenger and goods, terminated at Machynlleth, CR. station. **Region 13**

1882   **Bala-Blaenau Branch.** GWR. 25M. Absorbed F & BR **Regions 9 & 10**

1884   **Bethesda Branch.** L&NWR 4½m. Conveyed slate from small Bethesda quarries. **Region 1**

1888   **Glyn Valley Tramway.** Steamed and diverted to Chirk station, Cambrian Railways. **Region 15**

1904   **Tanat Valley Railway.** Steam S.G. 15m. **Region 16**

There were also several quarries which had short lines connecting them to a nearby road such as Llanfflewin (**Region 1**), Chwarel Fedw (**Region 5**) and Drum (**Region 10**).

Standard Gauge main lines which carried slate (e.g. the Cambrian to Aberdyfi), but were not built primarily for that purpose, are not included above.

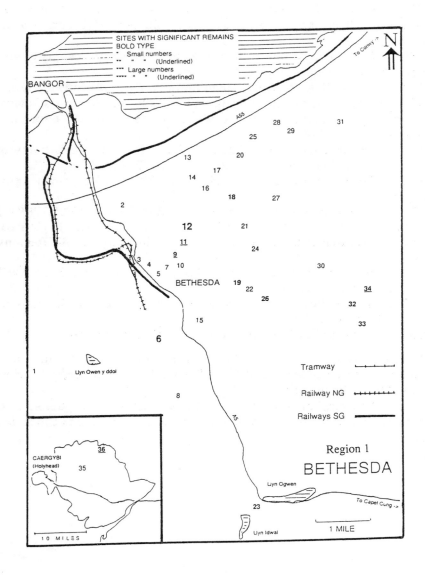

SITES WITH SIGNIFICANT REMAINS
BOLD TYPE
" Small numbers
" " " (Underlined)
"' Large numbers
"'' " " (Underlined)

BANGOR

To Conwy

N

28   29   31
25
13   20
17
14
16
18   27
2
12   21
11
9   24
3   4   7   10
5   30
BETHESDA   19
22
26   34
32
15   33
6

1
Llyn Owen y ddol

8

Tramway
Railway NG
Railways SG

Region 1
BETHESDA

CAERGYBI
(Holyhead)   35   36

10 MILES

Llyn Ogwen
To Capel Curig →

23   1 MILE

Llyn Idwal

BETHESDA
Region 1
Including quarries served by the Penrhyn Tramway (afterwards Railway) & L&NWR Bethesda Branch. Plus Anglesey, (Ynys Môn)

General

This region, the very heartland of slate working, was monopolised not only by the still active Penrhyn quarry which has dominated Welsh output for well over 200 years, but also by the power and influence of its owners. Penrhyn, the first quarry to be developed as an industrial unit, was a pioneer in the use of terrace working, in the use of balanced inclines and in the use of rails to reach a shipping point. Expanding from a coastal trade which dates from at least the 14th century, its slates roofed the buildings of the industrial revolution, both at home and abroad, and its price lists effectively set market rates for the whole country if not the world.

Although the quarry built houses and leased land for self-build on small holdings, many workers avoided quarry tenancy by living on non-Penrhyn land, where they were free to build Bethesda and other chapels, and develop settlements around them which came to epitomise Welsh quarry communities.

There were a few minor quarries to the North East of the Ogwen valley, some of which exploited speciality coloured slate, and all of which operated very much under the uneasy tolerance of Penrhyn.

However a feature of the area is the large number of tiny diggings by individuals and small partnerships during layoffs especially, the 1900/03 Penrhyn stoppage.

Transport

Traditionally material was carried to Hirael (Bangor) and to Aberogwen on pack animals, usually tended by girls.

At Hirael (589727) where boats were loaded over the beach, nothing remains; the nearby jetty being a much later structure. Aberogwen (613723) was developed as a shipping point by Penrhyn in the late 18th century. The road they made to it is still in use, but at Aberogwen itself the only traces of activity is the slate debris. The timber stathes are probably later.

Port Penrhyn was established at Pwll Cegin (pool) (592723) in 1790 to replace the rudimentary facilities at Aberogwen and in 1801, having abandoned the idea of a canal, the quarry was linked to the port by the horse-drawn 2'G. Penrhyn Tramway, which replaced the 400 horses and 140 wagons then being used, dramatically cutting transport costs. The civil work was good and the even spacing of the three inclines facilitated efficient working. Although the original round bar rail and semicircular wheel profile was unsuccessful, relaid on conventional rail it served the quarry for 75 years, finally carrying daily tonnages far in excess of its designed capacity.

It left the Coed-y-parc mills area (615663) to cross a minor road on the level (614666), from where it can be walked (traces of slate sleepers) a short distance to the head of the Cilgeraint incline. From here, almost all trace has been lost save for signs of an archway where the Dinas incline went under a minor road (607685). Close to the Llandygái roundabout a lane defines the route which, from there on is lost under the Llandygái Industrial Estate. The passage under the main road (594714) is still open. From there the route is defined by the curved wall of the Penrhyn Castle grounds. At the head of the Marchogion incline the drum-house and stables are in reuse as a dwelling. Near the foot of that incline there is a single arched bridge over the river Cegin; the route then passes under the later Penrhyn Railway (see below) to re-cross the Cegin by a fine three-arched bridge, and so on to Port Penrhyn. This final section from near Llandygái to the port took over the formation of an earlier, non slate, tramway. This line joined Abercegin with a flint mill on the Ogwen. This incline (severed by the L&NWR main line) is traceable.

In 1876 the horse/gravity line was superseded by the steam Penrhyn Railway (also 2' nominal G.) which operated until 1962. This left Coed-y-parc by a similar route but at a higher level, the slate embankment being still extant. The route is readily traceable curving around Tregarth, virtually interlacing the track bed of the later Standard Gauge Bethesda line. The viaduct at Felin-hen has vanished and, beyond there, the track is much overgrown. From near Maesgeirchen, where it passes under the main road, it is traceable to the nice little span over the track of the old tramway, and onto the steel and wood bridge over the Cegin which it shared with the Standard Gauge (Port Penrhyn branch), and on via an arch (now blocked) to the dockside. The Port Penrhyn sub-branch of the L&NWR, opened in 1852 (closed 1963), enabled transfer onto rail of slate brought to Port Penrhyn by the Penrhyn Railway and robbed the port of an increasing proportion of the quarry's output. It is readily traceable, including the bridge across the Cegin which was widened on its south-eastern side to accommodate the Penrhyn steam line.

The port itself, (SH593727) which was an industrial centre in its own right, remains relatively undisturbed, apart from the lifting of track. It continued in use, reached by lorries, for some years after both railways to it closed.

There are numerous buildings of interest, including an engine shed, offices, an unique circular lavatory, and the ruins of the writing slate factory.

The independent quarries were barred from Port Penrhyn and hampered at Aberogwen by being prohibited from maintaining stocks there. It was only after the Bethesda sub branch of the L&NWR opened in 1884 that effective transport was available to them, although no quarry was directly connected to it. Much of the line, which closed in 1963, is readily traceable to its junction with the main line near Llandygái.

Anglesey, Ynys Môn

For convenience, two small Anglesey quarries are include at the end of this section.

1)	SH589645	Chwarel Robin Jones
2)	SH611696	Chwarel Las
3)	SH613677	Dôl-goch
4)	SH617673	Cloddfa y Coed *
5)	SH619671	Coetmor
6)	SH620650	Penrhyn ***W (R)
7)	SH623671	Pantdreiniog
8)	SH626638	Cwm Ceunant
9)	SH626679	Moel Faban **
10)	SH628677	Ty'n-y-ffridd
11)	SH628683	Tan-y-bwlch **
12)	SH631693	Bryn Hafod-y-wern ****
13)	SH631708	Bronnydd
14)	SH633702	Ffridd
15)	SH634657	Braichmelyn
16)	SH636701	Dolpistyll
17)	SH640706	Nant Heilyn
18)	SH642697	Cwm Glas
19)	SH643672	Dr Hughes *
20)	SH645709	Crymlyn
21)	SH646688	Gyrn
22)	SH647667	Y Garth

23)	SH648604	Idwal *
24)	SH648680	Gallt-y-mawn
25)	SH648715	Yr Ogof
26)	SH652668	Afon Gaseg *
27)	SH657698	Pantydarren
28)	SH658723	Brechiau
29)	SH662720	Bontnewydd
30)	SH670675	Bera Bach
31)	SH675721	Bod Silin
32)	SH678663	Afon Wen *
33)	SH683655	Cwm Bychan *
34)	SH683664	Ochrfwsoglog *

Anglesey, Ynys Môn
| 32) | SH347892 | Llanfflewin |
| 33) | SH481925 | Llaneilian ** |

AFON GASEG SH652668
Small pit working alongside pre-existing track.
Remains Pit accessed by a tunnel; ruins of surprisingly numerous dressing sheds. Vestiges of a small, windowless building resembling a powder house, but its iron door suggests otherwise. (26)

AFON WEN SH678663
Underground. In 1905, 8 men working.
Remains Collapsed adit, rubbish runs, rail and tram axle on site, vestiges of buildings. (32)

BERA BACH SH670675
Unsuccessful trial.
Remains Run-in adit. (30)

BOD SILIN SH675721
Unsuccessful trial.
Remains Run in level. There is also some surface digging at 674721. (31)

BONTNEWYDD SH662720
Very small underground working, shaly material.
Remains Some traces of adit and dressing shed. The run-in level in forestry at 664710 may have been associated with this working. (29)

BRAICHMELYN SH634657
Trial.
Remains Traces of excavation. (15)

BRECHIAU SH658723
Small, unsuccessful?
Remains In forestry, some slight evidence of working. (28)

BRONNYDD SH631708
Trial.
Remains Small pit. (13)

BRYN HAFOD-Y-WERN SH631693
Owing to the unavailability of land downhill, this pit working could not be made self-draining. All material had to be up-hauled to the mill, and waste further uphauled to lengthy tipping runs. Also, the need to reuse a limited water supply (which had to be leated from Llyn Caseg) meant a less than ideal layout of the mill area.

Established around 1780, it was operated by the Pennants of Penrhyn, but abandoned by them in 1845 probably due to excessive working costs. Reopened and re-equipped by the Royal Bangor Slate Co, it closed in 1884 when the Pennants cut off the water supply.

Rock was raised from the pit, eventually 200' deep, by an incline. This incline was replaced by a second, and finally by a chain incline (all water powered?). From this final incline-head, rubbish could go by rail for tipping and good rock could be lowered to mills level. It is possible that this incline was powered to uphaul waste back up from the mill area. Pumping was also water-powered. Finished product was carted to Bangor.

In 1882 output was 2198 tons p.a. with 65 men employed, probably about half that of a decade before.

Remains The pit is now flooded and the buildings are ruinous, but otherwise it is relatively undisturbed. The incline landing platform, with traces of a horizontal sheave, is the most prominent feature with the rubbish runs fanning out from it. There are miscellaneous buildings alongside the short internal incline, one of which may have housed a water-turbine; near the foot of the short incline is a wheel-pit. Besides circular-sawn ends there are, in the overgrown part of the mills area, horizontal (hand?) sawn ends. The formation of at least one of the earlier inclines out of the pit is obvious. Bryn Hall, the owner's house, has a fine arched entrance gate and is still in occupation.

The long leat from the river Caseg to the two reservoirs is traceable, and the launder pillars and underground supply relief pipe are prominent. (12)

CHWAREL LAS SH611696
Pit, very small.
Remains Rubbish runs only. (2)

CHWAREL ROBIN JONES SH589645
Trial.
Remains Excavation. (1)

CLODDFA Y COED (Coed Ucha) SH617673
Hillside quarry, very small.
Remains Building ruins possibly associated with quarry. (4)

COETMOR SH619671
Mid 19th century adjacent to Pantdreiniog. From the late 1870s, it was used by the latter for tipping.
Remains All now obliterated. (5)

CRYMLYN SH645709
Underground, very small.
Remains Collapsed adit in gully; iron waste. (20)

CWM BYCHAN SH683655
Underground working, almost certainly 'unofficial' with a long and difficult journey to get product out. 2 men working part-time in 1905.
Remains Run in adit, some building remnants including a possible powder house. Another building nearby could have been sleeping accommodation. (33)

CWM CEUNANT SH626638
Small trials.
Remains Surface scratchings. (8)

CWM GLAS (Llywelyn, Moel Wnion) SH642697
Small, underground, late 1890s.
Remains Collapsed adit, trimming waste and a few finished slate. (18)

DÔL-GOCH (Coed y Ddôl) SH613677
Small pit, operated for few years after 1836.
Remains Depression in ground. Tip on far side of road. (3)

DOLPISTYLL (Ffridd Fedw) SH636701
Tiny, shallow excavation.
Remains Some trimming waste. (16)

FFRIDD SH633702
Putative quarry.
Remains Possible ground disturbance. (14)

GALLT-Y-MAWN (Chwarel Parry) SH648680 & 649681
Underground; may have been trials for slate or for metal.
Remains Collapsed adits. (24)

GYRN SH646688
Clearly unproductive; may have been an old metal trial re-investigated for slate.
Remains A number of shallow excavations around south and west of hilltop. (21)

DR HUGHES (Llidiart y Graeanyn) SH643672
Underground.
Remains Collapsed adit, rubbish run. (19)

IDWAL SH648604
Hone quarry.
Remains Traces of excavation and tips; buildings adapted as Youth Hostel. (23)

MOEL FABAN (Y Foel) SH626679
Partly underground, mid 19th century. Developed in the 1900s as co-operative in conjunction with Tan-y-bwlch; produced red and green slate. Unmechanised, but during co-operative era, material reduced in Tan-y-bwlch mill. Closed c1910.
Remains Diggings and 3 adits (2 open) to limited chambering; a fine grass-covered incline; traces of small buildings; tramway formation linking with Tan-y-bwlch. Also trial at 633682. (9)

NANT HEILYN SH640706
Small trial.
Remains Ground disturbance. (17)

OCHRFWSOGLOG SH683664
Little open working, perilously located in a cleft. Turf-roofed shelter. May have been worked in conjunction with Afon Wen.
Remains Working face and elaborate revetment. (34)

PANTDREINIOG (Cilfodan) SH623671
Pit/Underground; opened around 1850, it expanded during the 1860s/70s boom, with a steam hauled incline and pumping by hydrostats. By 1883 tonnage was down to 245 and manning to 13. Worked (with Moel Faban and Tan-y-bwlch) as co-operative from 1903 to 1911 with up to over 100 men. During this time a small mill was built and locos were introduced. Unsuccessfully re-started c1922 to produce slate powder.

After opening of L&NWR Bethesda branch, loaded at Bethesda for shipment at Deganwy.
Remains Site entirely landscaped, but some housing is still in use. (7)

PANTYDARREN (Afon Gam, Breichiau) SH657698
Pit. Doubtful if any saleable product was ever actually won.
Remains Run-in adit. (27)

PENRHYN SH620650
Terraced hillside quarry with some pit working.
Developed from a number of Take Note diggings dating from at least the 16th century, collectively known as Cae Braich-y-cafn. The present undertaking dates from 1782 when Richard Pennant bought out the existing leases. Within 10 years its 5 figure tonnages p.a. dominated the industry and by the latter part of the 19th century tonnages of around 100,000 p.a. were routinely produced. (In 1882 111166 tons with 2889 men). Apart from Dinorwig, it was several times the size of any other quarry. Following the 1900-1903 stoppage, manning never exceeded 2000.

By 1798 the problem of enabling a large number of men to work simultaneously was solved by the gallery system, whereby the working face was terraced out at 65'/70' intervals. Ultimately there were 21 such galleries, each with its own rail system. Movement downwards was mainly by self-acting inclines and upwards by water balance lifts. Latterly, some use was made of aerial ropeways. There was, and still is, some pit working.

Although water powered sawing commenced in 1803, it was confined to slab until 1912, when there was extensive electrification and an electric mill was built; thus there were virtually streets of *gwaliau* (dressing sheds) for the hand working of roofing slate.

Steam locomotives were introduced in 1876, and internal combustion units in the 1930's, the last of these being replaced by lorries in 1965.

Quarrying continues on a substantial scale although with modernised methods, and all movement being by specialist transporters and conveyors; their payroll is well below the post-WW2 peak of 1000.

Remains The quarry area has been much disturbed by working and road construction in recent years, but the gallery system pioneered here is still obvious. There are still several inclines and numerous buildings, including mills and rakes of dressing sheds. There are also very many artifacts still on the ground.

One of the water balance lifts is preserved near the main office, and there is at least one other on site.

The present mill, on the site of the old Red Lion mill and workshops, is equipped with diamond saws and is much automated; mechanical splitters are used, but most is done by hand. The original office block is still in use.

At Coed-y-parc (615663), which was a substantial industrial complex, there are several buildings in fair condition, but recent adaptation for reuse has made identification difficult. Much use was made of water power for the 1803 Felin Fawr sawing mill (which later had Hunter saws), the 1846 Felin Fach mill, as well as the extensive workshops. Until recently there were two fine internal water-wheels, the later one installed around 1906, and fed by inverted syphons.

This was the terminus both of the 1801 tramway and the 1876 railway. The ruins of what were the tramway stables, afterwards cottages, can be discerned. On the other side of the road the Ogwen Tile Works, later a slate mill, is now in industrial reuse.

On the hillside above and to the west is an extensive water supply layout.

There are many items of peripheral interest in the area, such as paths, steps, stiles, cottages (some with long allotment-like gardens) and the model village of Llandygái. (6)

TAN-Y-BWLCH SH628683

Pit/underground; established around 1805, it continued in sporadic use, including a period as a co-operative, until 1911.

Rock was up-hauled from the pit and reduced in a small steam mill. Later worked underground from the pit with a vertical shaft powered by a second steam engine. A constricted site made tipping a problem. Drained by a level emerging near Llanllechid church. Tonnage unlikely to have exceeded about 500 p.a.

Originally output carted; latterly used Bethesda station.

Remains Some buildings (in reuse), one with a slate sign 'Bangor Slate Co'; much tipping, tightly squeezed into a restricted space, there are the abutments of two rubbish run bridges and a stack of finished product on the stockyard.

The pit has partly run-in, obliterating any adits and any up-haulage arrangements. There is an unusually large engine house with an adjacent 13' x 13' stone lined shaft, now filled in. Possibly besides uphauling, it may have been used for pumping before the drainage level was cut. It is not obvious where the second engine, for saw power, was sited. (11)

TY'N-Y-FFRIDD SH628677
Very small hillside/underground, operated in the early 19th century.
Remains Virtually none. Also small digging at 629676. (10)

Y GARTH SH647667
Very small, underground; probably only a trial.
Remains Traces of two adits. (22)

YR OGOF SH648715
Small open working, some poor material possibly extracted.
Remains Surface scratching, with also 3 run in adits at 646716 and one at 645709 which may have been part of the same attempt. (25)

Anglesey

LLANEILIAN SH481925
There were several ancient diggings in the area, e.g. Ynys-goch (476925) & Porth yr Ysgaw (479930) and there was a letting in 1639 at Rhosmynach (unidentified), but this site was the only one seriously developed. It is remarkable for its complex tunnelling to facilitate loading into vessels and to dispose of rubbish, after attempts to use the tiny Porthycorwgl and Ogo'r Rhedyn were abandoned. Most work was done 1870-77 by the North Anglesey (Point Aelianus) Slate & Slab Quarry Co.Ltd.
Remains A series of cliff top workings with some traces of buildings. Records show that eight tunnels were cut, some seeking copper. The south-eastern working has a waste-disposal tunnel leading to a cliff face. Nearby, a spectacular stairway cut into the rock descends to a loading platform near sea level. The next working, accessed by a cutting, has in

its floor a slightly inclined (unguarded!) shaft, with a wagon jammed part-way down. This shaft drops to a ledge in a large artificial cave, apparently intended as a shipping place. A waste disposal tunnel (blocked by sea-bourn shingle), leading off this ledge is intersected by another tunnel from the open loading platform. There is also a waste disposal tunnel direct from the working. Under the more extensive, three level north-westerly workings, there is a blind tunnel near sea level.

Further on is a narrow rock cleft, widened in the original attempt to create a shipping point. (36)

LLANFFLEWIN SH347892

Pit working developed by the Llanfflewin Slate & Slab Quarry Co of 1874.

Remains Excavation, accessed through gently falling ground by a grand cutting. Quarry waste used to make a tramway causeway across Llyn Llygeirian to the road (349902). (35)

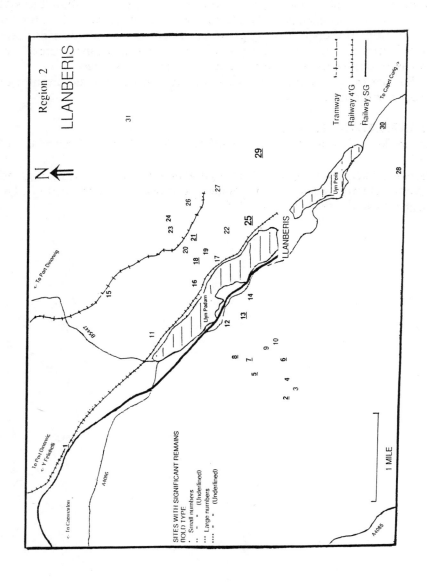

Region 2

LLANBERIS

N

SITES WITH SIGNIFICANT REMAINS
BOLD TYPE
·   Small numbers
·· "   "   (Underlined)
··· Large numbers
··· "   "   (Underlined)

1 MILE

Tramway   ⊢—⊢—⊣
Railway 4'G ⊢⊦⊦⊦⊦⊦⊦
Railway SG

To Caer Cong ›

30

28

29

31

27

26

23 24

25

22

21

20 19

18

17

16

15

14

13

12

11

Llyn Padarn

Llyn Peris

LLANBERIS

To Port Dinorwig

B5447

To Port Dinorwic
‹ Y Felinheli

To Caernarfon

Afong

Afon

Afon

1

2 3

4

5

6

7

8

9 10

LLANBERIS
Region 2
Including quarries served by the Dinorwig Tramway, Padarn Railway and L&NWR Llanberis Branch

General

This region, on the same Cambrian Vein as Bethesda, was also dominated by one huge quarry; Dinorwig, like Penrhyn, was landowner created out of ancient diggings. Unlike Bethesda, no single substantial community emerged, and the Dinorwig proprietors never exercised quite the influence over the locality and the trade as a whole, that was enjoyed by their counterparts at Penrhyn.

The principal settlements were Deiniolen and Llanberis, but many workers lived in the villages which grew up around chapels down valley. Everywhere, particularly on the hillsides, are the tiny stone-walled fields of their small-holdings.

There were few of the tiny individual workings seen around Bethesda, most of the ancient diggings on the south side of Llyn Peris being consolidated into sizeable undertakings.

Sadly no slate is now won here, but Llanberis is home to the magnificent Welsh Slate Museum which is constantly adding to its unique collection of exhibits and displays.

Transport

As at Bethesda, the dominant quarry was served by its own private railway and specially constructed port. Port Dinorwig (SH524678) was built at Y Felinheli in 1793, on the site of a disused tidal mill. Although roads were built which obviated pack horses and boating along Llyn Peris and Llyn Padarn, cartage remained difficult and costly.

The first line was the 1824 2'G. Dinorwig tramway. This left the quarry halfway up the present site, the first part of the route being lost in subsequent workings. It continued on the line of the present public road, which runs through Dinorwig village to the head of the Upper Cwm incline at SH579624. This is now a steep footpath which continues via a manoeuvring loop down the Lower Cwm incline, to stables at the lower part of Deiniolen. Its route towards Clwt-y-bont is defined by present streets before it swings right across fields. At SH565656 is the rebuilt smithy/stables which served the line (and which continued as a smithy until about 1930). The line is lost beyond here, but can be traced where it swings right off the B4547, and is defined by a line through trees to the head of the Garth incline near Garth Fach farm. The incline is largely lost in forestry, but slate sleepers can be found. The line is again lost by roadworks and the construction of the L&NWR, but the western portal of the tunnel which carried it under the A487 is visible in a field. The short stretch into Port Dinorwig is obvious.

Unlike the Penrhyn horse line of 1801, this line did not start at the lowest point of quarry working so uphauling was required and the fall of the line was much greater. The civil work was of questionable quality; the uneven spacing of the inclines hampered efficient working, the gradients were variable, and the use of slate sleepers caused maintenance problems. After only a few years, complete replacement was called for.

The new line, the Padarn railway, although not originally steamed, was laid out in 1842 for steam operation. Because of the limited power of locomotives then available, it was almost level to the head of an incline at the port. The unusual gauge of 4' was dictated by the then minimum size of engine.

It began at Gilfach Ddu, (where the 2'G. quarry wagons were loaded in fours onto carrier trucks). It ran alongside Llyn Padarn, passing three minuscule ancient diggings to the small Ladas & Boundary quarries and, via a curve (that was later straightened), past the foot of the Faenol quarry incline. The formation is now reused by the 2'G. Llanberis Lake Railway as far as Brynrefail, where the trackbed briefly becomes a road before passing under a road bridge, continuing on as a footpath to Pontrhythallt, where there is an engine shed. It again passes under a road, from where it runs alongside the formation of the Standard Gauge Llanberis branch. Between the two lines are the long, narrow sites of the Crawia & Pontrhythallt slate works.

The trackbed again passes under a road and swings right near Penrhyn farm. It may be followed with varying difficulty to a footbridge with high clearance to suit the original locomotives (one of which, together with some quarry artifacts, is displayed at Penrhyn Castle). Nearby is a fine carriage shed, for workmen's train stock.

The B4366 was crossed on the level at Saron and, after a mile, it swings left under a byroad to become a lane where there are railway cottages still in occupation. This lane led to the site of the large drumhouse/unloading shed at the head of the Penscoins incline. There is an engine/carriage shed, with a fine slate water tank. The 1895 date denotes the introduction of workmen's trains. Wagons were unloaded from the carrier trucks inside the drum-house and lowered down the 2'G. incline to Port Dinorwig. Originally, chains and an underfloor sheave were used, replaced by wire ropes and an overhead drum in the 1920s. Unfortunately this fine structure was entirely destroyed in the 1990s by the construction of the Felinheli by-pass. The portal of the now blocked tunnel where the wagons emerged at Port Dinorwig quayside can be seen.

This line gave Dinorwig an immediate competitive advantage over Penrhyn. Although the labour of loading and unloading wagons, and crewing them down to the port became increasingly burdensome, the line was not abandoned until 1962.

As at Port Penrhyn, there was a branch of the L&NWR to Port Dinorwig to enable slate brought down the Padarn line to be trans-shipped to the main line system. Opened 1852 and closed 1960, some of the trackbed is traceable.

In spite of the marina development, which followed closure as a commercial port in 1969, many buildings remain of what was an important industrial complex; including a slate factory, and the dry dock workshops which had a fine reputation for the servicing of steam yachts after Dinorwig's own slate steamers were sold.

Being a private line, the Padarn railway could not be used by the independent quarries. Although the 1830 turnpike obviated boating along Llyn Padarn, it was still a difficult journey to Caernarfon.

This dramatically changed after 1869 when the L&NWR Standard Gauge Llanberis branch opened. Either direct or via the mile long Ffridd incline system, almost all the quarries on the southern side reached the railway yard at Llanberis, enabling them to either use the national rail network, or gave them access to the slate quays at Caernarfon and Deganwy. The Ffridd incline crossed the village street on the level and curved north-west to exchange sidings. The lower end has been lost, but the upper part still makes a landscape feature.

After its 1964 closure, the Standard Gauge trackbed south-east of the Ffridd incline was made into the Llanberis by-pass, but the station has been preserved. To the north-west the railway formation makes a pleasant lake side walk, passing under a pretty accommodation bridge. Much of the rest of the route is readily traceable to its junction, to the south-west of Caernarfon.

1. SH536643 540641   Crawia (works) ** (R)
2. SH552600   Chwarel Fawr ** (R)
3. SH555595   Donnen Las

4.	SH555598	Brynmawr * (R)
5.	SH555604	Cefn-du ** (R)
6.	SH560600	Bwlch-y-groes ** (R)
7.	SH560605	Cook & Ddôl ** (R)
8.	SH560606	Glynrhonwy Uchaf ** (R)
9.	SH561602	Twll Coch (R?)
10.	SH562601	Caermeinciau
11.	SH563622	Pen Llyn
12.	SH565607	Glynrhonwy Isaf * (R)
13.	SH566603	Cambrian ** (R)
14.	SH572606	Goodmans * (R)
15.	SH572632	Glandinorwig (Works) * (R)
16.	SH574613	Boundary *
17.	SH578610	Ladas
18.	SH578615	Faenol ** (R)
19.	SH579613	Chwarel Isaf * (R)
20.	SH579617	Fronhyfryd
21.	SH581617	Chwarel Goch **
22.	SH582607	Allt-wen
23.	SH582619	Lloc *
24.	SH584619	Frondiron *
25.	SH586605	Vivian ****V (R)
26.	SH589616	Chwarel Fawr (R)
27.	SH591610	Allt Ddu (R)
28.	SH594576	Arddu *
29.	SH595603	Dinorwig ****V (R)
30.	SH601583	Gallt-y-llan **
31.	SH602628	Marchlyn

ALLT-DDU SH591610

Ancient pit/hillside working. Incorporated, with the old Adelaide digging, into Dinorwig in the early 19th century, forming with Chwarel Fawr a significant operation. Its tips and a mill, shared with Chwarel Fawr, were reached by two tunnels under the road.

Remains The main excavation to the east of the road, and the substantial mills area with buildings, inclines (including a transporter incline) and extensive rubbish runs to the west of the road, have all been completely landscaped. Fortunately, a nice powder house has been reconstructed and the one solitary original building has been rebuilt and extended to make an attractive dwelling. A track defines the tramway connection to Dinorwig, with the later steam line alongside it. (27)

ALLT-WEN SH582607
Putative site.
Remains In trees; possible ground disturbance. (22)

ARDDU (Gwaun-y-glo, Gwaun-y-tŷ) SH594576
A tiny open quarry consisting of two tandem cuts.
Remains Ruins of a dressing shed and other small buildings on upper level. The stocking area has several thousand finished slates, mainly doubles and small doubles. (28)

BOUNDARY SH574613
An ancient small open working, so named as it was at the limit of Dinorwig land. One of several lake side workings loading into boats, and much predating the Padarn Railway.
Remains Tiny dressing shed against a rock face. (16)

BRYNMAWR SH555598
Open quarry/pit; operated intermittently in the 1860s & 1880s. Taken over by Cefn-du in 1886. Steam possibly used for pumping and hauling. There was an attempted underground development a little to the north which would have acted as a drainage adit had connection been made with the pit. Product went out by the Ffridd incline. Output 1883, 160 tons.
Remains Virtually nothing other than the pit itself; some buildings and possible vestiges of the steam powered incline. The adit is lost in forestry, but there are extensive rubbish runs from it, and traces of some slate production. Nearby is a trial with distinctive purple waste. (4)

BWLCH-Y-GROES SH560600
Small open quarry/pit; operated in the 18th century revived during 1870s. Taken over by Cefn-du in 1886. Product carried by tramway to the head of the Ffridd incline. Output of a few hundred tons p.a.
Remains A surprisingly large pit with rubbish runs, and a very degraded tramway formation. Ruins of a barrack building to the west. (6)

CAERMEINCIAU (Cae'r Banciau) SH562601
A small and entirely unmechanised open quarry operated in 1870s and 1880s, on the site of a much earlier undertaking. No railed access, but may have carted to Ffridd incline. Output in 1883 of 300 tons; 12 men.
Remains Building traces, confused rubbish runs. (10)

CAMBRIAN (Ffridd Glyn) SH566603

Pits operating from the mid 19th century in conjunction with Goodmans, both amalgamating with Cefn-du in 1878. There was a tramway connection to the Ffridd incline. Output of around 1000 tons p.a.

Remains Pits; a network of tramway formations, rubbish runs, several collapsed tunnels and ruins of small buildings. One pit clearly produced red slate. (13)

CEFN-DU SH555604

Originated in 1802 when some little early diggings such as Cerrig y Pigia, Chwarel Huw Dafydd, Chwarel Morgan, Chwarel Owen, Chwarel y Maen etc., were amalgamated into the Cilgwyn & Cefn-du Co.

Consisted of several pits, with a locomotive tramway system basically on 2 levels. The upper one had tunnels to connect the various districts, and was connected by an incline to the lower level, which was in turn itself connected by an incline to the mills area. By 1879 there were said to be 4 steam engines, 2 water-wheels and a water turbine on the site. Latterly, electric power was used. Originally, product was carted to Caernarfon via Groeslon but, after amalgamation with the Goodman & Cambrian, the Ffridd incline was extended by 2 self acting pitches and a tramway connection was made to its head, with a loco from 1896. A substantial undertaking with an output (including associated quarries) of 5640 tons with 197 men in 1882. Reputedly a very poor waste to make ratio (45-1) accounting for the huge tips. Closed 1928.

Remains The pits and tunnels are much collapsed; there are several ruined buildings in the mills area including the remnants of a large mill, partly built of an unusual green country rock. The tramway formation to the Ffridd incline is obvious, near which are two barracks. The rubbish tips make a spectacular landscape feature. (5)

CHWAREL FAWR (Holland's) SH552600

The uppermost of the contiguous line of pit workings on the northern slope of Moel Eilio. In spite of its name, it was until the late 1860's very small. Material was originally carted to Caernarfon, via Waun Fawr. Later, it was connected by a tramway to the Ffridd incline but, after amalgamation with Cefn-du in 1883, the line was abandoned, material being taken by tunnel to this latter quarry for reduction. This tunnel also served as a drain, enabling deeper working.

Remains A large pit with very extensive rubbish runs. The tunnel which originally carried the tramway to the incline head has collapsed, but the tramway route is readily traceable. (There is a stock of slates alongside the tram route but this is from subsequent tip reworkings). There are no buildings, those in the pit area disappearing when the working was deepened following amalgamation with Cefn-du. The entrance of the collapsed connecting tunnel to Cefn-du is visible, and there is also a collapsed tunnel which carried a rubbish run. There are vestiges of a short incline, possibly associated with early workings. (2)

CHWAREL FAWR SH589616
Ancient hillside/pit, not to be confused with the above. Part of Dinorwig, its mill dating from at least the 1830s; its tips and inclines, reached by a tunnel, were shared with Allt-ddu. Also confusingly, it incorporated the old Chwarel Goch working, which had no connection with the later independent quarry at 581617.
Remains Comprehensively landscaped, and the road which was diverted around the pit has now been re-straightened. There are vestiges of a working face and, above the tips, of a trial. In the immediate vicinity and around Deiniolen village, the hillside right up to almost 1200' above mean sea level is divided by stone walls into the tiny plots whereby quarrymen supplemented their meagre wages.

On the mill site nothing remains; the tunnel emerged just below the trio of cottages at the western extremity of the mill site. (26)

CHWAREL GOCH (Twll Coch) SH581617
Hillside working.
Remains Pit to north of road, accessed by two tunnels (blocked); tips to south of road on several levels. Buildings adapted and in reuse as dwellings. (21)

CHWAREL ISAF (Tŷ Clwb) SH 579613
Pit working, connected to Faenol by tramway.
Remains Tramway formation; drainage tunnel. (19)

COOK & DDÔL SH560605
An amalgamation of two ancient pit workings; the easterly (Ddôl?) was abandoned early, the westerly was developed with a tunnel to a reduction area, finished product being carted out to the west. C1890 a steam mill was built at a higher level, reached from the old reduction area apparently by powering a redundant incline from the mill engine. A causeway was built across the pit to enable product to reach the Ffridd incline by a short self-acting incline. Output in 1882 was 631 tons, with

26 men, but more during the 1890s. In spite of a reputation for efficiency (a 13-1 rubbish to make ratio was claimed in 1905), it closed in the early 20th century.

Remains The older pit has a (collapsed) tunnel access to the east. Near the top of the western pit are the remains of the mill and other buildings; the causeway is a notable feature. At a lower level is the old working area, with the tunnel from the pit and the up-haulage incline to the mill above. There is an interesting building alongside the Ffridd incline which has a heavy slabbed roof and a fine fireplace. There are various dressing sheds including some in the pits, and extensive rubbish runs. Running down to the lower extremity of the site is the old track by which output was originally carted. (7)

CRAWIA/PONT RHYTHALLT SH536643/540641

Two works operating from the 1880s to the 1920s, producing writing slates and slab products from Dinorwig material brought in on the Padarn Railway. Finished product was loaded either onto the Padarn or the L&NWR.

Remains The Crawia works at 536643 has several buildings in reuse, as well as some remains of those on the other side of the L&NWR. Pont Rhythallt has vestiges of a building containing a water-wheel axle. Most of the leat which took water from the tail race of this wheel to Crawia is traceable, as is the formation of the tramway which connected the two works. (1)

DINORWIG SH595603

Hillside terraces. Established in 1787 when a group headed by landowner Assheton-Smith took over the pre-existing Take Note workings. These included Allt-wen, Braich, Bryn-glas, Bryn-llys, Chwarel Mynydd, Cloddfa Griffith Elis, Clogwyn y Gigfran, Diffwys, Garret, Hafod Owen, Harriet, Millington, Morgan's, Muriau, Sofia, Turner, Vaynol & Wellington, some being adopted as 'district' names.

By the end of the 18th century, operations had been consolidated into a series of terraces which would ultimately extend over 1800' vertically on more than 20 levels. From the 1830s there was a tramway system on each terrace, which generally had a slight gradient to favour loaded movement of trams. Steam locomotives were introduced onto the terraces in the 1870's, and internal combustion locos in the 1930's. At its peak, track mileage was said to exceed 50 (and Compressed air piping to exceed 15).

Although some downhill sledging to Llyn Peris continued until 1816, the use of self-acting inclines began in 1789, culminating in two main cascades; most pitches served two terraces, traffic from the intermediate terraces joining in mid pitch.

Since, in places, dykes of hard rock prevented orderly terracing, some material had to be uphauled from pits, several powered vertical lifts being used as well as several Blondin ropeways. Unlike the two-drum, three cable true Blondins which could lift from any point along the carrier catena, the lifting point of the single-drum, single cable Dinorwig version was determined by stops which had to be adjusted by a man crawling along the carrier-rope!

Ultimately there were more than a score of mills with a total of almost 500 saws, but few dressing machines. Extensive use was made of steam, and in 1905 they were one of the original users of the Cwm Dyli electric supply. By the late 1890s tonnage exceeded 100,000 and manning 3000. Afterwards output fell, but in the 1930s the payroll was still over 2000.

Closed in 1969 following a steep post WW2 run down.

Remains There is a great deal on this vast site and although much is no longer accessible, some of the western part, and all of the Vivian quarry (which was operated as a department of Dinorwig) is open to the public. The pumped storage scheme access tunnel and discharge point occupies the area of Wellington mill, and there has been some disturbance and tipping on the upper part of the site; but generally this reuse has ensured survival of many artifacts.

The magnificent 1870 workshop complex at Gilfach Ddu houses the main displays of the Welsh Slate Museum. Its extensive exhibits include the water-driven machine shop; its wheel, the largest in mainland Britain, although superseded by a Pelton wheel in 1925, is still in working order. Nearby is the Llanberis Lake Railway station which was where the quarry trucks were loaded onto the 4'G. carrier wagons. These arrived from the north-western side of the quarry via the adjacent A series inclines or from the south-eastern side via the Glan y Bala tunnel, now used as a cable route and near the portal of which is an unusually fine loco shed. Later the line was relaid around the bluff, its route being defined by the present road.

Near the arched entrance to Vivian quarry is a path partly incorporating steps made from slate sleepers of the 1824 tramway, leading up to Dinorwig village.

A little way off is the re-erected engine house and headgear which wound from the pit at Hafod Owen, which was near the now vanished Wellington mill.

On the hillside is the hospital building (open as a museum), beyond which is a large powder house, and behind which can be traced some vestigal earthworks of a rail line, intended to replace the 1824 tramway.

Behind and above Vivian quarry, the road from Dinorwig village which defines the route of the 1824 tramway past Chwarel Fawr and Allt-ddu quarries, continues as a private route past ruins of buildings and an electricity substation, to a large flat area from where a substantial block of mills have been cleared.

The main quarry was divided into 2 sides, Garret (north-west) served by the 9 pitches of the A series inclines, and Braich (south-east), served by the 10 pitches of the C series inclines. The several other inclines, around the middle of the quarry, were designated B.

The A series inclines brought material down to the Padarn Railway loading point near the Gilfach Ddu workshops. The lower drum-houses of the lowest 4 pitches have a pair of contracting shoes instead of the usual strap brake, and have stops and adjusters that are unique to this quarry, as are the double bar brake rods and finialled cast iron locking pillars. As was often Dinorwig practice, the drum-house walls and roof extend forward, and the backs are fitted with wooden pelmets to improve weather protection. Generally rails are still *in situ*, with cast check plates at the top and bottom of each pitch. The 2 lower pitches (A1 & A2) have commodious brakesman's cabins with fireplaces, and the upper one also has a contiguous office with a 'squint' window, to view approaching trains of waggons. At this latter point, a path is carried over the head of the incline by a nice cast iron bridge, and a wall bounding the track has heavy slabs cantilevered out, to provide shelter for men handling the waggons. Nearby too is the Anglesey barrack in the form of 20 dwellings, 10 on each side of a street some having the late occupants' initials incised at the doorway.

There is a sharp turn between A2 & A3, as the later A1 & A2 inclines replaced older ones that ran straight down. The 5 upper pitches are spectacular, but A5, A6 & A7 have been modified to carry cables, and the drum-houses demolished. The topmost (A9) has a very non-standard drum-house having a lean-to slabbed roof and two separate drums on a common axle, the drum barrelling being sheet iron. The brake too is curious, consisting of two curved wooden blocks on long timber uprights pivoted at ground level, but the control gear is standard Dinorwig. It is one of the few drum-houses on site (apart from the table inclines) that is of the remote type. Above this there is a small isolated development, not served by any incline but which had a ropeway; the upper sheave, with massive anchor block, is still in position. Near the top of this Garret side, the walls of the Garret mill still stand.

The middle of the central area is very much dominated by the big *Sincs*, accessed by tunnels. There are several inclines of the discontinuous B series, some being table inclines using pairs of standard drums on a common axle with the two brakes coupled together, the drum-houses being almost totally walled in with, unusually, jockey pulleys for the under-wound rope. Another incline is four-tracked with a double width drum-house having 2 co-axial, handed drums. Several inclines can be seen converted to single acting, with rubbish filled wagons acting as counterbalances. There are compressor houses, weighbridges, loco sheds and other buildings, as well as rail (properly chaired on the 'main lines', but bar type, often with slate sleepers, elsewhere) and numerous minor artifacts. Notable is a 'Caban' or messroom, still part furnished; a Blondin winding house having steel blast shutters and the winch *in situ*; and the remains of an unique all metal Blondin winding house and remnants of Blondin gear. Long flights of steps traverse this central area.

On the Braich side, the 4 tracked C1 & C2 inclines have been obliterated along with much of the lower levels, and C3, C4 & C5 inclines up to Australia level are much degraded.

The Australia mill still has its 36 Ingersol Rand saw tables, driven in pairs from a line shaft housed behind, which is virtually intact. It is of note that this mill, used right up to closure, had no dressing machines; all trimming being done by hand. Nearby is a compressor house with big Ingersol Rand compressors, one vertical, one horizontal, with D.C. control gear and, behind it, a large cooling water tank. There is also on this level a nice loco shed and a weighbridge complete with all mechanism.

Up from here, the C6 & C7 table inclines are unique in that the drums are underfloor in pits below the rails, the brakes being controlled, from cabins by a sort of ship's wheel, operating a rack through gearing. (This form of brake mechanism is to be seen on some A & B inclines). At C7 the usual cast iron/wooden drum has been replaced by twin sheet-metal drums. C8 has a conventional drum-house, but C9 drum-house which is a massive stone structure has, curiously, gear almost identical with A9. C10 incline, which has massive embanking, does not appear to have ever been completed. (29)

DONNEN LAS SH555595
Pit with tunnel access. (Outlier of Bryn-mawr?)
Remains Pit, dressing shed vestiges. (3)

FAENOL (Vaynol, Fachwen) SH578615

Pit/hillside working, developed by Shelton & Greaves (later of Llechwedd, Region 9) in the early 1830s. Later redeveloped by Assheton-Smith of Dinorwig and subsequently connected by incline to the Padarn Railway. Disused by 1912.

Remains Tipping run for the upper older working; weigh-house, some small structures, a bridge over a road and an access tunnel (blocked) to the lower working. On the wast bank a fine run of 7 dressing sheds (in reuse), weigh-house and other buildings. The incline is obvious, and the pre-incline road down towards the lake is traceable. (18)

FRONDIRION SH584619

Possibly an early shallow excavation.

Remains Some surface disturbance, considerable amount of fine trimmings. Building remains nearby may have a connection. (24)

FRONHYFRYD (Brynhyfryd) SH579617

Tiny early working.

Remains Pit only. (20)

GALLT-Y-LLAN (Hafoty) SH601583

Hillside quarry, opened about 1811 and operated intermittently over a long period on a restricted scale. Terrace working with central incline.

The ease of working and convenience to the road favoured economic operation, but with a high sulphur content, the product quality was poor. In 1882 90 tons was produced and 3 men were employed.

Remains Stone built incline formation and small building ruins. (30)

GLANDINORWIG FACTORY SH572632 etc.

Writing slate factory. The two storey building to the west of the road contained machinery for making the wooden frames viz; 3 saws, planing, morticing, tenoning, grooving and corner rounding machines and all equipment for wire binding the frame corners; also a slate planer, a sand-polisher and a device for ruling the slates. Another building held a vertical gang-saw for reducing logs to planks. Other buildings included stables, shoeing smithy, manager's house and a cowshed (!).

On the other side of the road the Caeffynnon mill had 2 sand-polishers, a machine for servicing the 7' dia. iron discs of the polishers, and 2 slate saws (1 handpowered?). 2 cottages adjoined.

Felin Uchaf at 578629 had a further two polishers and 2 saws, a slate drill and a 2 ton crane. Out of use by c.1900.

Remains The impressive main building which still has its water-wheel intact is in reuse. Caeffynnon, which has traces of the small Caerhun reservoir behind which supplied its water wheel, has been much extended as a factory. At Felin Uchaf, part of the site is occupied by the Deiniolen Band Room. Behind are the pillars for the launder which fed the internal water wheel. (15)

GLYNRHONWY ISAF SH565607

A pit working which grew out of a number of small diggings such as Bach, Fawnog, Ffynnon, Hir, Glan-y-Llyn, Gloddfa Ffordd, Gloddfa Ganol, Glyn Isaf, Twll Clai, Twll-y-chwil, Twll Glas, Twll Coch, Wen Fain. Some date from the early 18th century, accessed by boats by diggers living in Cwm-y-glo. It was extensively developed in the 1860's, becoming two large pits with a third smaller pit between them, all connected by drainage/tramway tunnels.

The extensive steam mills (electrified 1920) were to the north-east of the then main road, their equipment including at least one Hunter saw. A tramway from the easternmost pit passed under the road to the mills and continued under the railway to tip into the lake. A second line to the mills dropped from a higher level by incline to cross the road on the level. Some of the early diggings were pioneer users of internal rails and, in 1866, they were one of the first users of locos on the extensive rail network.

Several of the early diggings pumped but the unified quarry was largely self draining. With all downhill working and easy waste disposal, it made this an efficient unit achieving outputs of 40 tons per man year.

Product was carted to Caernarfon until c.1870 when it was connected to the northerly end of the Ffridd exchange sidings on the main line railway. Produced 1789 tons with 70 men in 1883 but later outputs were larger and after amalgamation with the Upper quarry, it became by far the largest on this side of the valley. Closed in the 1930's.

Remains The quarrying site was much disturbed by the Air Ministry occupation from 1940 to 1973, when a standard gauge rail network was laid. Subsequent tip working, landscaping and the laying out of roads for factory development have caused further obliteration. The western pit lying to the north of the Upper Glynrhonwy mills area, and separated from it by a tipping run, is relatively undisturbed; but the other two pits have been lost.

The mill buildings to the east of the main road, were extended for WW2 munitions manufacture and have since been further altered and rebuilt for industrial use. The portals of both the tunnels are extant. The tipping round is now a country park. (12)

GLYNRHONWY UCHAF (Premier, Glyn Ganol) SH560606

Pit, developed 1830s - 1860s by Shelton & Greaves, (later of Llechwedd, Region 9), incorporating older workings such as Chwarel Fain, Cloddfa'r Lôn, Glyn Ganol, Glyn Ucha.

Reopened 1870s and connected to the Ffridd incline, but after amalgamation with Glynrhonwy Lower this link may have been abandoned. Basically two tunnel linked pits in tandem, having a complex internal rail network with spectacularly located tracks, including some cantilevered along rock faces; partly loco worked from the 1890s. One of the few users of a chain incline in the area. Produced 2181 tons with 90 men in 1882. Closed in the 1930's.

Remains Above the road are the two impressive pits connected by a high level and a low level tunnel. There are traces of several early inclines. In the pit nearer the road is a fine wooden bridge. The tunnel under the road has been lost, as has the whole of the mills area to which it led. To the north is a big rubbish run; an abutment of a bridge to it across the road is extant. In the vicinity are a number of traces of small, early diggings. (8)

GOODMAN'S (Chwarel y Person, Coed-y-ddôl) SH572606

A small pit working developed in the 1870's and 80's from earlier diggings such as Greens, Potters, Twll Tomos Lewis, and Tŷ-du.

The pit was apparently pumped by water power and it had a small mill (steam?). Tipped into the lake by a tramway which crossed the road and the railway on the level. This line may have been used to take product to the railway.

Output of a few 100's of tons p.a. Closed about 1890.

Remains The site is now partly occupied by a modern factory. Some vestiges of tips and tramways. The lake side tip now forms a play area. (14)

LADAS SH578610

Early working and, like Boundary, accessed from the lake.

Remains Excavation only, alongside Padarn trackbed. (17)

LLOC SH582619

Small pit working.

Remains Pit and fine trimming waste, one building. Subsequent to closure, the site is cut through by a road. (23)

MARCHLYN SH602628

In the 1930s Dinorwig, due to dispersion and indiscriminate dumping, had become expensive to work. The motor lorry having freed quarrying from rail dependence, an abortive attempt was made to open up here as a 'Green field' site.

The idea was revived in the 1950's with major investment which included an electric mill. Never a success, it survived until Dinorwig's 1969 closure.

Remains Little on site apart from spoil runs. Buildings were mostly of Steel/timber and there was much disturbance during building of the Pumped Storage Station. (31)

PEN LLYN SH563622

Hillside quarry. Very small.

Remains Excavation only. (11)

TWLL COCH SH561602

Small pit working, exploiting a red slate occurrence. No mill on site, may have been connected to Ffridd incline.

Remains Scarcely any apart from rubbish runs and tramway formations. (9)

VIVIAN SH586605

Hillside quarry/pit, worked on 8 levels, 2 of which are now under water. Operated as part of Dinorwig, with which it shared all services. Being something of a 'show' quarry where distinguished visitors could be taken, the structures are particularly fine.

Remains A spectacular vertical gash in the hillside, with a shallow flooded pit, accessed through a nice archway, with working levels off to the north-west.

On these levels are a number of fine rakes of dressing sheds and other buildings, some with excellent slab roofs.

The main interest is in the inclines, in 5 tandem pitches, the lower 3 being table inclines, with much of the track and gear intact. The lowest incline has now been restored to full working order (albeit electrically powered!) The drum-houses, particularly of the lower inclines, are built and ornamented to an extravagant standard, the brake mechanisms being unusually interesting, of massive cast construction, operated via spur gears and 'ships wheel' controls, with elaborate remote control crimp sprags. The 4-6 incline is most unusual in that there is a continuous run from 6 down to 4, with tracks alongside from 5 down to 4 (giving four tracks on the lower part), both sets controlled from a double drum-house on level 6. A traverser enabled traffic using the 4-5 tracks to be aligned with the No 4 drum-house. On level 2 there is a rubbish run turning out towards the lake near the hospital.

At the foot of the main incline system, the lower pitch of which has been reconstructed to working order, is a short pitch at right angles to the rest, notable for its underfloor sheave gear and slate sleepers *in situ*. Inside the quarry a replica Blondin has been reconstructed on the original hillside mountings using a sheave from one of the twelve Dinorwig Blondins. There is also the Blondin winding house and the shed for the steam pump. Most of the site forms part of a country park and is freely accessible. (25)

NANTLLE
Region 3
Including quarries served by Nantlle Tramway
& L&NWR Tal-y-sarn Sub-branch

General

In this, the third major slate region of Caernarfonshire, were some of the earliest recorded slate workings. Although on an abundant continuation of the Bethesda/Llanberis veins, divided land ownership prevented the emergence of a dominant working. Almost all sites were small and constricted, forcing rubbish to be piled high behind vast revetments, and rendering much good rock inaccessible. Pit working involved pumping and uphaulage by Blondins and chain inclines. Shortage of water enforced much use of steam, further adding to costs. Thus, though their roofing slate tended to command a premium, few quarries were profitable.

Developed during the early 19th century on an Irish trade which went into recession in the 1840s, subsequently comparative prosperity only came during periods of high prices. This episodic nature meant that there was much unofficial re-working done by unemployed men. The numerous crude shelters of these 'Tip Lads' are a feature of the area.

Due to the small size of most units, there was little quarry housing or barrack accommodation. Some villages such as Pen-y-groes, Tal-y-sarn or Nantlle, were swelled by quarrying demands, but there was also extensive dispersed settlement in small holdings over a wide area. Some of these undoubtedly were unauthorised 'Tai Unnos'; occupations of common or Crown land, erected in the erroneous but rarely challenged belief that if a dwelling could be erected between dusk and dawn, the squatter had good title to it and to any land within 'an axe's throw'.

A beneficial effect of the small units was the absence of confrontational industrial relations, endemic in some larger quarries. In fact, both masters and men tended to unite against the owner/landlords of Penrhyn and Dinorwig, and several proprietors were actually active in Trades Union affairs.

Significant working continued post WW2, but now just one small quarry survives, operated by a family whose connections with slate in the area extend over two centuries.

Transport

Traditionally material was shipped at Foryd, (SH452586) but by the early 19th century most was going to Caernarfon, from 1828 via the 3'6" gauge horse-drawn Nantlle Railway, the first public railway built to serve the slate industry. (The 1801 Penrhyn and the 1824 Dinorwig lines being private lines serving only their respective quarries.)

In 1867 the L&NWR Caernarfon – Afon Wen branch absorbed the Nantlle Railway from near Caernarfon to Pen-y-groes. Nantlle, trucks being carried in transporters. In 1872 the Nantlle lines to Caernarfon quays were relaid Standard Gauge and a sub branch made to Tal-y-sarn. However the section from Tal-y-sarn to Penyrorsedd quarry survived until 1963 as the only British Rail horse-drawn line.

All the quarries on the northern side of the valley had direct connection, with some on the southern side reaching it via the short, but grandly named, Caernarfonshire Slate Quarries Railway which joined the Nantlle Railway about half a mile west of Tal-y-sarn. This line continued as a feeder to the L&NWR line until about 1914.

Those quarries with connection used 3'6" gauge trucks for product dispatch, but most, especially those with locomotives, used 2' gauge internally. Often trucks had double-flanged wheels loose on the axle, enabling them to be used for either gauge.

The route (or at least the final route, as it was moved several times when quarrying encroached) is readily traceable from Penyrorsedd to Tal-y-sarn, with a good run of slate sleeper blocks near the Penyrorsedd end.

The Tal-y-sarn/Pen-y-groes section (common to both steam railway and Nantlle), is now a road.

From Pen-y-groes to Caernarfon the Standard Gauge line is readily traceable, for the most part occupying the Nantlle trackbed. The notable exception is at Pen-y-groes where the horse line curved through the village streets, whereas the steam line ran clear of the village to the south. Nearer Caernarfon the L&NWR diverged leaving extant a fine Nantlle Railway bridge at Bontnewydd (SH480599), and the Coed Helen tunnel (SH482616).

The short route of the Caernarfonshire Railway is partly traceable.

The quay that served first the Nantlle Railway and, subsequently, the L&NWR harbour branch is now a car park below the castle. At Foryd, the old shipping point may be identified by the slate waste and mooring posts. The buildings probably post-date slate shipment usage.

John Williams, Rhyd-y-gro, splitting slates at Swch quarry, c1880? (Region 6)
By courtesy of Mr Griff R. Jones

Drumhouse, No.3 Incline Rhiw-bach Tramway 1930s? (Region 9)
By courtesy of Mr Griff R. Jones

Rhosydd quarry, 1920s. (Region 8)
By courtesy of Mr Griff R. Jones

The Mill, Bwlch y Slaters (Manod) quarry 1920s. (Region 9)
By courtesy of Mr Griff R. Jones

Bwlch y Slaters (Manod) quarry, 1920s. (Region 9)
By courtesy of Mr Griff R. Jones

Hunter Saw, Graig Ddu quarry. Date unknown. (Region 9)
By courtesy of Mr Griff R. Jones

Llechwedd quarry, c1890? The lower mill with the typical central water wheel
is now incorporated into the Visitor Centre. (Region 9)
By permission of National Library of Wales

Water Wheel Groeslon Works, c1950. (Region 3)
By permission of Museum of Welsh Life & Mr Roger Davis

Water Wheel, Glandyfi quarry, c1910? (Region 14)
By permission of Museum of Welsh Life

Splitting & Dressing, Penrhyn quarry, c1890? (Region 1)
By permission of Museum of Welsh Life

Wynne Quarry, probably 1920s. (Region 15)
By permission of Museum of Welsh Life

Mill Interior, Oakeley quarry. Early 20thC. (Region 9)
By permission of National Library of Wales

'Blondin' heads, Penrhyn quarry, 1930s? (Region 1)
By permission of National Library of Wales

Drilling for shot firing, Penrhyn Quarry. Early 20thC? (Region 1)
By permission of Gwynedd Archive Service

Deeside Mill, c1910? (Region 15)
By permission of Denbigh Record Office

Ventilation fanhouse, Croesor quarry, 1980. (Region 8)
Photo: Author

Blondin Towers, Penyrorsedd quarry, 1975. (Region 3)
Photo: Author

Ynys y Pandy Mill, 1990. (Region 7)
Photo: Author

Gorseddau Quarry, 1990. (Region 7)
Photo: Author

*Possibly unique remains of an Incline Bridge crossing a rubbish run,
Cwm Machno quarry, 1997. (Region 6)*
Photo: Author

Lavatory underground Cambrian quarry, 1995. (Region 15)
Photo: Author

Marine Donkey Engine operated by compressed air for
underground haulage. Braich-goch quarry, c1980.
Photo: Author

Signal Gong made from an old saw blade, head of 7-6 underground
haulage incline, Braich-goch quarry, 1980. (Region 13)
Photo: Author

Crab Winch underground, Craig Rhiweirth quarry, c1985. (Region 16)
Photo: Author

Fragment of the table of a handcranked circular saw,
probably a unique survivor, Darren quarry, 1980. (Region 13)
Photo: Author

Powder House interior, showing timber lining extant,
Morben quarry, 1997. (Region 14)
Photo: Author

Pantyrafon yard for Llechwedd loadings onto L&NWR (LMSR). Hydro power station
is behind storage sheds. Plas Waenydd, now Llechwedd offices, in distance, 1996.
(Region 9)   Photo: Author

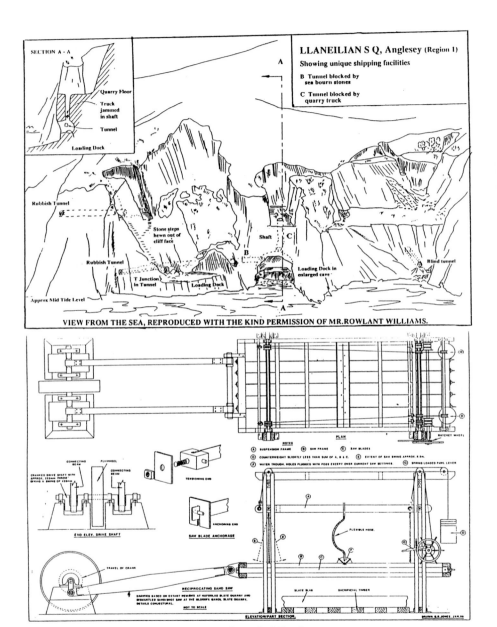

LLANEILIAN S Q, Anglesey (Region 1)

Showing unique shipping facilities

B Tunnel blocked by sea bourn stones

C Tunnel blocked by quarry truck

SECTION A - A

Quarry Floor

Truck jammed in shaft

Tunnel

Loading Dock

Rubbish Tunnel

Stone steps hewn out of cliff face

Shaft

Rubbish Tunnel

Loading Dock in enlarged cave

Blind tunnel

T Junction in Tunnel

Loading Dock

Approx Mid Tide Level

VIEW FROM THE SEA, REPRODUCED WITH THE KIND PERMISSION OF MR. ROWLANT WILLIAMS.

Layout of a typical Sandsaw
by Mr Griff R. Jones

ASCENDING: TRAIN DRAWN BY THE FAIRLIE LOCOMOTIVE, "LITTLE WONDER."

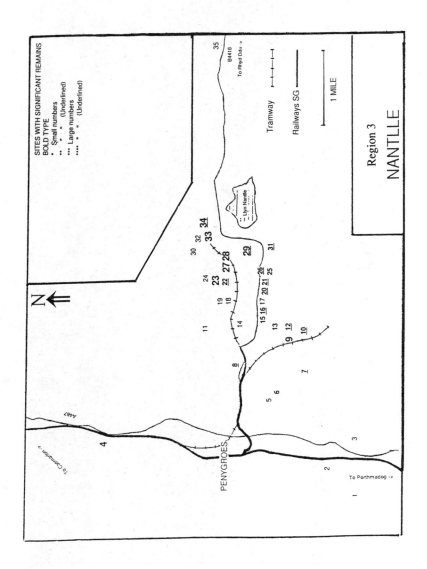

SITES WITH SIGNIFICANT REMAINS
BOLD TYPE
•   Small numbers
:   " " "   (Underlined)
••• Large numbers
••• " " "   (Underlined)

N ⟸

Tramway ┼┼┼┼┼┼┼

Railways SG ─────

1 MILE

Region 3
NANTLE

Llyn Nantlle

B4418
To Rhyd Ddu ->

PENYGROES

To Porthmadog ->

To Caernarfon ->

A487

1. SH458506 Foel Clynnog
2. SH464513 Gelli Bach
3. SH470508 Llwyd-coed
4. SH470551 Groeslon (works) ***WV (R)
5. SH477523 Bryn Castell
6. SH479522 Ty'n-llwyn *
7. SH482517 Tyddyn Agnes **
8. SH482526 Taldrwst ** (R?)
9. SH486518 Nant-y-fron *** (R)
10. SH489517 Fronheulog ** (R)
11. SH489540 Hafod-las
12. SH490518 Twll Llwyd **W
13. SH490522 Singrig
14. SH490530 Coed Madog
15. SH491522 Twll Coed *
16. SH491523 Tan-yr-allt ** (R)
17. SH493524 Plas Du (R?)
18. SH493532 Cloddfa'r Coed (R)
19. SH493533 Cefn-coed (R)
20. SH495523 Ty'nyweirglodd **
21. SH495524 Tŷ Mawr West **
22. SH496531 Cornwall ** (R)
23. SH496534 Tal-y-sarn *** (R)
24. SH496537 Alltlechi
25. SH497523 Tŷ Mawr Green *
26. SH497525 Nantlle Vale **
27. SH498535 Blaen-y-cae *** (R)
28. SH499535 Galltyfedw *** (R)
29. SH500532 Dorothea **** (R)
30. SH500540 Cilgwyn (R)
31. SH501526 Gwernor **
32. SH501535 Wern Ifan
33. SH502536 Pen-y-bryn *** (R)
34. SH510538 Penyrorsedd **** (R)
35. SH535532 Talmignedd

ALLTLECHI SH496537
Pit working, closed 1880s; later part of Tal-y-sarn; subsequently used by Blaen-y-cae for tipping.
Remains Tipped-in pit only. (24)

BLAEN-Y-CAE SH498535

Small open pit working, started about 1830. Incorporated Pen-y-ditch. Material was raised by Blondin to a mill to the west of pit, finished product going down the lower part of the westerly Cilgwyn incline to the Nantlle railway. Some tipping on the far side of that incline. Maximum of about 40 men employed, peak output around 800 tons p.a. Later became part of Tal-y-sarn. Closed 1930s.

Remains Pit, contiguous with Tal-y-sarn. Several buildings, an incline and an almost complete steam Blondin winder (possibly a unique survivor); wrecked wooden Blondin towers and gear, as well as some interesting trackwork. (27)

BRYN CASTELL SH477523

Tiny trial.

Remains Surface scratching. (5)

CEFN-COED SH493533

Small, served as a tip for Tal-y-sarn.

Remains Face and incline formation. (19)

CILGWYN SH500540

Developed out of a number of ancient small workings such as Cloddfa'r Bach, Cloddfa'r Dŵr, Cloddfa Edward Regiol, Cloddfa'r Eithin, Cloddfa'r Glynllyn, Cloddfa'r Clytiau, Cloddfa John Morris, Cloddfa Limerick (reflecting the area's substantial Irish trade?), Cloddfa'r Nant, Cloddfa Robert Roberts, Cocsyth Bach, Cocsyth Mawr, Faen-goch, Gloddfa Fach, Gwaith Newydd, Twll Cheinia, Twll-y-chwil, some dating from at least the 14th century. By end of 18th century, it was a substantial working with, by 1820s, horse-whim haulage.

Idle in the 1840s when there was much illicit working by trespassers, it was restarted in the 1850s and rapidly developed into a large undertaking in 4 pits with, in 1882, an output of 7430 tons employing 300 men. Districts had names such as Gwaith Newydd and Hen Gilgwyn.

Steam locos were used from 1876 around the south and east of the pits, as well as on the pit floors, with tunnels connecting the pits. Steam also drove the chain inclines and Blondins. The main mill was to the east with 3 other mills to the south.

Waste disposal space towards the valley floor was limited, so a long rubbish run took waste to the west. Later tipping was to the north, the tipping area (at 500548) being reached by a long horseshoe loop line.

When the Nantlle railway was opened, it was reached by an incline through Tal-y-sarn quarry which was also used by Fron (Section 5). In 1881, Fron traffic having been diverted to the N.W.N.G.Rly. and with tipping encroaching on the incline, a new incline was constructed some 200 yards to the east. Finally in 1923, a connection was made via the then disused tipping horseshoe loop line to the N.W.N.G.

Output declined steeply during the early 20th century. Final closure 1956.

Remains Buildings have been entirely demolished and the pits used for council rubbish disposal. The main tramway formations are traceable, some being reused as roadways. The 'Horseshoe' line is still a prominent feature. Both inclines are traceable. (30).

GLODDFA'R COED SH493532

Probably dating from the 17th century. Water-wheel pumping of the pit was augmented in 1807 by a steam pump, the first in the industry, (it fell into the pit ten years later!) In the 1890s having incorporated Pwll Fanog almost one hundred men were employed. Closed 1913, briefly revived c1930.

Remains Landscaped. (18)

COED MADOG (Gloddfa Glai) SH490530

Pit working opened early 19th century, output in 1883 2879 tons with 135 men. From 1877, internal loco worked tramway system with 3 De Winton engines. Chain inclines used. Closed 1908; revived briefly early 1920s.

Was connected to the Nantlle railway via the Gloddfa'r Coed quarry, but later had its own direct Standard Gauge connection to the L&NWR, the only quarry with that facility.

Remains Site completely landscaped. (14)

CORNWALL (South Dorothea) SH496531

Pit working opened 1867, but some working on site circa 1760, possibly by Cornish ex-copper miners. Blondin haulage to a mill on a rubbish bank. Output of 1040 tons with 70 men in 1882, increasing to over 3000 tons towards the end of 19th century. Connected to Nantlle railway. After 1899, tipped to south of the river Llyfni by a timber bridge (collapsed 1927). In Mid 19th century, became part of Tal-y-sarn. Incorporated into Dorothea 1921; finally closed 1957.

Remains Large flooded pit, several ruinous structures. (22)

DOROTHEA *(Cloddfa Turner)* SH500532

Pit working; districts had names such as Hen Dwll, Pen Dwyllt, Twll Bach, Twll Coch, Twll Fire (Twll Tân), Twll Ucha, Twll y Weirglodd, probably derived from earlier workings. Although not opened until the 1820s, it rapidly became the dominant undertaking in the area. By 1848 its 200 men were producing over 5000 tons p.a., which built up to a peak of 17442 tons in 1873. Even in the difficult times of the early 1880s, outputs were not much less with manning well over 500.

It was almost consistently profitable (until persistent flooding problems, commencing in 1884 and continuing into the 1920s, sapped profits), a most unusual record for a non-landowning slate quarry. There were ultimately 6 contiguous pits, the last being sunk in 1891.

At least 8 water-wheels were eventually used for pumping, haulage and mill power. Steam was introduced in 1841, and by 1864 there were three steam engines on site; in 1869 they were one of the first users of De Winton locos.

The first of 8 chain inclines, including 2 double and 1 triple, was installed in 1841 to uphaul out of the pit to the (ultimately) 8 mills with 42 saws. These replaced the horse whims and hand-worked turntrees hitherto used, and some survived until 1957. Further powered inclines on fixed formations, some transporter type, were required to reach the top of the huge revetted rubbish tips, which are such a prominent feature of the site.

Steam Blondins (ultimately 4) located on the rubbish banks to counteract the sag of the catenae which stretched right across the pit, were introduced in 1900, (converted to electric in 1959), and used until 1965 when a road to pit bottom was built.

In 1904 a large Cornish beam engine was installed to pump the pit, which by this time was 500 feet deep (replaced by electric pumps in 1951).

As the quarry expanded, the old Tal-y-sarn village was engulfed, some of the buildings being used for quarry purposes, and the Nantlle railway had to be re-routed further north. There was an extensive loco powered rail system both at ground level and on top of the waste banks. There were over 350 men in the 1930s but, post-WW2, half that number. In spite of much modernisation in the 1950s, including locally made diamond saws, it closed in 1970.

Remains The site is dominated by the lake formed by the flooded workings, (the depth of water is such that it appears as a single pit). The rubbish banks, with fine stone incline formations and magnificent revetments, make this a singularly impressive site. To the south are the ruins of a big integrated mill and many other buildings, and the remains of hoist gallows, landing platforms and haulage housings.

To the west is the Cornish Engine house which still has the engine, complete with boilers. To the north-east are some of the old village buildings, including the ruins of what was the Commercial Hotel. There are some fine archways, and on the old line of the Nantlle railway is a notable double arched retaining buttress. Nearby is a nice flight of cantilevered steps.

On top of the rubbish banks are tramway formations and several weighbridges. (29)

FOEL CLYNNOG (Foel Uchaf) SH458506

A mid 19th century working; pumping by water wheel; possibly had a mill. Employed 17 men in 1882, closed 1889 subsequently worked for stone.
Remains None from slate working. (1)

FRONHEULOG (Buarth Fotty, Fronlog) SH489517

Small pit working, dating from about 1840s. Output 1642 tons with 98 men in 1882. At 1930s closure, 36 men. Post WW2 worked intermittently for its green slates.
Remains Two pits. (10)

GALLTYFEDW (Alexandria, Victoria, Y Foel) SH499535

Several pit workings developed in mid 19th century incorporating the earlier Cae Ysgubor and Twll-mwg which, in turn, had incorporated very ancient diggings. Absorbed the old Pen-y-bryn site and in the 1920s, after amalgamation with Dorothea, a new pit was opened reviving the name Cae Ysgubor.

A steam incline raised block to a water powered mill with 6 saws, and there may have been additional saws in the open, an unusual but not unique practice in this area.

In spite of its size, output was a sporadic few hundred tons p.a. Product went out by an incline and track which crossed, and then made a junction with, the Nantlle Tramway. A rubbish run bridged the easterly Cilgwyn incline. Closed circa 1930.
Remains A crowded site with many ruined buildings, including an office with a patterned roof common on housing in the area. Incline formations, drum-houses, launder pillars and wheel-pit, and other structures; also a nice privy. Much, including the retaining walls, is on the point of collapse. (28)

GELLI BACH SH464513
Tiny pit working, possibly only a trial
Remains Pit itself. (2)

GROESLON SLATE WORKS SH470551
Established c1850s, to produce Writing Slates, from slab supplied via the Nantlle Railway. Originally water-powered by a wheel fed by a launder over main road, (removed to allow double decked buses to pass).
Remains Still in use as Inigo Jones works, producing high quality slab; besides usual saws (modern) and planers it has an interesting, possibly unique, sand-polisher and an enamelling oven. Visitors are welcome. (4)

GWERNOR SH501526
Open pit operated intermittently with up to 30 men from c1860 to 1915, with some occasional work to 1932. It is recorded that there was an 18' water-wheel, but water turbines (or Pelton wheels) appear to have pumped, wound the chain incline, and powered the 3 saws and a planer. Rubbish was tipped to the north of the public road. No rail connection; cartage to Tal-y-sarn.
Remains Flooded pit, ruins of small mill and abutments of rubbish run bridge. (31)

HAFOD-LAS SH489540
Putative early working.
Remains Nothing identified. (11)

LLWYD-COED (Eureka, Green Afon) SH470508, (& 470511)
Pit working, c1820; in 1883, 6 men produced 78 tons. Flourished in 1900s with over 20 men, but closed during WW1.
Remains Site cleared, used for tipping. (3)

NANTLLE VALE (Tŷ Mawr East, United) SH497525
Open pit/hillside working. Developed c1850; became one of the larger of the south side workings. Used, at various times, fixed ramp and chain inclines, and possibly vertical shaft haulage. Water power used for hauling (water balance?) and pumping, supplanted or supplemented by steam. 20 men employed in 1882 but only 150 tons recorded that year. Part was separately worked as Twll John Ffowc. Had an internal tramway system, but no external rail connection; material removed by cart. Closed around 1910.
Remains An interesting site. Several buildings including a nice rake of

dressing sheds and an engine house with chimney. There is a stone-lined pump shaft about 6'6" square with pump-rods. A haulage incline may have been water-powered. Alongside the engine house is the firebox and boiler of a semi-portable steam engine. Elsewhere on the site is a wheel pit and, nearby, a chimney for an engine and winder that were on ground now quarried away. This dated from about 1870s and was replaced in the 1890s by the now extant engine house. Near the pit, there are possible Blondin type bases. There is a well engineered access road. (26)

NANT-Y-FRON SH486518

Worked from about 1840; two pits in tandem, possibly with water-wheel uphaulage, with an incline down to a water-powered mill. Later, a third pit was opened below the mill level, with putative double acting water balance. Operated intermittently with tonnages of over 2000, with around 100 men during its 1890s/1900s heyday. An extensive internal tramway system connected to the Caernarfonshire Slate Quarries Railway. Closed circa 1915, but some very small scale working in the 1970s seeking the rich green coloured product.
Remains A number of buildings including a mill and a manager's house. Stone built incline, partly in a cutting. The lower incline has a curious tunnel through it for a water course and, associated with it, a stone covered leat. There are pillars that may be launder supports, and blocks that could be wire or chain incline anchorages.
In the mill area is an unusual excavated structure of unknown purpose. (9)

PEN-Y-BRYN SH502536

Site of 18th century diggings such as Cae Cilgwyn, David's Quarry, Herbert's, Owen's Quarry. The northernmost part was known as New Pen-y-bryn, and the north-western part as Twll Ismaeliaid. Unusually, originally used plateways. In 1836 it incorporated Cloddfa'r Lôn which comprised Dewi's Quarry, Hen Dwll, Twll Mawr (Middle Quarry), and Twll Balast. Its best days were the 1840s, when well over 6000 tons p.a. were produced. In 1882, employed 240 men producing 5083 tons. Eventually consisted of 4 pits with haulages up to a mill area with, from 1875, a locomotive tramway layout. At one time, 2 water-wheels were used for pumping, but later steam was used for pumping and winding. An early user of internal tramways (plateways?) and of chain inclines. Blondins utilised until the late 1930s. An incline, with an unusual drum buried under the crimpled down to the Nantlle railway of which it was one time the terminus, before being extended to Penyrorsedd. The

Nantlle line was diverted to the south along its presently traceable route as work at this quarry encroached. After 1836, owned by Dorothea, some tipping being done on Dorothea property. After 1887-95 closure, operated on a reduced scale with peaks of 166 men in 1902 and 144 men in 1922. Closed after a rockfall in 1950 (12 men then working). In 1963/4, Dorothea built roads and made some attempt to rework.

Remains Much of the eastern part of the site (Hen Dwll) has been covered by Penyrorsedd tipping, and the Twll Mawr & Twll Balast pits partly filled with water and rubbish. To the west, Galltyfedw has tipped onto the site. On the southerly, Cloddfa'r Lôn area, building ruins include a steam mill, winding-engine house and two wheel-pits, both possibly for pumping. On the northern, New Pen-y-bryn area, are the walls of a long mill, a barracks, and the chimney of a winding-engine house. A tunnel, one of several which gave access to the upper pits, is penetrable. Traces of incline formations, drum-house (with some gear), and several artifacts such as flat rods, vestiges of a bucket pump, a launder etc. are to be found.

Some tramway formations are traceable with the abutments of the rubbish run bridge onto Dorothea property. The final Nantlle railway route is a clear formation (with stone blocks), and the diversion from the original route can be seen. (33)

PENYRORSEDD (Nantlle) SH510538

Originally hillside galleries, developed from 1816 as a series of pits, producing five figure annual tonnages, with manning consistently exceeding 350 up to WW2. Some pits extended downwards to valley floor level, de-watered by a drainage tunnel. To raise material, two chain inclines and a vertical water balance were used, but these were replaced by six locally made Blondins. The first was originally steam powered, but finally all were electric, this quarry being in 1905 one of the first users of power from the Cwm Dyli station.

Between 1867 and 1896 four mills were erected on three levels connected by two incline pitches, with a third incline down to the terminus of the Nantlle railway. Ingenious use was made of limited water, including an inter-mill drive.There were extensive tramways in 2'G & 3'6"G, locos being used on the former gauge from the mid 1870s. In spite of a proposal to make a connection with the N.W.N.G.Rly, the Nantlle line was used until its 1963 closure, after which product went out by road.

In spite of modernisation in the 1960s, work ceased in 1978. Re-opened in the late 1980s with a re-equipped mill and a road down into

New pit, it closed again in 1997.

Remains There are 4 pits extant (William, Ellen, Eureka and New). Other old workings such as Arthur, Hen Dwll, Twll Caled, Twll Mawr, Twll Shafftydd & Twll Shed, have vanished under tipping, and the Ceunant y Glaw working is under the mills area. There are some tunnels in the quarried faces and, to the north, are several shafts which were cut to investigate the rock.

Most of the Blondin towers, which were such a feature, have gone, but the electric winding houses and the complex pulley arrangements which enabled the towers to be moved as work progressed, are extant. The lately used mill and other buildings are on the upper level.

The middle level has the ruins of a large mill originally water driven, later electrically powered, which for long had unique hydraulic-feed saw tables and an unique example of a De Winton planer. Adjacent was a 'specials' department. On the lower level are further buildings, including two partly demolished mills, offices and a hospital. Some buildings have signs of late renovation.

The drum-houses and inclines are in unusually fine condition, with track on the ground and hinged wooden crimp sprags. There are pleasing 'sentrybox' type banksman's shelters. Brake gear is conventional except for the use of pulley and weight counterbalances for the levers.

At the Nantlle railway terminus, at the foot of the lowest incline, are stables etc. associated with the line, including a building with a wheel-pit alongside, where horse feed was prepared.

The fine war memorial which stood outside the quarry hospital has been re-erected in the village, where many of the houses were quarry owned. (34)

PLAS DU SH493524
Small pit, hived off from Tan-yr-allt; portion worked for a time by Singrig as Dolbebi East.
Remains Pit, tip and building traces. (17)

SINGRIG (Dolbebi West) SH490522
Small unmechanised pit working. Tipping area extended across public road by a bridge. Not rail connected although, c1900, this was proposed.
Remains Dressing sheds, abutments of the road bridge. (13)

TALDRWST (Caernarfonshire Quarry, Llyn-y-coed) SH482526
Several small pits, which at times operated independently as Taldrwst Upper, Taldrwst Lower, Taldrwst West, Twll Malawi. Had two water-

wheels; may have been connected to the C.S.Q. Railway.
Remains Ground disturbance, possible vestiges of buildings. (8)

TALMIGNEDD SH535532
Hillside quarry.
Remains Forestry and other work has obliterated all but some traces of inclines. (35)

TAL-Y-SARN (Caernarfon & Bangor) SH496534
Pit working, incorporated ancient diggings such as Cloddfa'r Onnen Fach, Cloddfa'r Onnen Fawr. Parts were named Chwarel Goch, Cloddfa Fawr, Tal-y-sarn Bach, Twll Ffactri, Twll Mawr, Twll Pen-ditch, Twll Pen-parc. By the late 1790s, had 100 men with 40 carts handling over 1000 tons p.a. By 1829 a water balance was in use and de-watering by rag & chain pumps. By 1845, 6000 tons was exceeded, but later dramatically dropped.

Flourished again in the late 1870s when over 500 men were employed; 1882 tonnage 8210, with 400 men. Chain inclines were steam powered and had locos on the internal rail system from c1880, but reverted to horse working by end of 19th century.

Connected to Nantlle railway by incline. As it developed, the railway was resited further south. Very little working post WW1; closed 1926, worked by Galltyfedw until early 1930s.
Remains Flooded pit, numerous buildings including a mill, drum-house, possible dwelling, and traces of engine house(s). (23)

TAN-YR-ALLT (Caernarfonshire Slab) SH491523
Pit which incorporated Chwarel William Jones; opened in 1805 with material uphauled to the north, and a mill later built on waste on the far side of a public road. Worked intermittently, the 87 men of 1877 and 78 of 1904 were probably exceptional peaks. Some very small scale working up to 1980s. Was connected to Carnarfonshire S Q R via Fron Heulog. Stated to have had up to three water-wheels (one for pumping?). Later, part hived off as Plas Du.
Remains Flooded pit. Some sheds from late working; uphaulage incline formation, and vestiges of early buildings, including possible barracks, several wheel-pits and abutments of bridge across road. (16)

TWLL COED SH491522
Small hillside working producing green slate, was originally part of Tan-yr-allt; operating in the 1970s.

Remains Some modernised buildings, with H Owen & Sons saw table; Williams Porthmadog (Greaves type) dresser. (15)

TWLL LLWYD SH490518
Small hillside working, was part of Tan-yr-allt, operating on a small scale in the 1990s, using virtually pre-19th century methods of crowbarring rock.
Remains Small modern building with locally made diamond sawing machine. Interesting 'home-made' sawing machine on old lathe bed. Warehouse type weighing machines once common in small quarries. (12)

TYDDYN AGNES SH482517
Small pit working, active in 1860s/70s; may possibly have used water power. At its height up to 20 men, but in the 1900s as few as 2.
   Directly connected to C S Q R which passed through the site.
Remains Some building ruins and tramway formations; pit part filled with refuse. (7)

TŶ MAWR GREEN SH497523
Small pit working, formerly part of Nantlle Vale.
Remains Some small buildings. (25)

TŶ MAWR WEST (Tal-y-sarn West, Welsh Green) SH495524
Pit and hillside quarry developed into open pit. Access to pit by an open cut; later, as work progressed downwards, by Blondin. Active in 1860s with up to 40 men employed, but later very much fewer. Material reduced in a small mill and taken to the road by a long, shallow incline. Closed 1930s.
Remains Pit, adit and shaft. A number of buildings, mill, Blondin bases and concrete machinery base, possibly for late oil engine. Remnants of an interesting 'lash up' balanced wire incline, used in late re-working of tips. The fine, embanked incline is now much eroded. (21)

TY'N-LLWYN SH479522
Extremely small pit working.
Remains Pits and vestiges of buildings. To the south-west, several trials. (6)

TY'NYWEIRGLODD (Vale, Cockle Bank, Dorothea West) SH495523
Early 19th century pit/hillside working producing green and red slate. Worked intermittently with occasionally up to 100 men. Haulage incline

which may have been water powered, was replaced by a steam Blondin. The mill to the north-west of the pit was later powered by a gas, then an oil, engine. Product sent out by road, via an incline. Closed 1953.

Remains Site used for bulk fill; some vestiges of buildings and a house that clearly predates the quarry. Some concrete bases. Wheel-pits and vestiges of a haulage incline. The apparent tramway formation to Fronheulog is, in fact, a road built shortly before 1950s closure. (20)

WERN IFAN SH501535

Small early working.

Remains Small depression (behind buildings at terminus of Nantlle railway). (32)

CWM GWYRFAI
Region 4
Including quarries by the North Wales Narrow Gauge Railway

General

In this region working the Cambrian veins between Llanberis and Nantlle, the quarries were in two groups. A series of mostly small workings along Cwm Gwyrfai, and a compact cluster on Moel Tryfan contiguous with the Nantlle quarries. Both groups suffered isolation until the opening of the North Wales Narrow Gauge Railway, after which several particularly in the latter group became relatively important producers.

The development of the Moel Tryfan quarries swelled villages such as Rhosgadfan and Rhostryfan, with many dispersed small holdings very much following the Cwm Nantlle pattern. In Cwm Gwyrfai, Betws Garmon and Waunfawr became centres of quarrying settlement.

Few survived much beyond WW1, but there was some working in the Tryfan area until the 1970s.

Transport

Until the belated availability of the railway, Caernarfon could only be reached, at best, by cart. Opened in 1877 (final extension 1881 to Rhyd-ddu), the exclusively loco worked North Wales Narrow Gauge Railway was never a commercial success. Its opening coincided with the collapse of the slate market, so tonnages fell short of expectations. Had this line reached Caernarfon it might have been fared better, but its termination at Dinas, on the L&NWR Caernarfon-Afon Wen branch, entailed costly double handling of traffic for Caernarfon port. Also, this encouraged distribution via the main line network, rather than by coastal shipping, thus accelerating that port's decline.

Traffic dwindled during the first years of the new century and, apart from the Bryn-gwyn branch, the line was moribund by the time it was incorporated into the Welsh Highland Railway in 1923. This short-lived (closed-1937) development, which provided an extension to Porthmadog, was the product of various ambitious schemes to provide a network of narrow gauge railways, possibly powered by hydro generated electricity,

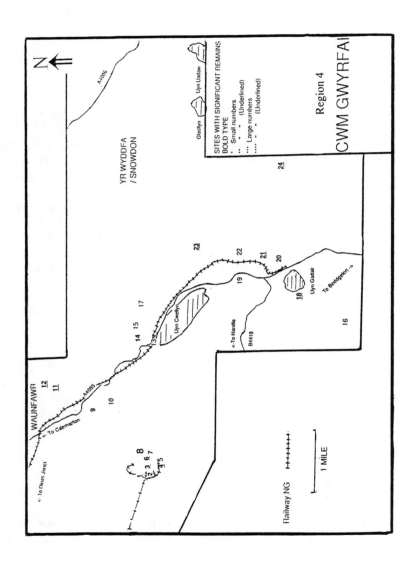

Region 4

CWM GWYRFAI

SITES WITH SIGNIFICANT REMAINS

BOLD TYPE
. Small numbers
.. " " (Underlined)
... Large numbers
.... " " (Underlined)

Glaslyn   Llyn Llydaw

YR WYDDFA / SNOWDON

WAUNFAWR

Llyn Cwellyn

Llyn Gadair

To Beddgelert →

To Nantlle

B4410

To Caernarfon →

To Rhyd-Ddu →

A4085

A4086

Railway NG +++++++

1 MILE

N

the most notable being the Porthmadog, Beddgelert and South Snowdon Railway which was, in the early 1900s, responsible for the never-used bridge and formations at Beddgelert. The WHR carried little slate traffic as, by 1923, the post-war mini-boom in slate had collapsed.

The old Standard Gauge route has been relaid in 2′ from Caernarfon to Dinas, with the intention of reviving the whole length of the WHR.

The NWNGR may be readily traced throughout its length. Several bridges remain *in situ*, albeit undecked, most being of a standard, steel pattern. Near Rhostryfan was the Tryfan junction for the Bryn-gwyn branch, which served the upper Nantlle valley quarries, and in fact carried most of the NWNGR's traffic. It consisted almost entirely of one impressive incline. From the head of this incline, three sub-branches led to various quarries. The first, which curved around the north of Moel Tryfan to Alexandra quarry, is particularly spectacular. End on to the Bryn-gwyn incline was the connection to Moel Tryfan quarry, and the third turned southwards to meet the foot of the Braich incline. This was extended in 1923 through Fron village to Fron quarry, and connected with Cilgwyn quarry (Region 3) via a spur off its horseshoe tipping line. All the system is readily traceable, with some rail visible at a road crossing in Fron village.

The main line continued from Tryfan junction to Cwm Gwyrfai where, just beyond Waunfawr, a spur swung north over the river. This branch intended to serve an ironstone mine, connected to the Treflan quarry incline.

At Betws Garmon another branch, readily traceable, ran south to Hafod-y-wern quarry.

Further on, Glanrafon quarry incline was connected by a triangular junction, and beyond, Rhos Clogwyn quarry was originally incline connected, but later a ropeway was used.

At the Rhyd-ddu terminus of the NWNGR a connection was planned to Llyn y Gadair quarry, but was never completed.

1. SH510552 Braich ** (R)
2. SH512549 Old Braich * (R)
3. SH513556 New Crown **
4. SH515548 Fron ** (R)
5. SH515551 Pretoria
6. SH515559 Moel Tryfan ** (R)
7. SH518556 Brynfferam *
8. SH519562 Alexandra *** (R)
9. SH530571 Hafod-y-wern * (R)

10. SH532565 Tŷ Coch
11. SH538582 Garreg Fawr ** (R)
12. SH539584 Treflan ** (R)
13. SH552552 Castell Cidwm
14. SH552562 Plas-y-nant * (R?)
15. SH553562 Brynmanllyn
16. SH557500 Bwlch Ddeilior
17. SH562565 Lefal Fawr
18. SH564519 Llyn y Gadair **
19. SH570533 Bryncwellyn
20. SH573526 Ffridd *
21. SH576530 Rhos Clogwyn ** (R)
22. SH577547 Bronyfedw
23. SH581540 Glanrafon ** (R)
24. SH600521 Bwlch Cwmllan **

ALEXANDRA (Cors y Bryniau) SH519562

A substantial open pit working with steam powered mills etc. and, from 1876, an extensive loco worked internal tramway system. Opened in the 1860s, from early diggings such as Y Foel. At its peak it produced 6000 tons p.a., employing over 200 men. Worked sporadically after W.W.1 and closed in the late 1930s but, after amalgamation with Moel Tryfan, extraction continued until the mid 1960s, all reduction taking place in the Moel Tryfan mill. Finished product was taken away by a most spectacular 'Himalayan' line down to the head of the Bryn-gwyn incline of the NWNGR.

Remains The gem of this site is the sinuous railway formation, with tipping area part way down. The road for bulk working the pit has much degraded the site. There are ruins of a double mill, generator house, Blondin bases and winding houses; possible traces of a water balance and various other structures. (8)

BRAICH (Braichmelyn, New Braich) SH510552

Pit developed from the old Bwlch-y-llan quarry, which had 18th century origins. Said to have experimented with wind-power for pumping in 1827. Substantially expanded in the 1870s with steam for mill drive, pumping and incline haulage, with a locomotive for internal movement. After a peak of 2614 tons with 124 men in 1882, output declined. Closed 1913, but some work was done in the 1920s.

Remains Large flooded pit with vestiges of a pumping engine house, and a cutting for pump-rods; ruins of a mill and other buildings. A nice incline with steps alongside leads to a lower-level working area with several dug-out shelters from tip reworking. A further incline, with remains of drum, makes connection with the Fron branch of NWNGR. There is a small trial at 501549 (with tip on far side of road) that may be associated with this quarry. (1)

BRONYFEDW SH577547
Trial only.
Remains Small excavation. (22)

BRYNCWELLYN (Cwellyn, Clogwyn Coch) SH570533
Small pit working, one pit accessed by a cutting, the other by a tunnel. Tipping on far side of the main road. Cart transport possibly to NWNGR.
Remains Little apart from pits. Ground disturbed by road and forestry. (19)

BRYNFFERAM SH518556
Two hillside workings in tandem, the upper deepened into a pit accessed by a tunnel from the lower working, which itself was accessed by a tunnel.

Worked sporadically from mid 19th century to early 20th century 1883 output of 252 tons with 18 men probably was an exceptional peak. Some attempt to re-work in late 1920s and 1940s. May have used NWNGR by carting to Fron.
Remains Pits and two tunnels; building vestiges on original working level of upper digging. On spoil at lower tunnel level is a sawing building with internal combustion engine base. There is a nice stone-lined cutting which formed an earlier access to the lower digging. A cart track leads to the road. (7)

BRYNMANLLYN (Caergwynion) SH553562
Very small hillside quarry; if anything was produced, it may have been carted to Plas-y-nant. Closed before the NWNGR opened.
Remains Working face only. (15)

BWLCH CWMLLAN (West Snowdon) SH600521
The original pit, possibly dating from the 1840s, had a small water powered mill reached by a tunnel. Later, probably following re-opening in the 1870s, a fresh excavation was made at a higher level with a new mill. Product went down to the access track by two inclines in tandem. Later a

third mill seems to have been built with a further access tunnel possibly obviating a chain incline. Until the NWNGR was opened, output was carted to Caernarfon.

Tonnages were moderate, mainly slab, and cannot have justified the large volumes of overburden which had to be removed, let alone the investment on site works and the cart road to Rhyd-ddu. The 1877 tonnage of 850 and around 50 men was probably about its peak, and by its 1914 closure its output with a dozen men would have been a quarter of that.

Remains On the upper site there are substantial remains of a mill, with a prominent wall which carried a launder for the water supply. There are two drum-houses built of country rock. Back from the upper one there is a chamber for an underfloor sheave predating the conventional drum-house. The lower drum-house appears to have had an overhead horizontal sheave.

On the lower site there is the small mill and wheel pit, some tramway formation, vestiges of the third mill and a weighbridge. Lower down there is a rake of barracks that would appear to date from a later period of working.

Above the site are the dams of two tandem ponds of conventional 'three ply' construction. There is also a small holding reservoir for the lower mill. At the top of the site, where the access track ends, there is some isolated excavation which may have been very early working.

There is a nice slate slab bridge on the access road that has been reinforced with 'T' bulb rail, and with what may have been round bar rail. There is also some bull head rail nearby. (24)

BWLCH DDEILIOR SH557500
A small pit working accessed by a cutting; may have employed up to 30 men but by 1883 output only 160 tons with 7 men. Material carted to Caernarfon. May have briefly used the NWNGR.
Remains Almost nothing. Site disturbed by forestry work. (16)

CASTELL CIDWM (Chwarel Goch) SH552552
A small hillside/pit operating in the mid 1870s; a dozen men producing a poor, irony slate.
Remains Very little owing to subsequent hard-core extraction. Vestiges of buildings, access track at original level; also a later track alongside the lake. Water available on site, but no evidence that water power was used. (13)

CILGWYN

Although this quarry was, latterly, a user of the NWNGR, it was for most of its long history very much part of the Nantlle scene. Therefore it has been included in Region 3. The formation of the 1923 connection from the Cilgwyn 'Horseshoe' tipping line to the head of the Bryn-gwyn incline, is clearly traceable.

FFRIDD (Ffridd Isaf) SH573526

Very small open working, close to Rhyd-ddu station but closed before the NWNGR was built. Possibly up to a dozen men.

Remains Distinctive slot like working; quite a lot of spoil for such a small site; two buildings now in reuse and an exceptionally fine powder house. (20)

FRON SH515548

Pit worked intermittently from the 18th century and developed mid 19th century. After amalgamation with Old Braich in the 1860s, the workforce was generally around 70-100 using a steam mill, (with 8 saws), which replaced or supplemented a water powered mill. Possibly had a water-balance haulage, later replaced by a chain incline. Production in the early 1880s well exceeded 1000 tons p.a., but then declined sharply. After a mid 1920s boost, when it was connected to the NWNGR, it survived on a small scale to post WW2.

Remains Extensive rubbish runs and retaining walls. Tunnel to Old Braich lost. Vestiges of several buildings including possibly two mills, one with wheel-pit and launder pillars. (4)

GARREG FAWR SH538582

A small pit working, possibly dating from the early 1800s, with a separate, later, underground development. Operated sporadically with up to 30 men; by 1883 was down to 6 producing 160 tons; closed shortly afterwards with revivals up to c1930. Output originally carted to Caernarfon. Work on an incline to the NWNGR was started, but probably never completed.

Remains An interesting site. There is a drum-house type building (for the incline that was or was not built?) which has been made into a two storey office or dwelling. There is also another two storey structure built to resemble a tiny 'castle'.

Apart from the usual dressing sheds, there is a brick building associated with the last working. (11)

GLANRAFON SH581540

Open quarry which, with the coming of the NWNGR, developed into the largest in the valley, producing 1725 tons with 92 men in 1882, increasing to over 400 men during the ensuing few years. Consisted of one big and several subsidiary workings. As the main working deepened, material may have been raised by a water balance, pumping being by flat rods from a remote water-wheel. At first, block was taken by incline to the large mills area (double mill with a central wheel), but later a tramway tunnel was cut, which also partly obviated pumping. Later a second, lower, tunnel was made.

From c1880 there were several locomotives in use. A short, followed by a longer, incline went down to make a triangular junction with the NWNGR. Closed c1915.

Remains Clearance and reworking have left only scant traces of the mill, its launder pillars, and other structures. There is an incline, possibly powered, for tipping. The access tunnels have collapsed. Below the site is the pit for the big pumping wheel, and some traces of the rod supports.

The most notable relics are the two storey barrack, and a large shed part way down the incline. The fine incline formations make a prominent feature. (23)

HAFOD-Y-WERN (Victoria) SH530571

A small working developed, with the coming of the railway, into a 100 plus man operation. Originally a hillside working, it deepened into three pits accessed by tunnels. Material was brought down by incline to a mill at valley floor level. Following some years of very small scale working, it closed in the mid 1920s. A branch of the NWNGR ran right to the mill.

Remains The site has been much disturbed by bulk excavation and clearance. Almost everything in the mills area has gone. There is the much decayed formation of one incline with a ruined drum-house at its head. The upper part of this incline was abandoned, and one can see how it was broken into part way down to serve an intermediate level. No drum-house was used for this truncated section, but a brake lever suggests that underfloor sheaves were used and may still remain buried. There are vestiges of a second incline and a small reservoir.

The railway branch track-bed is still prominent. (9)

LEFAL FAWR SH562565

Putative site of, at least, trials.

Remains Possible scratching. (17)

LLYN Y GADAIR (Gader Lake, Gader Wyllt) SH564519

A most interesting little site working at various times by open quarrying, pit and underground. Run as quarrymen's cooperative between 1883/6, with about 12 men. Worked sporadically up to WW1. Revived underground 1920/2 with 30 men. Prior to being able to load onto the railway at Rhyd-ddu, output was carted to Caernarfon.

Remains Several open faces, one developed into a pit with a two way incline to a mill which is built on top of an earlier structure. Two wheel-pits (pumping, haulage, and mill drive?) with a massive leat embankment.

At the back of the site is an open working with a small mill, the power source for which is unclear. It has a rubbish run, with some Hudson track *in situ*, and an incline down.

At the lower level is a relatively large, uncompleted, mill behind and above which is an unfinished tramway to an underground working that was never properly developed. There are ruins of several dressing sheds and other buildings, including a possible office. There is also a trial 200 yards to the east.

Overlaying a rubbish run from early open workings to the lake is the part-completed exit causeway, which was intended as a tramway or a railway branch. Part way along is a forge with a ramp up from it. At the far end are squat pillars for a projected bridge over marshy ground. (18)

MOEL TRYFAN SH515559

A modest pit working which expanded rapidly in the 1880s following rail connection. By 1882, 81 men were producing 1880 tons, which became almost 5000 tons p.a. by the mid 1890s. Material was taken by tunnel to a substantial mills area; loco hauled from the early 1870s.

Finished product went down a long incline to the Bryn-gwyn drum-head. Worked in conjunction with Alexandra until the 1970s.

Remains At the head of the fine incline are the ruins of a large steam mill and other buildings. The tunnels from the main pit (now contiguous with Alexandra) and a small pit have been lost. Above is a cleared area, believed to have been the site of a second mill; a few buildings partly stand, and there are vestiges of a possible ropeway system. (6)

NEW CROWN SH513556

A partly underground 1930s attempt to make a 'greenfield' opening. Success was very limited.

Remains The main working is on two levels; an initial working and an adit below, chambered up to break into the floor above. There are investigative tunnels off, including one that is 125 yards long.

The walls of a mill with a base for an internal combustion engine are standing. At 515555 is a curved slot working, with a culverted drain under the access cutting, and a small building (weigh-house?) on the rubbish run. Lower down the site is a run-in adit, probably a trial. The other run-in adits nearby are from much earlier Moel Tryfan trials. There are rail fragments on both sites, but presumably inter-site and external transport was by lorry. (3)

OLD BRAICH (Braich Rhyd) SH512549
A pit working not to be confused with Braich quarry. Older and developed earlier, it amalgamated with Fron 1868, after which a tunnel eliminated pumping and uphauling. Disused by the early 1900s.
Remains Pit with traces of chain incline. Mill in reuse. (2)

PLAS-Y-NANT (Garmon Vale, Plas Isaf) SH552562
Small hillside quarry, opened mid 19th century and closed around 1889, recorded as employing 28 men and producing 672 tons in 1883. An incline led to a small mill. Loadings were made onto the NWNGR at Plas-y-Nant Halt, possibly via a feeder tramway.
Remains Very little, apart from some small buildings, including a nice powder house and an incline formation. (14)

PRETORIA SH515551
Two small diggings worked by Brynfferam in the 19th century, with an attempt at re-opening in the early 1900s. Output trifling.
Remains Pit and collapsed access tunnel and, at lower level, an open working reached by a cutting. Much spoil, but no buildings. (5)

RHOS CLOGWYN (Clogwyn y Gwin) SH576530
An open pit working developed in the 1880s. A tunnel brought material to the substantial mills area. Originally, finished product was taken down an incline to be carted away. When connection was made with the NWNGR, this incline became disused and the output was trammed out on the level to a short incline to a siding, closure coming only a short time afterwards. When the quarry was revived on a small scale in the 1920s, slates appear to have been made in the quarry itself, possibly using a portable saw. Product went out through a second, lower, tunnel and down to the railway by a short ropeway. Final closure in the 1930s.
Remains The 'old' substantially built incline is a prominent feature, but the mills area has been entirely cleared. The two tunnels are open, and

the tramway and incline to the railway is obvious. At the lower level is the base of the ropeway down the railway and, inside the quarry, a late date dressing shed, with much trimming waste around. (21)

TREFLAN (Y Dreflan) SH539584

An open pit working, operating up to the mid 1880s, and, sporadically, later. Probably a maximum of about 30 men employed, producing around 7/800 tons p.a. Material was brought from two pits by tunnels to a dressing/mills area. Latterly, finished product went down an incline to a branch of the NWNGR.

Remains The two tunnels lead into the workings. Near the upper one is a fine stone office/workshop, probably adapted from an earlier dwelling. Near the lower tunnel is an extensive working area that has been totally cleared except for one small building. At the highest point of the site is a curious structure some 10' x 6½' x 13', open at the front at ground level and at the back at 'first floor' level. Its purpose is unknown. There is water available on site, but there is no evidence that it was used for power. What appears to be a leat is actually a channel to divert surface water from the workings.

There is the substantial incline down to valley floor level, with a little smithy near where it crosses a road. There is an adit from a trial probably associated with this quarry at 552587. (12)

TŶ COCH SH532565

A series of four unsuccessful underground trials.
Remains Traces of excavations. (10)

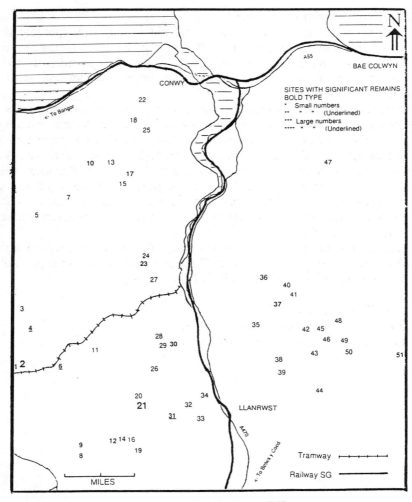

Region 5   LLANRWST

LLANRWST
Region 5
Including quarries served by Cedryn Tramway

General

The north-easterly extremity of the Caernarfonshire Cambrian veins outcrop on either sides of the lower Conwy valley. In spite of the sparseness and poor quality of the occurrences, the availability of the river as a transport route meant that the region was once the source of a significant proportion of Welsh output.

The quarries to the east of the river were tiny and ephemeral, yielding at best a coarse slab or block. Those to the west generally produced a better product but, apart from a few in the vicinity of the lakes, were very small. Although most were open quarries, the first Welsh underground workings were in this area.

The abundant availability of superior slate, and easier transport elsewhere, caused the region's early decline, there being little significant output after the 1880s.

Dispersed over a wide area, the small and mostly short lived quarries had little social or economic impact on this predominantly agricultural and lead mining region. Indeed Cedryn and Cwm Eigiau, the two largest units, were mainly manned by barrackers from Bethesda. Trefriw was the only settlement to substantially expand due to slate, but this was because of its function as a shipping point.

Transport

Any slate not for local use was carted to the river, mostly to Trefriw which was a quite substantial port, handling in the 1830s around 3000 tons of slate p.a. (much from further up valley, region 6). Some loadings were also made at Tal-y-cafn. The river boats occasionally ventured along the coast, but most transshipped at Conwy.

The L&NWR which reached Llanrwst in 1863, being on the wrong side of the river from the productive quarries, brought little benefit.

The one notable tramroad was the 2'G. line from Cedryn & Cwm Eigiau to the riverside near Dolgarrog. It functioned from the early 1860s to c1888.

The Eigiau to Cedryn mill section is traceable, and from near the Cedryn mill it becomes a road. This road does not strictly follow the tramway route, as it was in fact the bed of a temporary steam-worked line for the construction of the Eigiau reservoir, substantially following the old tramway route, but making a diversion to avoid a short incline at 745664 near Pwll-du, where there are some excellent stone embankments.

The line reached the head of a 3 pitch self-acting incline at 765672. This incline was rebuilt as a single pitch haulage incline for the Eigiau reservoir construction. It made use of the upper 2 pitches of the slate incline, but since the lowest pitch of the original incline turned slightly northwards, a new lower portion was built to achieve a straight run. It was afterwards further reused in conjunction with the Cowlyd water-works railway, for the building of that reservoir, the incline and railway being retained for maintenance purposes until c1980. The shed for the incline haulage engine is extant, and the engine shed is still in use as a workmen's hut. The railway formation now forms a trackway.

The bridge under the road of the more modern incline survives, but the tunnel which took the earlier line under the road, and the track across the marsh to the riverside, has been obliterated.

The incline formation also serves as a pipe route for the Dolgarrog works Hydro-electric plant, and a feature of the area is the water supply for this plant. Near Cedryn quarry is Llyn Eigiau, now much reduced in size following the 1926 dam collapse. The breached dam and the consequent rock strewn scour can be seen. This reservoir is connected to Llyn Cowlyd by a tunnel, from where overground pipes run to the works. Coedty lake is also part of this scheme, and its pipeline joins the main pipe near the head of incline. There is a network of catchment leats which illustrate, on an enlarged and modern scale, the sort of leatwork that was associated with the water supply for many quarries.

Particularly at Trefriw, there are vestiges of wharves at the shipping points.

1. SH699634 Caerhun
2. SH702635 Cwm Eigiau *** (R)
3. SH702663 Dulyn
4. SH705654 Melynllyn **
5. SH706709 Nant Canolbren
6. SH719635 Cedryn ** (R)
7. SH726717 etc. Bwlch y Ddeufaen
8. SH736594 Bwlch y Geuallt *

9. SH736596 Clogwyn William *
10. SH738733 Tal-y-fan *
11. SH741643 Siglen
12. SH742601 Manod *
13. SH743733 Ffriddlys
14. SH746602 Cornel *
15. SH748723 Ffridd Ddwy Ffrwd
16. SH751601 Cynllwyd
17. SH755727 Coed Mawr *
18. SH756757 Llechan Uchaf
19. SH757597 Tal-y-llyn *
20. SH758620 Hafod Arthen
21. SH759618 Clogwyn y Fuwch ***
22. SH759762 Waun y Fedwen
23. SH759687 Rowlyn *
24. SH760688 Pen-lan
25. SH760745 Trecastell
26. SH767630 Cefn Cyfarwydd
27. SH767672 Porthllwyd
28. SH770647 Ffridd
29. SH773642 Ardda
30. SH775642 Cae Rhobin *
31. SH776612 Pen-y-ffridd **
32. SH782618 Pontycarw
33. SH788610 Gwydir
34. SH802627 Cae Ffynnon
35. SH811652 Penbryncaled
36. SH817673 Pennant
37. SH825654 Cefn Madog *
38. SH826634 Hen Ffridd
39. SH827627 Henblas
40. SH827666 Pennant Ucha
41. SH829663 Gwern-bwys
42. SH831651 Ffridd Uchaf
43. SH834637 Cefn Coch
44. SH835624 Rhwng y Ddwyffordd
45. SH838650 Chwythlyn
46. SH840646 Nant-y-wrach
47. SH841727 Gofer
48. SH843657 Wenlli
49. SH844642 Liberty

50.   SH851638 Lydan
51.   SH881635 Tyddyn Uchaf *

ARDDA *(Pen-y-cefn, Tylcia)* SH773642
A tiny hillside working, possibly first quarter of 18th century.
Remains Three excavations and access track. (29)

BWLCH Y DDEUFAEN *(Cae Coch)* SH726717
Also 720720 & 716721. Tiny workings without surface shelter of any
kind; probably worked on an 'as required' basis.
Remains Excavations only. (7)

BWLCH Y GEUALLT SH736594
Very small open working.
Remains Rock face with signs of hand drilling; quantity of trimming
waste. Only vestige of a building is some distance away, and may have
been unconnected. (8)

CAE FFYNNON SH802627
Tiny digging, shaly material
Remains Excavation. (34)

CAE RHOBIN *(Conway Vale)* SH775642
A small and primitive open quarry on a difficult site, with workings
tramming to a mills area. Intermittently worked over many years with
final closure in the 1920s. The present public road provided access.
Remains Two buildings, one sunken with steps access and a stocking
area in front; the other with engine holding down bolts, and possibly
contained a saw. Much waste and trimmings, some tramway formations.
Two small pillars of unknown purpose. Possibility of water power but no
evidence of its use. (30)

CAERHUN SH699634
A fraudulent hiving off of a useless part of Cwm Eigiau in 1866, but
never separately worked.
Remains NW workings of Cwm Eigiau. (1)

CEDRYN SH719635
Hillside and possibly underground workings on four levels, developed
c1825 from a remote vernacular site. A road built in 1830 provided
access until superseded by the tramway in the 1860s, the incline and

mill dating from about the same time. Following very mixed fortunes when up to about 50 men were employed, it closed in 1870.

Remains On the site itself, a few ruined dressing sheds etc. A well engineered cart road rises past a rake of barracks to the original working. The incline has a collapsed drum-house part way down, where it was truncated to suit later lower working. A third working was reached by a tunnel. The embankment that connected to the mill across the valley is obvious, but the wooden bridge over the river has gone.

The mill is ruinous; there is a wheel-pit alongside and mountings, apparently subsequently raised, for the drive shaft. Circular as well as sandsaws may have been used; the Hunter-sawn ends now on site were probably carried down from Cwm Eigiau. There is an unusual rubbish disposal trackway. Alongside the mill there is a small reservoir and some leatwork. The tramroad can be readily traced. (6)

CEFN COCH (Pen y Gloddfa) SH834637
Possibly not slate.
Remains Pit at roadside. (43)

CEFN CYFARWYDD SH767630
Trial only?
Remains Excavation. (26)

CEFN MADOG SH825654
A small shallow working. Surprisingly, an 1867 sale listed a 10 hp steam engine, 2 saws and 2 planers.
Remains Rubbish runs, tramway, mill building in reuse. (37)

CHWYTHLYN SH838650
(Also 837652) Tiny diggins for crude flags.
Remains Excavations only. (45)

CLOGWYN WILLIAM SH736596
Tiny open working on a shelf on cliff face. An abortive 1920 re-opening proposal included a ropeway.
Remains Dressing areas with stock of 13 x 7 slates; at foot of rubbish are a number of slabs, possibly intended for the production of hones. (9)

CLOGWYN Y FUWCH SH759618
Possibly the first underground working in Wales. The series of openings up the hillside and the use of cut-and-cover entrances are redolent of

Lakeland practice, and it is tempting to attribute this to William Turner a Westmorland man who operated here in 1798-1800, prior to making his mark at Blaenau.

An unusual site with workings on 6 levels, going into a near vertical scarp on steeply sloping ground. Until c1820 when a transporter incline was built, material was sledged down to road level for carting to Trefriw. In spite of producing a small irony and perishable slate, work continued into the 20th century. Output around 200/300 tons p.a.

Remains At the lowest level there is a working area and a chamber going straight in from the rock face, accessed through waste tipped from above by a cut-and-cover tunnel. Just above, at foot of incline, is a building and above this is the non-productive Level 2. Level 3, a considerable distance above, has a twisting strike tunnel leading to some pillared chambering that just breaks into level 4. Outside there are several dressing sheds, those beyond the incline were reached by a bridge.

Level 4 is chambered in for some 300'; at the far end there are footboards still *in situ* for a roofing tunnel development. Underground there is small forge and on the surface there are several buildings, including a small smithy and the remains of the remote type drum-house at the head of the main incline.

Level 5 has, underground, largely been chambered out from level 4. On the surface, buildings include a curious circular construction with a rock 'bench' around the inside, possibly a powder store. There are traces of a slideway down to Level 4. Level 6 has some traces of small buildings; underground it has been chambered through from below. There are some further trials above. There is some Thomas Hughes rail on site, and reputedly some of the lines were plateways. (21)

COED MAWR SH755727
Small hillside quarry, shaly material, early 20th century?
Remains Some buildings with brick quoins. (17)

CORNEL (Mynydd Deulyn, Coed-y-fron) SH746602
A small hillside quarry developed downwards into a pit. Unmechanised until an oil-engined diamond saw was installed during an attempt at revival c1920. Transport by cart down valley.

Remains The pit has been partly worked down to the level of the (collapsed) access tunnel. A nice weigh-house has been rebuilt. The office buildings are now a dwelling, with the base of an oil-engine alongside.

There was a Hone mill at Hafod Arthen (SH759620) which may have dealt with product from this quarry. (14)

CWM EIGIAU SH702635

A small hillside quarry dating from c1827. Repeatedly re-developed from the 1850s with up to 60 men employed. In 1865, an extension of the Cedryn tramway replaced carting. In spite of considerable effort and expense, output remained well under 1000 tons p.a. Closed in 1874.

Remains A most interesting site. Workings on 5 terraces with an incline, (which apparently over lies an older incline) to a mill area, with some exploratory work above drum-house level. This incline, in turn, seems to be overlain by a later level route. A curious short incline may have been a temporary uphaulage which, it has been suggested, was made self-acting by loading rubbish into down going trucks.

There are traces of at least 4 water powered mills on the site; the one alongside the massive leat embankment, which seems to have had circular saws, and probably being the earliest (mid 1850s?); followed by one in front of it which had sandsaws, drive being carried by unusual external shafting. The third, (1860s) mill, which had at least one Hunter saw, is at an angle to it and may have been intended to be steam driven, but could have been driven via crown gears from the No.2 mill shafting. The final mill is on the other side of the pit of the 30′ wooden water wheel, but was probably never completed. There are some small supply reservoirs and leatwork. There is a barracks, workshop, powder house and traces of several other buildings. During successive operating periods undoubtedly redundant structures were robbed to build new ones, making it difficult to interpret the site.

At least one cast iron Thomas Hughes sleeper and several lengths of rail have been found. A curious relic for such an isolated site is a rock cannon.

Beside the tramway formation to Cedryn, the earlier cart road is traceable. (2)

CYNLLWYD SH751601

Trial.
Remains Excavation. (16)

DULYN SH702663

Possible trials for hones?
Remains Excavations. (3)

FFRIDD SH770647

Tiny underground trial.
Remains Run-in adit. (28)

FFRIDD DDWY FFRWD SH748723
Trial.
Remains Surface scratching. (15)

FFRIDDLYS (Craig Celynin) SH743733
Putative site.
Remains Possible ground disturbance. (13)

FFRIDD UCHAF SH831651
Tiny open quarry.
Remains Two excavations. (42)

GOFER SH841727
Rather bigger than most of the shaly diggings in the area.
Remains Roadside digging, also little working at 838726 that may be part
of the same small enterprise. (47)

GWERN-BWYS SH829663
Hillside quarry, shaly product.
Remains Excavation and rubbish runs. (41)

GWYDIR SH788610
Open quarry, latterly used for building stone. Just possible that it
produced slate earlier.
Remains Quarry face, much overgrown. (33)

HAFOD ARTHEN SH758620
Small Hone quarry.
Remains Quarrying site now obliterated. Mill now incorporated into a
dwelling. (20)

HENBLAS SH827627
Small flag quarry.
Remains Excavation only. (39)

HEN FFRIDD SH826634
Tiny open working.
Remains Digging at roadside. (38)

LIBERTY SH844642
Very small.
Remains Slight traces of excavation. (49)

LLECHAN UCHAF SH756757
Possibly very ancient site.
Remains Excavation, tips, collapsed adit. (18)

LYDAN SH851658
Tiny shaly digging.
Remains Small pit. (50)

MANOD (Clogwyn Manod, Crafnant) SH742601
Partly underground, operated late 19th century, briefly revived in the early 1900s.
Remains On the upper level, a working that was subsequently worked out from below; some small buildings including a round powder house. On the intermediate level there are 2 dressing sheds; a large opening, broken into from below and with a small tunnel leading off; beyond is a pit. At the lowest level, a collapsed tunnel and the remains of a hand sawing shed.

There are nice, well engineered, tracks to the road from all three levels. (12)

MELYNLLYN SH705654
This was a hone quarry exploiting a high-grade, close-grained slate. Operated in mid/late 19th century and revived in the 1900s, closing in 1908.

From a tiny underground working, rock went by a reputedly wooden-railed tramway to a sawmill. There, after splitting to about a ½" thickness, slabs were sawn into rectangles, typically 6 to 8" x 1½ to 2", and hand-finished into stones, for sharpening razors and scalpels. About 6 men produced only a dozen tons per year, but this was offset by the high value of the product, which was sent to London via Tal-y-cafn Station.
Remains Adit, tramway formation and building ruin, containing the crank mechanism of the one sandsaw. (4)

NANT CANOLBREN SH706709
Several small pits, trials only?
Remains Traces of digging. (5)

NANT-Y-WRACH SH840646
Extremely small shale digging.
Remains In forestry. (46)

PENBRYNCALED SH811652
Tiny digging for flags.
Remains Excavation. (35)

PEN-LAN SH760688
This quarry was the subject of doubtful promotions circa 1860; it is highly unlikely that any saleable product resulted.
Remains The location is conjectural, but is likely to be this adit which penetrates a mere 6 to 10', with no obvious means of access. (24)

PENNANT SH817673
Roadside quarry, building block?
Remains Excavation. (36)

PENNANT UCHA SH827666
Hillside quarry, building block?
Remains Excavation and rubbish runs. (40)

PEN-Y-FFRIDD (Llanrhychwyn) SH776612
Open quarry, partly underground, operating late 18th century to 1865. Finished product carted via Llanrhychwyn to Trefriw quay.
Remains A very early example of underground working, and may even have predated Clogwyn y Fuwch. Site now forested, the only structure is a smithy(?) in fair condition. Stated never to have had any railed transport but a set of wheels on an axle were found on the site. An eerie series of chambers in the original working face, dip down on 5 levels; pillars are so slender as to virtually form one vast cavern. Much fallen rock from old face and from roof.

There are no barracks on site, but it is believed that a house in Trefriw was used from the 1820s to house men living a distance away. If so, this is a very early example of proper barracking, as opposed to men sleeping rough in quarry buildings. (31)

PONTYCARW (Tai Isaf) SH782618
Small, possibly only a trial.
Remains In forestry. (32)

PORTHLLWYD (Dolgarrog) SH767672
Small slab quarry.
Remains Tiny face. (27)

RHWNG Y DDWYFFORDD SH835624
Tiny shale digging.
Remains Excavation. (44)

ROWLYN SH759687
Although a company was floated around 1860 to exploit this
underground site, it is unlikely that much, if any, saleable product came
out.
Remains Excavation with tip; run-in adit; vestige of building, (forge?).
Well engineered track. (23)

SIGLEN SH741643
Possible trial.
Remains Excavation only. (11)

TAL-Y-FAN SH738733
A tiny, primitive quarry, possibly 16th century; two small faces worked.
Remains Two dressing sheds, another tiny building and a powder house.
The power-drilled holes are from the early 1900s, when it was
temporarily revived with about 6 men. In spite of its comparative
insignificance, there is a well engineered road to the site. (10)

TAL-Y-LLYN SH757597
A small, long abandoned, open working; going into an overhang, accessed
by a cutting.
Remains Large trees growing out of rubbish runs; vestiges of one, or
possible two, dressing sheds; access track. (19)

TRECASTELL SH760745
Open quarry, possibly not slate.
Remains Excavation only. (25)

TYDDYN UCHAF SH881635
Although this seems to have only produced block for building (1880s?),
sawing appears to have been planned.
Remains Small digging; some stonework suggests attempt at using water
power. (51)

WAUN Y FEDWEN SH759762
Trial.
Remains Small pit. (22)

WENLLI SH843657
Very small; block for local use?
Remains Tiny pit. (48)

BETWS-Y-COED
Region 6
Including quarries served by L&NWR Dyffryn Conwy Branch

General

This region, in the valleys of the Machno, the Lledr and the Llugwy which all confluence with the Conwy at, or near, Betws-y-coed, mostly worked the north-eastern extremity of the Blaenau Ffestiniog Ordovician veins, with those to the north of Dolwyddelan finding outliers of the Cambrian rock.

Until well into the 19th century the quarries in the region were very small, most catering only for local needs.

The development of better and more abundant occurrences during the 19th century led to significant long term quarrying at Dolwyddelan, Capel Curig, Penmachno and, to a lesser extent, at Betws-y-coed itself.

As in the lower Conwy valley, activity was too disparate for any significant quarrying communities to develop, other than Dolwyddelan. However, the hamlet of Cwm Penmachno was almost entirely created by slate as was the remarkable little Rhiwddolion settlement, the latter now surviving almost exclusively as holiday homes.

Transport

Traditionally, all product going out of the area was faced with the long cartage to Trefriw, the highest point of practicable navigation on the Conwy; yet several units managed to thrive.

From 1868, quarries such as Rhos and Cwm Machno could load onto the L&NWR at Betws-y-coed, helping them to survive to the mid 20th century era of lorry transport. The 1879 extension of the railway up the Lledr valley to Blaenau Ffestiniog benefited the Dolwyddelan quarries, (which up to 1810 did not even have a road!), although only Ty'n-y-bryn had direct rail connection.

Although there were several railway proposals, such as lines from Hafod Las and from Cwm Machno to Betws-y-coed, the sole quarry lines were the Rhos/Foel tramway which led to a loading point at Pont Cyfyng, and the short cross-valley line of Chwarel Fedw.

1.   SH683479 Cwm Ddynhadog

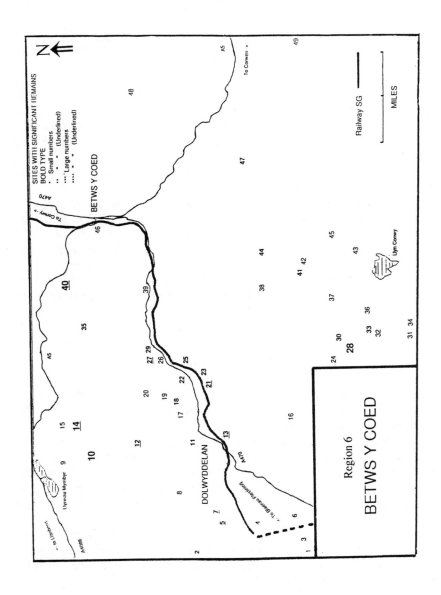

SITES WITH SIGNIFICANT REMAINS
BOLD TYPE
. Small numbers
: " " (Underlined)
… " " Large numbers
…. " " (Underlined)

BETWS Y COED

Region 6

BETWS Y COED

Railway SG

MILES

2. SH683520 Chwarel Owen Parry *
3. SH687486 Chwarel Gethin **
4. SH697497 Moel Dyrnogydd
5. SH698512 Hendre **
6. SH699487 Bwlch Gorddinan *
7. SH700514 Coed Mawr **
8. SH709530 Ffridd
9. SH716569 Bryn Engan
10. SH717556 Foel ***
11. SH721521 Chwarel Ddu *
12. SH722540 Penrhiw **
13. SH726519 Pompren **
14. SH729564 Rhos ****
15. SH729568 Cae Gwegi
16. SH732492 Cwm Penamnen
17. SH734523 Llan
18. SH735526 Chwarel Sion Jones *
19. SH738529 Adwy'r Dŵr
20. SH740539 Ffridd Bryn-moel
21. SH742521 Ty'n-y-bryn ** (R)
22. SH744528 Prince Llywelyn *
23. SH746522 Penllyn *
24. SH748472 Glyn Aber (tunnel)
25. SH748525 Chwarel Fedw *
26. SH748528 Buarthau
27. SH749537 Rhiw-goch **
28. SH751470 Cwm Machno ***
29. SH752539 Ty'n-y-fallen *
30. SH755474 Sŵch *
31. SH756452 Foel Rudd
32. SH756464 Foel
33. SH756466 Rhos-goch *
34. SH758452 Tan-y-rhiw
35. SH767558 Bwlch-gwyn *
36. SH769464 Hafodyredwydd
37. SH777476 Penybedw
38. SH779499 Moel Pen-y-bryn
39. SH779533 Chwarel Glyn Lledr
40. SH779562 Hafod Las ****
41. SH783483 Pen-y-bont *
42. SH786482 Llechwedd Oernant

43.　　SH790469 Bryniau Duon
44.　　SH792498 Hafod Dwyryd *
45.　　SH793476 Afon Oernant
46.　　SH797552 Beaver Pool
47.　　SH819509 Hwylfa *
48.　　SH849545 Bryn-haul
49.　　SH862492 Rhyd-goch

ADWY'R DŴR SH738529
Small underground working, possibly associated with the Prince Llywelyn quarry.
Remains Collapsed working; flooded access tunnel. (19)

AFON OERNANT SH793476
Trial only.
Remains Digging and run-in adit below. (45)

BEAVER POOL (Llyn yr Afanc) SH797552
A small hillside working, possibly active around 1850s.
Remains Possible vestiges in forestry. (46)

BRYN ENGAN SH716569
Open quarry with adit to limited chambering.
Remains Dressing shed, small building, and tiny annexe with fireplace. Thomas Hughes rail on the ground. (9)

BRYN-HAUL SH849545
Putative site.
Remains No evidence of slate working. (48)

BRYNIAU DUON SH790469
Trial.
Remains Digging and 2 run-in levels. (43)

BUARTHAU SH748528
Unsuccessful trials?
Remains Possibly three disturbances in forestry. (26)

BWLCH GORDDINAN (Ffridd y Bwlch) SH699487
(These names may also have been applied to Chwarel Gethin.)
Underground; almost certainly an unsuccessful trial, possibly in

association with Chwarel Gethin.
Remains Adit. (6)

BWLCH-GWYN (Chwarel Rhiwddolion, East Arfon) SH767558
Open quarry of moderate size, operating late 19th/early 20th century. Material trammed some 150 yards to a mill which may have been water-powered. Product, predominantly slab, was carted to Betws-y-coed.
Remains Site is now in forestry but some buildings are discernable, including the old Bwlch-gwyn farmhouse that was reused for the quarry operation. Outside of the afforested area are the abandoned dwellings of the quarry village of Rhiwddolion, which included terraces and a chapel. This community outlasted the WW1 closure of the quarry, the quarrymen finding alternative employment in Blaenau Ffestiniog.

There is a delightful slate flagged path leading from the village to the chapel and quarry. Much of the access road is traceable. (35)

CAE GWEGI SH729568
Trial, attempting to reach the Rhos vein.
Remains Short adit and spoil. (15)

CHWAREL DDU (Bwlch y Beudy, Dolwyddelan) SH721521
A small open working, developed into a pit on three floors with a trial underground. At least late 18th century but anecdotally much older. Operated sporadically until the 1850s when, for a few years, reputedly up to 70 men produced some 700 tons p.a., with steam for hauling and pumping. During this time the road to Blaenau was cut through the tip. Idle until the 1920s, when a few men worked, using an oil engine.
Remains During roadworks in the 1980s, the site was landscaped, obliterating the winding house, the vestiges of dressing sheds, and the abutments of the tip bridge. At this time, relics of iron sheathing for wooden rails, and also a *Dog-bone* Thomas Hughes sleeper, were found. (11)

CHWAREL FEDW (Y Fedw) SH748525
An open working; material was brought down a short incline and across the river Lledr by a causeway and bridge; latterly into the Prince Llewellyn mill. Cartage to Trefriw. Closed by 1889.
Remains Site and incline now almost lost in forestry. The incline is cut by a forestry road, and the rail underpass is blocked. There are drum-house walls, and vestiges of several dressing sheds. The causeway and (rebuilt) bridge are a prominent and pleasing feature. (25)

CHWAREL GETHIN (Chwarel Andreas, Chwarel Ifan Lloyd, Gorddinan, Crimea) SH687486

A small underground quarry active over several short periods from the 1840s to 1900s, with around half a dozen men. Carted to Dolwyddelan, latterly via the road built to service the construction of the railway tunnel.

Remains On 3 levels. Upper; an old open working, later adit and chambering; small building. Middle; adit and chambering, partly breaking out to daylight; a roofing shaft comes up from below. Lower; adit is run in. The much degraded and tipped over incline formation possibly had a horizontal sheave. Ground disturbance to the north may have been an earlier working. No mill; the circular sawn ends on the tips date from the early 1900s when a saw bench with a portable engine was in use. (3)

CHWAREL GLYN LLEDR SH779533

Possible site.
Remains Lost in forestry. (39)

CHWAREL OWEN PARRY SH683520 (etc.)

Three separate trial adits; the middle one seems to have possible yielded product.
Remains Traces of a small building. (2)

CHWAREL SION JONES SH735526

Small open pit.
Remains The modernised house may have been connected. (18)

COED-MAWR (Ty'n-y-ddôl) SH700514

A small open pit with a short, intermittent life from about 1870. Haulage up and pumping possibly originally by water-wheel (source of water uncertain, but said to be by inverted siphon from Ceunant Ty'n-ddôl); later by steam engine on the rubbish bank. Unlikely to have had any mill. Transport by cart down valley.

Remains Several buildings including engine house and a forge. A curious small square aperture penetrates the retaining wall alongside the incline formation, presumably for the pump pipe. (7)

CWM FYNHADOG SH683479 etc.

Open quarry; probably no significant product.
Remains Hillside excavation. Also, traces of an associated underground trial at 675475. (1)

CWM MACHNO SH751470

Basically two hillside workings, the lower deepened into a pit with some underground extraction. There were three mills, successively water-wheel, turbine and internal combustion powered. The extensive rail network used locos.

Originally known as Tan-y-rhiw, it operated almost continuously from at least 1818 to 1962, employing upwards of 100 up to WW2; it only finally closed due to lack of skilled manpower. A remarkable record since, although there were several proposals for rail connection (the most bizarre being through Rhiw-bach, Region 9, via their drainage tunnel), output had to be carted, initially to Trefriw wharf, and later to Betws-y-coed station. In the 1900s a traction engine replaced horses; later steam, and then motor, lorries were used.

Remains The mills area has been landscaped, leaving only two small buildings and part of one mill standing. The remarkable crenallated boundary wall has gone, and some tips removed so as to fill the pit of the lower working obliterating its uphaulage, which latterly was air-winch powered. The inclines which served the terraces of this lower working are much degraded, but one drum-house and a fine revetted tramway formation survive.

The most prominent feature is the big slate-paved trwnc incline which brought block to the mills from the upper working and, due to lack of tipping space, doubled as an uphaulage for rubbish from the lower working. Near its head is the pit of the water-wheel which originally wound it. Alongside is the formation which carried a balance tank, after it was converted to a water-balance. This formation, which is pierced by a fine accommodation arch, is twice as long as the trwnc ramp, suggesting that a sheave was used to increase mechanical advantage. At its head is a massive structure, with access steps, which carried the header tank. As well as fabricated pipe, there are some wooden launders.

The four inclines connecting the levels of the upper working are in good order, some with drums etc.; one has remnants of a wooden bridge. There are vestiges of several superseded inclines. On an intermediate level there are parts of a tripod crane and, nearby, an adit (roof dropped a few yards in) has been doored as a store.

There are several other buildings on these upper levels, including a hydro-compressor house with piping.

Above the site is the bed of Llyn Pen-rhiw which provided the water supply. A late trial at 748468 is lost in forestry.

Much of the village, including several rows of single-storey cottages, some still in occupation, was quarry property. (28)

CWM PENAMNEN SH732492

This was the centre of a number of trials; probably only the one directly on the hillside behind (Chwarel David Hughes) was productive.

Remains Besides the small mound of waste at this point, and the open quarrying behind, there are traces of work on the forested hillside ½ mile to the north; several about 2/300 yards to the south; and two to the south-east on the eastern side of the path. (16)

FFRIDD SH709530

Possible trial for hones, could be associated with Pen-rhiw.
Remains Trifling excavation. (8)

FFRIDD BRYN-MOEL SH740539

Trial.
Remains Possible adit. (20)

FOEL (Bryn Cyple, Tredir, Moel Siabod) SH717556

Open quarry, c1835; developed around 1860 on five levels with tunnel access to the pit on two levels. There were two mills on the site itself, the upper one being powered by a water-wheel, possibly with a sandsaw; a lower one, which may have supplanted it, had a turbine or Pelton wheel driving circular(?) saws. Due to water shortage, a further mill was built at Pont Cyfyng (735570) equipped with sandsaws, possibly later replaced by circular saws.

Material went out by an incline to a tramway which led, via further inclines, to the road; an extension passed under the road to the Pont Cyfyng mill. After the lower mill was abandoned, this extension was truncated and turned to serve a loading point at 734572, from where product would have been carted to Betws. Closed in the 1880s but continued to trade, renting their inclines to the Rhos company.

Remains At the lowest level there is a small mill building with vestiges of the turbine supply and some other structures, including a possible barrack; also a tunnel to the pit. Above, connected by an incline, there is another working level with ruins of a small mill with launder pillars and a wall screening the wheel which, unusually, is traversely sited. There are some other structures including a forge. There are a number of dressing sheds, the most notable being a rake of three with cantilevered slab roofs. A second tunnel has, like the one below, been blocked to keep the pit flooded up as a water supply for Rhos. At this level is a possible horse-whim circle, and a substantial rubbish-run that has been resited to enable the workings to progress. There are several much degraded internal inclines, and a further possible barracks.

There is some interesting leatwork on the hillside above, and a small reservoir that was seemingly inadequate to supply either of the on-site mills.

The main tramway is traceable past the vestiges of a third barracks, and past the Rhos reservoirs to the head of a two-pitch incline, with conventional drum-house. The lower pitch, steeper and shorter than the upper one, has a remote type drum-house and the two pitches are connected by a neatly excavated swan-neck loop. The roadside buildings and dwellings at the foot of the incline are undoubtedly connected to the quarry.

Below the road is the ruin of the Pont Cyfyng mill, with a pit for a breast shot wheel. There are massive slate bases for the reciprocating sand saws. The old incline down under the road is not traceable. (10)

FOEL SH756464
Small hillside working, latterly worked by Cwm Machno; reached by an access track known locally as 'Burma Road'.
Remains Excavations and tips. (32)

FOEL RUDD SH756452
A series of small open diggings.
Remains Shallow pits. (31)

GLYN ABER SH748472
Not a quarry, but the end of the Rhiw-bach drainage tunnel. (See region 9)
Remains The excavation waste and some quarry waste form a now afforested platform. Underground, there are rails *in situ*. (24)

HAFOD DWYRYD (Pen-y-bryn) SH792498
Small, but had a water-powered sandsaw.
Remains Some traces of buildings. (44)

HAFODYREDWYDD SH769464
Tiny underground working.
Remains In forestry; rubbish and access track traceable. (36)

HAFOD-LAS SH779562
A terraced working, deepened into a pit. Opened in the 1850s; by the late 1860s it was producing up to 1400 tons p.a. of mainly slab, with around 50 men but, except for a few early 20th century years when building

block boosted the tonnage to over 2000, later output was very small. After WW1 closure, it was re-equipped in the early 1920s with air-drills being used for the first time, but finally closed 1929. In spite of its small size it was lavishly equipped with up to 10 Hunter saws, 6 circular saws, 2 sandsaws and eventually, a diamond saw, as well as planers and polishers. It was one of very few quarries to enamel on site.

A tramway to Betws-y-coed station was planned but never built.

Remains At the top of the much degraded quarry area is a collapsed hoisting derrick. On the uppermost level 6, a tunnel takes a tramroad formation past a weigh-house, to the head of an incline down to level 5. This has a chamber for underfloor sheaves. The tramroad formation continues past dressing sheds to the head of an incline down to level 4. This level 6/4 incline has an unsually narrow drum-house. Just above it is a quaint powder house with slate slab roof and slate floor.

Below, on level 5, is a similar tunnel with a formation leading past a weigh-house and the head of the level 5/4 incline, passing under the level 6/4 incline to a tipping area. The underfloor sheaves of the level 5/4 incline (which has vestiges of longitudinal wooden sleepers), are complete with the two remote control levers (offering a self-wrapping action in either direction of operation).

Level 4 is the main mills area. It has a similar tunnel from the workings as level 6, and a cut and cover tunnel through waste. There is a weigh-house and traces of a complex tramway layout, and a most elegant pair of mills. Both depart from the conventional layout in having a double roof, the earlier (1863) having fine pillars and lintels to support the roof trusses. The later (1866) mill has an iron gantry to support the roof and to hold line shafting; it also has the most unusual doorways.

Between the two mills is a wheel-pit (later holding a Pelton wheel, afterwards an electric motor), an underfloor shaft tunnel, which also acted as a drain, runs the length of both mills and continues to an extension to the older mill.

Behind the newer mill are the launder pillars and walls of an additional water-wheel. In front of the mills is a commodious stocking area, the remains of store sheds, and a pair of unique enamelling furnaces with elaborate ducting.

At the end of the newer mill is the much older drum-house of the main exit incline. Uniquely it does a double duty, having been adapted to be powered from the mill line shafting (some of the mechanism is *in situ*). This enabled the incline to uphaul block from level 3, which was opened up in the 1920s. Beyond the drum-house is a forge and workshops.

At the opposite end of this level is a cleared area which was the site of the 'London' mill, a 1901 sheet metal structure. The adjacent house (with fine slate lined food store), was converted from a forge which also housed the mill's electric motor.

Alongside is an old 6 to 5 incline.

On level 3, there is another tunnel from the quarry, a weigh-house with much of the mechanism intact, a building which may have housed a crusher and compressor, and the intermediate landing stage on the exit incline. Below is the abortive level 2.

There are traces of a watercourse from Llyn Elsi which supplied the water-wheels. The 24" pipe, which is prominent on the ground, supplied the Pelton wheel, powered the generator near the foot of the main incline, and provided a water supply to the town. Near the top of this run of pipe is a penstock with a curious slate gasket.

Some of the housing at main road level was built by the quarry. (40)

HENDRE (Glyn Lledr, Cwm Ddynhadog) SH698512
Small hillside working deepened into a pit, yielding a characteristic black slate. Opened circa 1840; water-power was used for haulage and, presumably, pumping. At some time a horse-whim was used for uphauling rubbish. Closed early 1900s. Transport by cart down valley.
Remains Flooded pit with uphaulage incline and possible traces of a pump. Alongside the incline is the pit for the winding wheel. Nearby is another wheel-pit alongside building ruins which could have been a mill, but were probably a rake of dressing sheds, the wheel being for pumping. There are launder pillars apparently fed from a shallow reservoir, dammed by partly using a natural rock outcrop. At the highest level are the centre-stone and curved wall of the horse-whim circle which uphauled the rubbish that formed the extensive tips to the west. (5)

HWYLFA SH819509
A tiny pit, literally a cottage industry; probably worked on an occasional, as required, basis.
Remains Apart from the shallow pit, there are the ruins of a cottage with a big peat style fireplace, and a 'workshop' alongside. There is a peat excavation nearby. (47)

LLAN SH734523
Very small open working, possibly only for building block.
Remains Quarrying face. (17)

LLECHWEDD OERNANT SH786482
Tiny pit; unsuccessful trial?
Remains Excavation only. (42)

MOEL DYRNOGYDD SH697497
Tiny scratching.
Remains Almost nill. (4)

MOEL PEN-Y-BRYN SH779499
Trial?
Remains Excavation. (38)

PENLLYN SH746522
Hillside quarry on three levels opened in 1875 as an extension to Ty'n-y-bryn, whose mill it used, and to which it was connected by an incline and tramway. Closed 1924.
Remains Excavation, incline and some buildings. Sandsaw blades are woven into a nearby fence. (23)

PENRHIW (Moel Siabod, Llwyn Graeanig) SH722540
A hone quarry which operated intermittently from the mid 19th century to WW1, with about half a dozen men. Material was taken from the open working to a water-powered mill with a sandsaw, and possibly a polishing machine. Finished product was probably taken out via Capel Curig.
Remains On upper level; the, blocked, open working, which from adit below met. Tramway formation, with rail on ground, to mill at 723542. The water-powered mill, which has a fireplace (forge?) contains remnants of a sandsaw; a room behind has plummer blocks in the ground. There are two tiny lean-to buildings. Nearby is an almost complete (7') sandsaw blade, and one end part with 2 fixing holes. The tip contains many part finished hones. (12)

PENYBEDW SH777476
Trial.
Remains Run in adit. (37)

PEN-Y-BONT SH783483
Probably unsuccessful trial.
Remains Two collapsed adits, one of which has two small buildings nearby; very steep access track. (41)

POMPREN (Pont Bron Bedw) SH726519

Two pits opened c1840, and developed in the 1870s with water-powered sandsaws. Prior to there being tunnel access to the pits, uphaulage may have been by horse-whim. Later a water-powered incline raised rubbish. Output of c100 tons p.a. was carted to Dolwyddelan; closed pre-WW1.
Remains Pit with haulage incline; mill ruins with wheel-pit and launder pillars, and some other buildings; vestiges of tunnels. (13)

PRINCE LLYWELYN (Bwlch Cynnud, Y Foel) SH744528

Open hillside quarry and pit from c1820, with some underground working. An incline led to the original 1840s steam mill which later used a 30' water-wheel. It had 4 horizontal sandsaws, and a second 1890s water turbine mill brought the total of machines to 10 sandsaws, 6 dressing machines and 3 planers. These also dealt with slab from Chwarel Fedw, brought across the valley by a tramway on the still extant causeway. Steam used for pumping. May have uphauled from the pit by water-balance.

Output in 1882 of 1685 tons, mainly slab, with 74 men, some of whom barracked on site, but may have been more in earlier years. Closed in 1934, and was possibly the very last user of sandsaws. Product carted successively to Trefriw, Betws-y-coed and Dolwyddelan.
Remains Virtually nothing; site has been used for bulk fill and is almost entirely cleared and afforested. The pit is flooded, and adits are inaccessible. Some traces of the incline. A garage is close to the site of the original mill. Associated cottages are still occupied. There is a reservoir behind the site, and very extensive leats. (22)

RHIW-GOCH (Brandreath) SH749537

Hillside quarry, opened in the 1860s and deepened into a pit; accessed by adits with some limited underground working. Block was sawn in a water-wheel powered mill. In the mid 1870s a much larger mill was built, but possibly never completed. It had a central wheel which may have been replaced by a water turbine. Following 1890s closure, it reopened in 1904 in conjunction with Ty'nyfallen, to which it was connected by a tramway. It is believed that, most unusually for a slate quarry, a steam powered reciprocating shot-saw was used. Production is unlikely to have ever approached four figures; closed 1908.
Remains Massive pit with some limited chambering off it. A tunnel led to the original mill (now incorporated into a farm building). The large, newer mill lower down the site, has only the walls of one half standing. There is further tunnel access to the pit at this level, and another tunnel

lower down; there are traces of a water balanced incline. Near the bottom of the site is a drainage adit that is big enough to suggest that material removal was planned.

There are several other buildings including a powder magazine. A tramroad formation leads in from Ty'nyfallen. The access road, which crosses a stream by a nice bridge, was intended as an exit incline. There are two reservoirs above the site. (27)

RHOS (Capel Curig, Rhos y Goelcerth) SH729564

A large pit working with extensive use of water-power; opened in the 1850s. Produced 1285 tons with 45 men in 1882.

At first, material was trammed out of the working via a short tunnel (which was later opened out as a cutting) to the nearby mill area.

As work progressed downwards, a haulage system was powered by the 30' mill wheel which probably also pumped. There was a second 18' wheel at the mill, which possibly predated the larger wheel which may have been installed when the mill was doubled in size.

Later, a drainage tunnel was cut permitting the use of a water balance, and providing a ready route out for waste. This waste was consolidated into a platform incorporating a wheel-pit with the intention of constructing a new mill at a lower level to avoid up haulage.

Later the water balance was abandoned and a further 18' wheel (that may have come from Nantlle) was inserted into the mill wheels supply to operate a chain incline.

In 1919 a 40' Wheel (ex Cyffty lead mine?) was installed, working off the mill tail-race to power a compressor.

At some time, another tunnel was started from the pit bottom but was never completed. Locomotive power was used; a De Winton worked from the 1880s to around 1930. A tramway connection was made to the Foel inclines, and finished product being carted from Pont Cyfyng. Final closure came in 1952.

Remains The pit is of an impressive size. The headframe of the water balance is in place (the balance tank is on the opposite side of the quarry), but the incline itself has been quarried away. There are some traces of the later chain incline with its wheel-pit inserted onto the main mill wheel supply, with associated sheave mountings etc.

The fine mill, some 300' long, has the wheel behind, at right angles. This wheel has a mounting for some secondary duties, possibly pumping and winding. There are also traces of the earlier, smaller wheel. The mill building has a series of alcoves along one side for dressing. As frequently the case in quarries working Cambrian rock, no dressing machines were used. There is an adjacent lavatory over the wheel tail-race.

From the mill tail-race, a carefully built stone channel with penstock leads to the big wheel-pit for the compressor.

At the lower end of the drainage/rubbish tunnel is the area intended for a new mill, with the wheel housing towering up. Although never used, it is believed that a wheel was actually installed.

On the commodious mill area is a big stocking ground and several other buildings including a workshop/forge and a weigh-house, with its mechanism pit converted to a locomotive inspection pit. There is some underground leating for water pumped out of the pit. Nearby is a rake of barracks/dwellings, part of which latterly housed a diesel generator.

Immediately behind the uppermost wheel is a small holding pond and, behind that, the lower reservoir which has a three-ply dam, reinforced by bridge rail and slate slab. The upper reservoir, latterly supplied from Foel quarry, still holds water.

The tramway and inclines are readily traceable. (14)

RHOS-GOCH SH756466 & 756468
Two hillside quarries with some slight underground development. Opened around 1830, later forming outliers to Cwm Machno.
Remains Both workings are on two levels, with some tentative tunnelling at 756466. Small buildings include weigh-houses and some relatively modern structures. There are vestiges of inclines, one connecting the two sites, the other lowering to a tramway to Cwm Machno mills. Traces of access tracks. (33)

RHYD-GOCH SH862492
Putative site; unlikely to be slate.
Remains Obvious quarry face. (49)

SŴCH SH755474
A compact underground working operated in conjunction with Cwm Machno. Rock from an adit was trammed to a short incline to the mill(s).
Remains The adit is only just identifiable due to later Cwm Machno tipping. The incline is clear with a leat alongside. The mills area is in agricultural reuse; the walls and a wheel-pit suggest two mills. The office and adjacent dwelling are in good order. There are traces of launder pillars, and a possible uphaulage for mill waste. (30)

TAN-Y-RHIW SH758452

Tiny open pit worked for a few years from 1828.
Remains Excavation and tip. (34)

TY'N-Y-BRYN (Bwlch y Llan, Lledr Vale) SH742521

Developed c1860s as a re-start of an earlier working. It consists of a pit
on 5 levels accessed by tunnels, and connected by inclines to a water-
powered mill. Though supplemented by conventional saws and probably
a Hunter saw, the original sandsaws remained in use, dealing with
Penllyn blocks up to 1924.

Output, including Penllyn, may have neared 2000 tons p.a.
Originally, material was carted to Trefriw for shipment, but later there
was an incline to a siding at Dolwyddelan, making it the only quarry in
the region to have direct rail connection. Closed c1914.

Remains 4 inclines and ruined drum-houses; a number of dressing sheds
and other buildings, and remnants of a weighing machine. Tips have
been used for bulkfill leaving little in the mill area, other than machine
bases and a wheel-pit. There are still vestiges of the tramway and the
incline from Penllyn, and the connection to Dolwyddelan station. (21)

TY'NYFALLEN (Lady Willoughby, East Rhiw-goch) SH752539

A small underground working started by Joseph Kellow of Croesor
(Region 8) in the 1870s; developed, with little apparent success, in
connection with Rhiw-goch in the early 1900s.

Remains Two adits. The lower one having very limited chambering
attempts; some rail on ground. The upper, with adjacent dressing shed
and drum-house, has several small workings breaking out to a bank, and
a steeply inclined shaft downwards with some rail *in situ*. The incline
formation joining the two levels is much degraded. The tramway to
Rhiw-goch now partly forms the access road to the farmhouse. (29)

PENNANT/GEST
Region 7
Cwm Pennant, and coast from Borth-y-gest to Cricieth, including quarries served by the Gorseddau tramway

General

In this region where the Caernarfonshire Cambrian veins peter out into isolated outcrops, most slate workings were small and scattered; few served more than temporary local needs. Only in Cwm Pennant, which thrusts north for some five miles from Dolbenmaen, were there any sizable quarries, few of which were successful.

As a result the economic and demographic impact of the industry, except in Cwm Pennant, was minimal.

Transport

Other than some output from Cwm Pennant which was carried northwards over Bwlch Ddeilior to Caernarfon, all product went south. Prior to Porthmadog becoming available in the late 1820s, shipment was at Pwllheli, Cricieth or Ynys Cyngar.

There were plans to connect Hendre Ddu, and possibly others on the western side of Cwm Pennant, by a rail line to Cricieth, but the only slate rail line actually built was the 8 mile, 3'G. Gorseddau Tramway, opened in 1857 to connect the Gorseddau quarry with Porthmadog. Constructed to a very high standard, it is notable for the fact that, apart from the Nantlle Railway (which ran over almost level terrain), it was the only horse-drawn quarry to seaport line never to have used inclines.

The formation remains traceable almost throughout its length from the quarry, past the Ynys y Pandy mill, to Penmorfa where the road crossing has been lost in roadworks. It is defined by a lane through Penmorfa, drops down in front of the scarp to behind Tremadog, where there was a reversing loop. From there, after crossing the main road, it used the trackbed of the old Tremadog Ironstone tramway (now a footpath to Porthmadog) alongside the old Tremadog canal. In Porthmadog, the line followed the line of Madog street to the port itself. The section south of the main line railway was reused in the early 1900s as part of the non-slate Moel y Gest tramway.

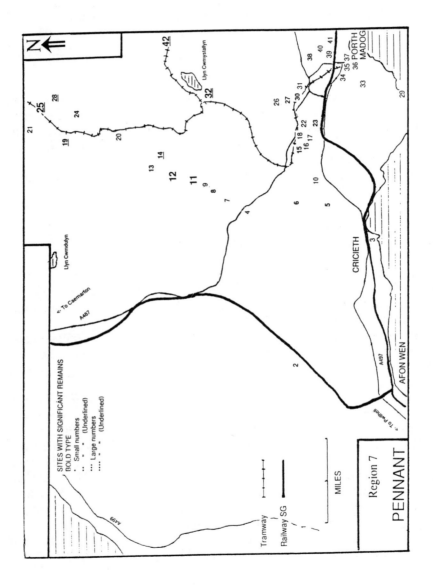

SITES WITH SIGNIFICANT REMAINS
BOLD TYPE
  . Small numbers
  . " "   (Underlined)
  ... Large numbers
  ... " "   (Underlined)

Tramway
Railway SG

MILES

Region 7
PENNANT

Llyn Cwmdulyn

← To Caernarfon

A487

A499

Llyn Cwmystallyn

CRICIETH

AFON WEN

A497

→ To Pwllheli

PORTH
MADOG

In 1875 the then defunct line was relaid in 2'G. and extended for 4 miles from near the Ynys y Pandy mill to the Prince of Wales quarry. It had one De Winton locomotive, but it is doubtful if it had much use. In fact, latterly, traffic was so sparse that trucks were hand pushed to Porthmadog.

Following a further, very short-lived 1 mile extension to serve the Cwm Dwyfor metal mine, the whole system was out of use by the early 1890s. The extension line to the Prince of Wales can be readily traced and it can be seen that, though the trackbed is sound, the bridges etc. are much inferior to the original works. Indeed, if the mine extension is followed (via a delightful cutting) an even poorer standard of construction is evident.

1.	SH394407	Pont Rhyd-goch
2.	SH454407	Foel Isaf
3.	SH497378	Marine Terrace
4.	SH506428	Tyddyn Mawr
5.	SH507394	Mynydd Ednyfed *
6.	SH508407	Ymlych *
7.	SH510427	Ysgubor Gerrig
8.	SH516437	Dôl Wgan *
9.	SH518439	Prince Llywelyn
10.	SH519393	Pencraig
11.	SH519444	Hendre Ddu ***
12.	SH521451	Moelfre ***
13.	SH525461	Chwarel y Plas
14.	SH532448	Isallt **
15.	SH534399	Garreg Felen *
16.	SH536397	Bryneglwys
17.	SH538396	Coed y Chwarel
18.	SH538397	Cambrian Railways
19.	SH538495	Dolgarth **
20.	SH541469	Cwm Llefrith
21.	SH541505	Cwm Dwyfor
22.	SH542398	Cloddfa Sion Prys
23.	SH544390	Bron-y-foel *
24.	SH548483 etc.	Moel Lefn *
25.	SH549498	Prince of Wales ****(R)
26.	SH550409	Tŷ Cerrig
27.	SH550433	Ynys y Pandy (Mill) ****V
28.	SH552408	Penmorfa *

29. SH553495 Princess **
30. SH554365 Ynys Cyngar
31. SH554406 Ty'n-y-llan * (R)
32. SH555372 Garreg Wen
33. SH559388 Moel y Gest
34. SH559393 Penrhyn Llwyd
35. SH561389 Tu Hwnt i'r Bwlch
36. SH562372 etc. Pen-y-banc
37. SH562386 Tyddyn Llwyn
38. SH564406 Cwm Bach *
39. SH566382 Garth
40. SH567386 Morfa Lodge
41. SH572385 Ynys Tywyn
42. SH573453 Gorseddau ****(R)

BRON-Y-FOEL SH544390

Small open quarry; 18th century or earlier, probably closed by mid 19th century. Could have been one of the first in this region to ship slate by sea.
Remains Little apart from the actual excavation. The house that was associated with the quarry is still occupied. The track by which output was carried in animal panniers to Ynys Cyngar survives as a footpath. (23)

BRYNEGLWYS SH536397

Putative site.
Remains Possible excavation. (16)

CAMBRIAN RAILWAYS SH538397

Very small, c1870.
Remains Excavation; possible building, much overgrown. (18)

CHWAREL Y PLAS SH525461

Small pit working. Material carted to the road at Plas y Pennant.
Remains Upper working with dressing shed. Lower working, that is accessed by a tunnel, does not seem to have produced. (13)

CLODDFA SION PRYS SH542398

Tiny scratching from circa 1880.
Remains Obliterated by forestry. (22)

COED Y CHWAREL SH538396
Small, early working.
Remains In forestry, almost obliterated. (17)

CWM BACH (Tan-yr-allt) SH564406
An abortive 1921/23 development.
Remains Bases of temporary buildings; zigzig access track. (38)

CWM DWYFOR (Blaen Pennant) SH541505
Almost certainly only an 1880s trial.
Remains Adit and rubbish run. All the buildings etc. pertain to the metal mine. (21)

CWM LLEFRITH SH541469
Possibly trial only. (1880s?)
Remains Adit and rubbish run. (20)

DOLGARTH (Dôl Ifan Gethin, Pennant Vale) SH538495
Precipitous hillside working on 3 levels; the upper level was almost certainly not productive. Opened in the 1870s, it was possibly closed by 1880. Material taken from hillside workings by a balanced incline to a water-powered mill on th valley floor. Finished product carted down valley.
Remains Two levels have dressing sheds and tramway formations to the head of a steep incline, which has a substantial, remote type, drum-house.

Near the foot of the incline is a massive rectangular structure of unknown use.

The mill building is an 'add on' to a pre-existing building; another building (dwelling?) is in agricultural reuse. Notable is the long, slate covered, tail-race to the river.

There were reputed attempts to mine copper on this site. (19)

DÔL WGAN SH516437
Early 18th century open working.
Remains Virtually nothing other than the pits themselves. (8)

FOEL ISAF SH454407
Putative trial.
Remains Nothing located. (2)

GARREG FELEN SH534399
Possible slab quarry.
Remains Ground disturbance? (15)

GARREG WEN SH555372
Tiny scratching (1880s?)
Remains On caravan site; barely traceable. (32)

GARTH SH566382 & 568383
Small open slab workings.
Remains Possible vestiges. (39)

GORSEDDAU SH573453
A small early 19th century working most spectacularly, but unsuccessfully, developed in 1855 on a 'no expense spared' basis into a multi-level hillside quarry. Besides the extensive workers' housing and the railway to Porthmadog, a huge water-powered mill was built at Ynys y Pandy (550433), with a reservoir and extensive water courses.

In spite of this investment, and the employment of 200 men, it took until 1860 to reach a brief and relatively derisory peak output of 2148 tons, which had dwindled to almost nothing by its 1867 closure. Except for some small, sporadic, activity in the 1870s it has been idle ever since.
Remains Four terraces were served by a single central incline; three levels above these do not seem to have produced at all. There is a separate small level served by its own short incline, near the bottom of which is the collapsed adit of an underground trial. Indeed, it is immediately apparent that the orderly layout of extraction to the north-east, tipping to the south-west, was abandoned in a frantic search for useable rock. The best known feature, the curious overhanging curved wall, was built to prevent the huge quantities of bad rock that was extracted, from overwhelming the tramway.

Incline bridges over the terraces have two apertures. The larger one accommodated the 3' gauge wagons which carried finished roofing slates and blocks for the mill down the incline; the narrower bridge was for the 2' gauge rubbish wagons that were used only on the terraces. Also to be seen on the terraces are pieces of slate which have been drilled as makeshift sleepers for Thomas Hughes rail.

There are several dressing sheds, blast shelters etc. on the worked levels. Near the foot of incline there is a small barracks and a stable; in the latter is a slate slab with 1" diameter holes, possibly for drill testing. There is a curious absence of weigh-houses.

In some working faces are borings of up to 3" diameter which, on an unpowered site, suggests the use of a hand-cranked Dixon drill.

The trackbed of the 3' gauge tramway that took material to the mill passes a grove of trees, the site of the manager's house; behind are the vestiges of the 18 pairs of houses (the uncompleted village of Treforus), laid out in 3 'streets', which were built for the workforce. One can trace the covered leats that brought water from a catchment pond to these dwellings and to the manager's house.

This trackbed continues to, and past, the magnificent 3 storey Ynys y Pandy mill. (42)

HENDRE DDU (Prince Llywelyn) SH519444

Early small scale pit working, developed in the 1860s with a mill (steam?) and an incline to the valley floor. More than 60 men were employed, but annual output was well under 1000 tons.

Following 1872 failure, it re-opened with around 20 men with a new water-powered mill at the foot of the incline. An earlier proposal for a tramway to Cricieth was revived, but not proceeded with. Following a reservoir collapse in 1875, it survived to about 1880. An attempt to re-open in 1898 met with little success.

Remains At the original highest level there are barracks with unusually tall windows, dressing sheds, and a weighhouse. Below are vestiges of the original mill and a weighbridge. The incline, which has several spurs leading onto it, is in fair condition, and has a small reservoir alongside. Only the foundations remain of the roadside mill, which may have been of wooden construction. On the old access track is a nice powder house.

In the main working is some investigative tunnelling. There are a number of other smaller workings nearby, some of which may have been productive, and one of which was used as a reservoir. (11)

ISALLT (Chwarel y Llan) SH532448

A small hillside quarry, operating around the 1840s-50s. Material was lowered by incline to a working area where there may have been a mill. As work deepened into a pit, access was by a tunnel.

Remains Very little, apart from the incline formation and some ruined buildings. At the earlier, higher, level there is a surprisingly long tramway bed for tipping. The tunnel has collapsed.

The substantial and level construction of the access track suggests that it was intended as a tramway, but no evidence has been found that rail was laid. (14)

MARINE TERRACE SH497378
Small open working.
Remains Quarry face behind houses. (3)

MOELFRE SH521451
Developed in the 1860s on the site of earlier slate diggings and copper trials. As the working deepened into pits, material was taken out first by a cutting, then by tunnels and finally by uphaulage, to an adjacent mill. Finished slate was taken out by incline. Later a new, lower, tunnel provided access and drainage; material was taken out through this and down a new incline to a mill on the valley floor. It originally employed 60 men but only produced around 600 tons p.a. and, handicapped by a long cartage down valley, failed after a few years. Revived around 1870 on a smaller scale. Closed about 1880, but some work was done in the 1930s.
Remains Two pits (one water filled), linked part way down by a cutting and, at pit bottom, by a now blocked tunnel. One side of the dry pit is elaborately walled and has an unusual cantilevered slab stairway. At pit bottom is the later drainage/access tunnel. Traces of a gallery in this pit may have been from earlier copper mining. At the top of this pit are traces of a water-wheel powered chain incline, with iron fixing bolts showing where a launder may have fed the wheel. The slate-lined tail-race from this wheel leads down to a working area with a mill, weigh-houses etc. A nearby tunnel also connects to this same pit. Not far away, another tunnel connects to the 'wet' pit.

At a lower level are traces of the tipped over original incline; the later reservoir has a stone lined leat passing between the pillars of the drum-house of the incline down to the lower mill. Launder pillars lead to the site of the overshot wheel of this later mill, now in reuse. In the river near this mill are the remains of a small undershot wheel, probably for agricultural use.

There are two disused water turbines on the site which generated electricity in post-quarrying days. One, said to be an ex-Hendre Ddu item, was fed by a diversion of the water-wheel leat; the second by an iron pipe. A third generator, fed by plastic piping, is still in use.

Above the site is a reservoir, a powder house, and another building that predates the quarry operation.

The access road to the site has been diverted and extended to serve an early 20th century quartz working. On that track are two adits that may have been late attempts at underground quarrying. (12)

MOEL LEFN SH548483 & 550489 & 551488
Probably trials only.
Remains Tiny buildings on first two sites; relatively large rubbish runs.
(24)

MOEL Y GEST SH559388
Small open quarry, long abandoned.
Remains Rockface. Not to be confused with later stone quarry near the top of the hill (with incline). (33)

MORFA LODGE SH567386
Very small working circa 1880.
Remains Area built over. (40)

MYNYDD EDNYFED (Cloddfa) SH507394
A pit working producing a poor product; on the western extremity of the slate occurrences. Possibly 1840s; closed by 1880.
Remains No buildings; some pits and rubbish runs. The access track now forms the road to the Golf Club, and can be traced across the course. (5)

PENCRAIG SH519393
Very small pit.
Remains Development now obscures the site. (10)

PENMORFA (Allt-wen) SH552408
Hillside quarry with incline that crossed, but did not directly connect to, the Gorseddau tramway. Operated from 1820s to 1870s.
Remains Incline and excavation; remains of a building that just possibly might have been a mill. (28)

PENRHYN LLWYD SH559393
Putative site; possibly not slate.
Remains Ground disturbance. (34)

PEN-Y-BANC (Borth-y-gest) SH562372/562374
Very small open workings. Possibly only block for building, circa 1870s.
Remains Slight depressions in ground. (36)

PONT RHYD-GOCH SH394407
Putative slate site.
Remains Slight vestiges of extraction. (1)

PRINCE LLYWELYN SH518439

A tiny hillside working whose name was applied to the later, and much bigger, Hendre Ddu whose access track it shared.

Remains Pits only. (9)

PRINCE OF WALES (Cwm Trwsgwl) SH549498

An old open working which carried finished product to Rhyd-ddu. Some development in the 1860s when, possibly, three levels were worked. Vigorously opened up in 1873 when the extension of the Gorseddau Tramway to the mill gave ready access to Porthmadog. Four further levels were started, served by twice extending the main incline. At the peak, 200 men were employed producing 5000 tons p.a. Closed 1886, but there was some small scale working up to 1920. As was then usual, all reduction of roofing slate took place on the terraces, slab only being dealt with in the mill.

Remains A particularly interesting site whose layout closely replicates Gorseddau, i.e. extraction to the north-east, tipping to the south-west, with the incline in the middle. On each working level there were a number of buildings including weigh-houses and dressing sheds etc.; one level had a particularly fine rake of such sheds, and a barrack block without fireplaces (possibly portable stoves were used). There are several weigh-houses. The well engineered incline has remains of its final, upper drum-house, and traces of the two earlier drum-houses that were abandoned as the quarry was extended upwards.

On the lowest working level is evidence of some underfloor leatwork and adits, some open, leading to very limited chambering.

The little building behind the reservoir, was the workshop, possibly a reuse of a pre-existing structure.

The stretch of level tramway, from the foot of incline past the reservoir, is a prominent feature as is the lower incline drum-house. One can see traces both of work begun to raise the height of the dam, and the formation of a little tramway to serve that work. At the foot of the lower incline is the compact mill, which has very pleasing archways and a wheel-pit alongside with a row of launder pillars adjacent.

The track bed of the tramway to the south has some interesting little bridges and embankments and immediately to the north, on the subsequent extension to the Cwm Dwyfor mine, is a deep, curved cutting. (25)

PRINCESS SH553495

A small and remote hillside working of the 1880s as an outlier of Prince

of Wales, with some attempt at underground extraction. Material was carried down to Prince of Wales.
Remains Some ruined dressing sheds and other buildings. At a lower level, there is an adit from which apparently no useable product was taken. The track down to Prince of Wales quarry is traceable. There are some pieces of Thomas Hughes rail. (29)

TŶ CERRIG (Allt-wen) SH550409
Small working; possibly only buildings stone.
Remains Excavation. (26)

TYDDYN LLWYN SH562386
Flooring flags produced in 1830s-40s?
Remains Almost none. (37)

TYDDYN MAWR (Dolbelmaen) SH506428
Tiny open quarry.
Remains Excavation only. (4)

TU HWNT I'R BWLCH SH561389
A small and early working with cart access.
Remains Almost nothing, some traces of retaining walls for cart track. (35)

TY'N-Y-LLAN (Cae-crwn) SH554406
Hillside quarry connected by incline to the Gorseddau tramway. Possibly building block only.
Remains Excavation and incline. (31)

YMLYCH (Braich y Saint) SH508407
Small hillside working. 1840s?
No remains identified. (6)

YNYS CYNGAR SH554365
Traditional loading place; also an anchorage for the transshipment of Blaenau slate that was boated down the river Dwyryd in pre-Porthmadog times. Some extraction nearby to the east, but probably only shales for rough building block.
No remains. (30)

YNYSTYWYN SH572385
Small workings around a knoll.
Remains One tiny face now occupied by a building. (41)

YNYS Y PANDY SH550433
The unique mill for Gorseddau quarry. Worked c1855-1867; subsequently occasionally used as a public hall.
Remains This impressive structure has been conserved by the Snowdonia National Park. On two main floors, with an attic (storage?) and part basement (Workshop?), it is more redolent of a mid 19th century gasworks, retort house, or engineering building, than a slate slab mill. It is unknown why such an expensive to build and difficult to work design was adopted.

It contains a pit for a large breastshot wheel, and a deep shaft trench running the length of the building (extended outside for shaft maintenance). There is a fine water tunnel that was linked by a traceable leat from Llyn Cwmystradllyn. Besides traces of rubbish tramways on the ground floor, both main floors are linked by tramway formations to the Gorseddau tramway.

Contemporary accounts as well as an examination of the small amounts of waste from its trifling output, suggest that saws, planers and polishers were used. Which floor the machines were on is disputed but, since it is unclear how the wooden upper floor could bear the weight, or how water would be carried to the saws and polishers, or how slurries could be drained, it is inevitable that the machines were on the ground floor, despite the absence of evidence of mountings. The upper floor was presumably intended for the hand finishing of fine products and, possibly, writing slates. (27)

YSGUBOR GERRIG SH510427
Tiny scratching circa 1880.
Remains Possible ground disturbance. (7)

GLASLYN
Region 8
Croesor, Beddgelert & district,
including quarries using Croesor Tramway

General

Most of the slate workings in this region were small; many around Beddgelert dated from the 1870s when it was confidently predicted that the area was to be the 'New Penrhyn'. Although their success was limited, Beddgelert and hamlets such as Nanmor did briefly become partly slate dependent.

Much greater success was found in the Croesor valley where, on the western flanks of the Moelwyn, quarries, several of them large, exploited the Ffestiniog veins, resulting in the creation of the village of Croesor and the augmentation of others such as Llanfrothen.

Quarrying had ceased by WW2 but, controversially in these environmentally aware times, we may again see slate quarrying at the head of Cwm Croesor.

Transport

Prior to the building of the Porthmadog Cob at the beginning of the 19th century, which enabled the reclamation of the Glaslyn estuary, a few quarries in the south-west of the region had reasonable access to navigable water but all others were isolated. New roads, such as the one from Penrhyndeudraeth to Llanfrothen eased communications, but quarries still had an expensive cartage to Porthmadog.

Railways for the area had been mooted from the middle decades of the 19th century. The slate quarry traffic that would arise from the Beddgelert area had been often cited in proposals, and the plethora of quarry openings in the 1860s and '70s was spurred by the 'imminence' of railway connection (which did not actually happen until 1923!).

The more substantial quarries near the head of Cwm Croesor packhorsed down that valley by the still extant track, or down Cwm Maesgwm. Briefly, around 1860, Rhosydd reached the Ffestiniog Railway via Cwm Orthin.

Apart from the Hafod-y-llan tramway, the one rail link actually built

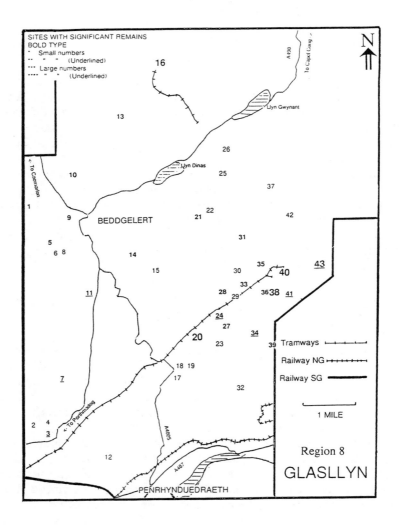

SITES WITH SIGNIFICANT REMAINS
BOLD TYPE
* Small numbers
** " " (Underlined)
*** Large numbers
**** " " (Underlined)

16

13

A498

To Capel Curig

Llyn Gwynant

26

Llyn Dinas

25

37

< To Caernarfon

10

1

9   BEDDGELERT

22
21

42

31

5
6 8

14

15

35
30   40   43

33
28   36 38 41
29

24
27
20   34
23   39 Tramways
Railway NG
Railway SG

11

7

18 19
17

32

1 MILE

< To Porthmadog

A4085

2   4
3

12

A487

Region 8

GLASLLYN

PENRHYNDUEDRAETH

132

was the notable 2'G. Croesor Tramway of 1864. Horsedrawn, it linked Rhosydd, Croesor, Fron-boeth, Parc and other minor quarries to Porthmadog. It operated until the mid 1930s and, never being officially closed, unofficial use in Cwm Croesor itself may have continued into the 1950s.

The line is traceable throughout its length. It starts at the head of Cwm Croesor with the spectacular Rhosydd and Croesor inclines, the highest single pitch inclines in the industry, reaching the valley floor via the Blaen-y-cwm incline which also served to carry the pipes of the Croesor quarry power station.

Part way along the valley floor it met the foot of the Pant Mawr/Fron-boeth incline. This incline was originally in 2 pitches, from the top of which it was connected to Pant-mawr quarry by another finely engineered tramway. In about 1886, when the Fron-boeth quarry was much developed as a downwards extension of Pant-mawr, the upper pitch was abandoned and the lower pitch extended upwards some 100'. From this new incline head, a line ran along the hillside to an unique tunnel (now blocked near the north-western end) into Cwm Maesgwm.

Near Croesor village was the loading point for the little Croesor Bach quarry where, due to the unavailability of land south of the river, it passed over the second of three delightful bridges. The Parc (Hen Dwll) branch joined immediately after the third bridge.

A fine stone embankment led to the top of the two-pitch Parc incline. The lower drum-house is ruined, but the upper one has been converted into a house.

Near the foot of these inclines was the Parc quarry branch junction; from there the formation runs across level ground to join the clearly defined route to Porthmadog, which was reused by the Welsh Highland Railway.

1. SH571485 Meillionen *
2. SH573409 Porth Treuddyn (old site)
3. SH578408 Porth Treuddyn (new site) **
4. SH579409 Fron Olau
5. SH579472 Cwm Cloch *
6. SH581466 Cwm Cŷd
7. SH582420 Aberdunant **
8. SH582468 Goat
9. SH584476 Bronhebog *
10. SH584496 Gwernlasdeg *
11. SH594453 Dinas Ddu **

12. SH598394 Braich Gwilliad
13. SH599514 Cae'r Gors *
14. SH605466 Cwm Caeth *
15. SH611458 Dôl Friog
16. SH613524 Hafod-y-llan ***
17. SH616421 Brondanw Isaf
18. SH619426 Brondanw Uchaf
19. SH620426 Brongarnedd
20. SH626436 Parc *** (R)
21. SH629481 Berth-lwyd *
22. SH631484 Gerynt
23. SH632436 Hafoty
24. SH632444 Parc (Slab) ** (R)
25. SH632490 Blaen-nant
26. SH632499 Castell
27. SH633442 Llidiart yr Arian * (R)
28. SH633448 Bryngelynnen *
29. SH636446 Garreg Uchaf
30. SH637457 etc. Crib-lwyd
31. SH637463 Gelli **
32. SH638418 Hafod Boeth
33. SH639452 Croesor Bach *
34. SH643434 Hafod Uchaf **
35. SH643462 Cnicht **
36. SH646448 Cefn-y-braich * (R)
37. SH651485 Llyn Llagi
38. SH652448 Fron-boeth *** (R)
39. SH653437 Cwm Maesgwm *
40. SH657457 Croesor *** (R)
41. SH658446 Pant-mawr ** (R)
42. SH658476 Cwm y Foel
43. SH664461 Rhosydd **** (R)

ABERDUNANT SH582420

A tiny short lived late 19th century underground working, employing about 12 men. Revived for a few years in the early 1900s, with four men making slab. This later working was close to the boundary fence and all material, including waste, had to be uphauled to mill level by an incline powered by an extension of the underfloor mill shaft.

Remains Wheel-pit and mill with pit for the incline winder. The later, and lower, work chambers up through the original adit, and out to daylight. Besides the incline up to the mill a second, possibly uncompleted, uphaulage incline runs up past a small rake of buildings. How this incline was, or was intended to be, powered is unclear. In view of the small output, a hand winch is a possibility. (7)

BERTH-LWYD SH629481

A small unmechanised hillside working on two levels, which may reflect two brief periods of mid 19th century working. Output under 200 tons p.a.

Remains Upper level has a back-to-back dressing shed of a pattern rarely seen other than in north-east Wales. Another building could have been a powder store. The lower working cuts into the floor of the upper working, and on this level are vestiges of the rake of three dressing sheds. Behind it is an abortive attempt at an opening. There are traces of access tracks and a leat, possibly to feed farm machinery.

The servants' cottages opposite the meticulously restored house may have been used by lodging quarrymen. (21)

BLAEN-NANT SH632490

Possible trials.

Remains Traces of excavation. (25)

BRAICH GWILLIAD SH598394

Putative site.

Remains Nothing traceable. (12)

BRONDANW ISAF SH616421

Tiny open quarry that is said to have employed 10 men in the early 1920s, producing 60 tons p.a. Slate quality was described as poor. Direct access to road.

Remains Face and base of a possible shed. (17)

BRONDANW UCHAF SH619426

Extremely small. Reported to have employed 5 men in 1836. Material taken down a slide to the road.

Remains Excavation and vestiges of slideway. (18)

BRONGARNEDD SH620426

Small pit; employed 10 men around 1820, producing 70 tons p.a. Crude incline or slide to road.

Remains Face and traces of ramp. (19)

BRONHEBOG SH584476

Small underground working.

Remains Four collapsed adits; vestiges of buildings but site now heavily overgrown. (9)

BRYNGELYNNEN SH633448

Tiny underground working circa 1860, reputedly with about 5 men.

Remains Traces of adit; possible vestiges of dressing shed and of bridge over river. (28)

CAE'R GORS (Dorlan Ddu, Cae Gors) SH599514 etc.

Early 1870s underground workings which failed to fulfil the expectations that this area then promised.

Remains At location above; a collapsed adit, a dressing shed, and a tiny shelter with shelf. At 594512; collapsed adit and, nearby, a most curious keyhole plan underground shelter. The circular portion of 8′ diameter is vaulted over, and the 18″ wide x 10′ long 'tail' is covered over with slab. Its purpose is unknown. At 593516 there is a collapsed adit and a tiny half-underground shelter. At 592519 there is a collapsed adit and vestiges of a tiny shelter. Some good quality trimming waste is on the ground at each location. (13)

CASTELL SH632499

An underground working, certainly 18th century, and possibly much older.

Remains Adit slant collapsed; quite extensive rubbish runs on the opposite side of the road. (26)

CEFN-Y-BRAICH (Braich y Parc) SH646448

Hillside terraces; in 1877/83 about 20 men were employed, producing 240 tons p.a. Product described as brittle. Became part of Pant-mawr/Fron-boeth, its two open workings being designated levels 19 & 20.

Remains Working faces and tramway formations connecting to Fron-boeth incline system. (36)

CNICHT (Clogwyn y Darren, Drws y Darren) SH643462 etc.

A tiny underground working spectacularly located some 800′ above the valley floor. Material was possibly carried on men's backs down a pathway, but at some time a crude ropeway may have been used.

Operating in 1860s with 6 men producing 20 tons p.a. An attempt was made to develop in the early 1870s.

Remains At the short adit is a tiny dressing area with a double shed with fireplace; alongside is a number of slates. Some 6m below is a substantial platform that appears to have been a stocking area and loading platform. The zigzag path is now much eroded by scree. Below, almost at valley floor level, are some possibly associated building ruins and traces of what may have been the lower termination of a ropeway.

A few yards to the east is the unsuccessful 1870s Deufaen scheme. It is only the merest surface scratching, but is notable for the uncompleted incline formation and the substantial loading platform at its foot, from where another much degraded zigzag path leads down. (35)

CRIB-LWYD SH637457 & 639460
Abortive underground trials; perhaps attempts to reach the Cnicht vein by an easier route.

Remains Both adits are open to dead headings, the southerly one ending in a face partially drilled for shot firing. There are other collapsed adits at 631454, 632457 and 634457. There is a building nearby which may have been connected with these diggings. (30)

CROESOR SH657457
A substantial underground quarry, employing up to 300 men, (around 70 in barracks). It is unusual on many counts. It never had any significant surface workings; in employing forced ventilation; in the number, for its size, of steam engines used; for the ingenuity of its engineering; and in the small volume of its rubbish tips (due to a vigorous policy of back-filling worked out chambers).

Working with mixed fortunes from 1846, it closed in 1878. Re-opening in 1895 under the energetic management of Moses Kellow, it produced 5/6000 tons p.a., but declined rapidly during the early years of the 20th century. For a short time century, Kellow patent rock drills were produced on site. The quarry finally closed in 1930.

The water-powered mill (28′ wheel), with about a dozen saws was built in the early 1860's. A 1866 extension with 12 to 14 saws had a 39′ wheel operating totally underground from the tail-race of the first, with a 13hp steam engine back-up. Shafting was underfloor, as was the rubbish tramway. The water-wheels were replaced by Kellow with a Pelton wheel, driving through overhead shafting, and later electrified.

Underground working was arranged on seven floors. At the far end of the access tunnel (floor A), an incline went up the dip of the vein to floors B, C and D Up, and with another incline going down to floors B and C Down, with a further incline joining C Down with D Down.

Several steam engines were used for pumping, ventilation and possibly haulage, including a steam turbine (on level D Up). Much attention was given to ventilation, a Guiblas fan being installed in a stone fan-house near the adit. Besides this, one of the several vertical shafts out to bank was used to experiment with waterblast ventilation.

Apparently these vertical shafts were at one time used to water-balance the A-C Down incline, and to counterbalance the A-D Up incline, via ropes and pulleys.

In the mid 1890s compressed air drills were used, with a water-powered compressor. Partially electrified in the late 90s, a full scale 250 kW 40cps AC hydro-electric plant was opened in 1904, with a small DC supply for excitation and for lighting the manager's house. The pioneering AC loco had a 90hp motor as did the winder, the mill drive used 10hp motors.

Finished product was originally carted to the Ffestiniog Railway at Penrhyndeudraeth, but after 1864 the Croesor Tramway was used, reducing the carriage cost to Porthmadog from 7/10½ (39p) to 2/6½ (12.5p) per ton.

Remains There are few traces of the mills which at closure contained 18 saws, 18 dressers, a Kellow saw capable of cutting up to 12″ thicknesses, and a Kellow patent rapid-return planer. There is now no trace of the exceptionally fine fan-house.

Immediately below the tip can be seen the small mound of spoil from an uncompleted lower adit and, near it, the outline of a balance track used in its construction. In the valley below, near the foot of the incline, there are the traces of the small compressor house which provided air for the scheme, with some sign both of the water pipe run to it, and the air-pipe run from it. Above, on the hill, are traces of the vertical shafts, an extensive leat system, traces of the pipe which superseded it when the Pelton wheel was installed, and the washed-out reservoir dam. Further off is an old digging sometimes referred to as Upper Croesor.

Underground the 440 yard long access tunnel is of unusually large bore with, part way along, one of the vertical shafts coming down from above. At its far end the tunnel widens into a large marshalling area. There are several buildings and artifacts associated with the post-WW2 use as an explosives store. The incline down is flooded up to adit level and the massive masonry of the haulage winch, installed for explosives handling, hinders access to the incline up. To the right is a large flooded chamber, with a collapsed bridge to workings beyond. To the left are two blocked tunnels.

Outside, near the adit, the incline with ruined drum-house is a prominent feature. Nearby is the ruin of the barracks, but the row of 8, [Blaen-y-cwm], cottages on the valley floor have vanished.

There is (1998) a proposal to replant the power station near the foot of the Blaen-y-cwm incline of the Croesor Tramway, and to renew the feed pipe from Llyn Cwm-y-foel. (40)

CROESOR BACH SH639452
A small underground unmechanised working, hand dressing being done in shelters adjacent to the adit. Said to have employed 12 men in the late 1860s, but they only produced 40 tons p.a. A cart track led to Pont Sion Goch, where slate was loaded onto the Croesor Tramway.
Remains Collapsed adit; ruins of dressing sheds; tramway formation traceable, slate waste on ground at Croesor Tramway loading point. Three other trial adits are on the hillside above. (33)

CWM CAETH (Aberglaslyn, Nanmor) SH605466
A small open working with a small water-powered mill. Product carted via Nanmor village. Said to have employed about 12 men and to have worked between 1876-79.
Remains Tunnel into pit. Several buildings much altered for agricultural reuse. (14)

CWM CLOCH SH579472
Tiny underground working; undoubtedly unsuccessful, although 20 men were reportedly employed c1870.
Remains Collapsed adit; ruins of one small building; traces of an access track. (5)

CWM CŶD SH581466 &583465
An almost certainly unsuccessful trial.
Remains Two collapsed adits. (6)

CWM MAESGWM SH653437
Very small working.
Remains 3 adits, 2 collapsed; vestiges of 1, possibly 2, dressing sheds. (39)

CWM Y FOEL SH658476
Small underground working on an inaccessible site. Said to have employed 5 men in the 1820s, producing 20 tons p.a. Finished product may have been man carried down to Cwm Croesor.

Remains Collapsed adit. Trial at Llys Dafydd-y-foel (656471) may have been associated. (42)

DINAS DDU SH594453

Small hillside quarry with some underground workings, having a small tramway network and a water-powered mill. Output carted to Porthmadog. Little activity after about 1870.

Remains A dwelling occupies what was possibly the site of an office. The mil,l with its wheel-pit, has been used as a source of stone for nearby farm structures. A nice stone cutting leads to the working area. The adit is open for a short distance. There is some leatwork. (11)

DÔL FRIOG (Ty'n y Chwarel) SH611458

Open pit, stated as active in 1865 with 10 men producing 40 tons p.a.
Remains Virtually nothing; site in forestry. (15)

FRON-BOETH SH652448

Underground, an ambitious 1886 enterprise to extend the Pant-mawr workings. Never very successful, but up to 50 men were employed, with activity tapering off in the early 1900s.

Adits to chambers developed below the Pant-mawr workings were served by a short, single-acting table incline, which brought material down to a steam powered mill. Finished product was taken along a contour chasing incline to the head of a long, stone embanked incline. From the foot of this incline, a 500 yard tunnel led to Cwm Croesor, where the line turned up valley to a point above the head of the lower pitch of the Pant-mawr incline. This lower pitch was extended, and the upper pitch abandoned.

In the early 1890s a further mill was built at the tunnel entrance, possibly to deal with Cefn-y-braich material, and in anticipation of downward development of the main workings. This mill was nominated as Level 22 in a continuation of the Pant-mawr and Moelwyn numbering sequence.

Remains The upper mill, at Level 18, has evidence of 3 saw tables and 3 dressing machines having been installed, although the building is large enough for twice this number. Alongside the mill is a large Lancashire boiler, apparently used for water storage and which may have originally been used in the Pant-mawr mill.

The short incline, which has a slate lined channel running alongside, may have been water balanced to enable product to be dispatched via the Pant-mawr incline before the tunnel route was built.

There are various buildings on site and, part way along the tramway, the foundations of an elevated office structure.

There are a number of adits, some blocked, some wet, leading to chambering in rather poor rock. There is much backfilling, including some in the adits.

The drum-house and incline (which also served the Cefn-y-braich workings) down to the lower mill are in good condition, but the lower mill itself is very ruinous.

At the lower mill (647446) is the entrance to the tunnel, which can be pentrated for much of its length. Oddly, there are two chambers part way along it. From its northern end, in the Croesor valley, the line can be traced to where the lower Pant-mawr incline was extended to meet it. The drum-house has some brakegear, and there are rope-support rollers *in situ*. (38)

FRON OLAU SH579409
Tiny pit working, which may have been worked in conjunction with Porthreuddyn.
Remains Excavation only. (4)

GARREG UCHAF SH636446
Tiny pit; probably only a trial c1820.
Remains Slight excavation. (29)

GELLI (Craig Boeth, Bwlch Batal) SH637463
An isolated, part underground, working active for a few years from about 1860, when 50 tons were produced by 8 men. Finished product was carted via Croesor village.
Remains There are some small ruined buildings on the site and, some distance away, a small dwelling that may have been connected with the quarry. However, the main feature is the barracks, with workshops and smithy in a lean-to at the rear. The underground workings, basically on two levels, can be entered for a short distance. Above and behind the site is an adit that seems to have been a trial. The cart track is traceable. (31)

GERYNT (Gelli Iago) SH631484
A moderate sized open pit working, from which material may have been raised by horse-whim. A gravity incline led down to a large water-powered mill. Active around 1870 with 30 men employed, producing 200 tons p.a. Finished slate was taken by wagon to Porthmadog, part of the journey possibly on the Croesor Tramway.

Remains Unusually for a pit working, the uphaulage incline is a ramp rather than of the chain type, but the method of power is unclear. The incline formation down to the mill is extant, but the mill site was levelled in the early 1990s. (22)

GOAT SH582468
A tiny short-lived working, circa 1870; 5 men.
Remains Two adits in tandem, the lower one certainly unproductive; both collapsed. Vestiges of an access track. (8)

GWERNLASDEG SH584496
Open quarry late 1870s; unsuccessful due to falling prices and lack of transport.
Remains Excavation and rubbish runs; traces of buildings and access track. (10)

HAFOD BOETH SH638418
This was a metal mine, but there is a report of it being a slate operation employing 12 men who produced 50 tons p.a. in the 1860s.
Remains Nothing that can be identified as slate working. (32)

HAFOD UCHAF SH643434
A compact underground working with several adits in a little valley, and with a water-powered mill. Active in the 1870s with 12 men producing 60 tons p.a.
Remains Adits on 4 levels, the lower ones collapsed. There are traces of a dressing shed at the highest level; below is a neat smithy with a dressing shed backing onto it. There are sawn ends nearby suggesting possible use of a hand-cranked circular saw. At the bottom of the site are ruins of a mill, but it seems unlikely that machinery was ever actually installed.

There are trial adits to the east and west of the site. (34)

HAFOD-Y-LLAN (Cwm y Llan, South Snowdon) SH613524
An early hillside/pit working, developed in the 1840s. Tramways and inclines brought material to a water-wheel powered mill, finished product being sent out via a short tramway to the Cwm y Llan cart road which also served copper mines.

Emboldened by the proposals to lay a railway along Nant Gwynant, there was considerable expansion in the late 1870s. The mill was extended and converted to turbine power, and the workforce increased to 50.

The most notable part of this development was the construction of a tramway, down to Pont Bethania, of truly heroic proportions. From there, material was carted to the Croesor Tramway for conveyance to Porthmadog, latterly using a steam traction engine. Closed 1880s.

Remains There are a number of workings at several levels, dispersed over a wide area and connected by two inclines. There is an interesting archway where one tramway was carried over another, and pieces of drilled slate seem to be tramway sleepers. Lower down are the ruins of a number of buildings, including the mill; the route of the turbine feed pipe can be seen on a redundant incline. Since the mill extension was on the far side of the wheel-pit and the launder pillars still stand, it may be that the wheel was retained to supplement the turbine. There are traces of at least two dwellings; a barracks and, unusually, an unhoused weighbridge.

The bed of the original tramway runs to what was a cart road, now forming part of the Watkin path to Snowdon.

The really notable feature is the later tramway. From the site it gradually descends for ¾ mile, via impressive stone embanking, cuttings, and a rock-cut shelf, to the head of the upper incline. On route, it cuts an earlier tramway (which brought ore from the Braich yr Oen copper mine to the Lliwedd Bach Mill), on which can be seen a fine run of stone block sleepers.

The precipitous upper incline has a ruined drum-house with brakeman's hut, and part way down are the abutments of a bridge where it crossed the cart-road.

From the foot of this incline, the line runs for ¼ mile to a further drum-house and hut at the head of the lower incline. This incline is shorter, and also has traces of a bridge where it crossed the cart-road; at its foot are the stables and sheds (now in agricultural reuse) for the carts that were used to convey slate along Nant Gwynant. (16)

HAFOTY SH632436

Open quarry operating around 1875/76 with 17 men producing 100 tons p.a. Possibly had a water-powered mill. There was a proposal in 1904 to develop this site by tunnelling through from the Parc workings.

Remains Site afforested; some traces of buildings including possible mill. (23)

LLIDIART YR ARIAN SH633442

Hillside workings, with some underground trials. Latterly worked in conjunction with Parc (Slab), this name being applied to the combined unit.

Remains There are two open quarry workings, one of which may have been extended underground. At a lower level, there is a run-in adit.

There are extensive shallow rubbish runs, and the formation of the tramway connection to the Parc (Slab) mill. The stone embanked formation, running in front of the workings, is the old road down valley to Llanfrothen. (27)

LLYN LLAGI SH651485
A small and remote underground working with half a dozen men apparently operating without any above ground shelter of any kind.
Remains Collapsed adits. (37)

MEILLIONEN SH571485
Small underground working employing about 10 men.
Remains Site now in forestry. Vestiges of a small building at collapsed adit. It is possible that a formation down the hillside was, or was intended as, an incline. (1)

PANT-MAWR SH658446
Underground, sited some 1500' above sea level. Operating from c1850 in chambers under, communicating with, and with levels numbered sequentially with, the Moelwyn quarry (Region 9). Finished product was taken down on pack animal via Moelwyn's traditional route down Cwm Maesgwm, to be loaded on the Ffestiniog Railway at Penrhyndeudraeth. In the 1850s, a small mill was built with incline connection. In 1863 there was a big development with a fresh incline to the mill being built and, partly using a pre-existing track, a spectacular tramway was constructed on a rock-cut shelf to the head of a two pitch incline down to the Croesor Tramway.

A steam engine was installed in 1878 but, the following year, its up to 100 workforce was idle until it was partly re-opened in 1886 on amalgamation with Fron-boeth. As late as 1905, 2 or 3 chambers were still being worked by about 4 men.
Remains Several adits on various levels are penetrable to chambers in the steeply dipping vein. The inclines from the adits, the compact mill with its impressive retaining wall, and other buildings are extant, but the main feature is the tramway that gently climbs round the shoulder of the hill to the top of the 1000 ft incline, the highest two pitch incline in any slate quarry system. The drum-house is ruinous, but the upper pitch can be traced down to the embanked inter-pitch manoeuvring loop, which led to the lower pitch before it was extended for reuse to serve the Fron-boeth tunnel line. (41)

PARC *(Ceunant Parc)* SH626436

A compact underground operation in a narrow valley, opened around 1870 with up to 50 men. Under Moses Kellow's management many innovations were introduced, and had not his energies been diverted to Croesor in 1895, there would have been others, including the wide use of compressed air.

Chambering was on 7 floors (4 above, 2 below the adit) connected by an underground incline powered by an 80hp hydraulic engine. Hydraulics were also used for the Kellow drills, and for injector pumps. There were two water-powered mills which contained 6 saws, 3 dressers and 3 planers.

Although output was modest (351 tons with 15 men in 1883), concentration on specialities such as *Parcro* patent ridging, brought relatively good returns.

Finished product was taken by a short incline to a bridge across Afon Croesor, then by a further short incline to make a junction with the Croesor Tramway at the foot of the Lower Parc incline. Closed 1920.

Remains Several buildings are in reuse or in good condition, and the unusually ornate office is now a dwelling. The river is so extensively bridged by massive slabs as to be virtually culverted. At the north-eastern end of the site is a building with a wheel-pit and a slate bedded, powered incline with rope-score marks, and a flight of stone steps alongside. The building contains a compressor base and offcuts of the patent ridging.

Opposite is the collapsed adit, near which is a lavatory and the ruins of the main mill, powered by a launder from the tail-race of the upper wheel. The leat which fed the mill before the ridging mill was built, is traceable. There is another building, now in reuse, and a large stocking area. The rubbish runs are extensive.

At a higher level is a blocked adit which seems to have served purely for rubbish disposal.

Save for vestiges of the drum-houses, the tramway branch has been almost obliterated. (20)

PARC (SLAB) *(Garth Llwynog, Hen Dwll)* SH632444

Open pit working. In 1870, 20 men were employed almost exclusively on slab. Finished product was taken out via a branch line which joined the Croesor tramway at Croesor village.

Remains Pit, part flooded. There is an incline down to the vestiges of the mill which was cut through by the present road. On the south side of the road are rubbish runs, and the pit of what was one of the largest wheels in the industry, which was fed by a wooden launder. This wheel may have also powered the incline to uphaul finished product back up to the Croesor tramway. It is also possible that it pumped as well, although an Injector pump may have been used latterly. Nearby is a tiny building with what appears to be a small wheel-pit which may have been a compressor house.

There is a very nice cutting for the connection to the Croesor tramway, and a children's paddling pool has been made from a holding pond. (24)

PORTH TREUDDYN (Pantillan) SH573409

Open quarry, 18th century; took slate, perhaps by horse sledge, to a shipping point near the present main road, which represents the limit of the tidal estuary prior to the building of the Cob in the early 1800s.
Remains Working and rubbish runs; building that may have unconnected with the quarry. (2)

PORTH TREUDDYN SH578408

This working, which dates from the mid 19th century, possibly went partly underground. Material was taken by incline to a water-powered mill near the road. Due to the lack of water, this quarry was an early user of steam. Output was carted to Porthmadog. Ceased in the 1870s.

Much of the product was, to be more accurate, Tremadog Grit, which is a very hard rock used for slab esp. steps (e.g. main entrance Plas Tan-y-bwlch).
Remains There is, apart from the diggings itself, some walling and a possible adit. The incline is much collapsed but at its foot is an unusual mill building, now in reuse, with a wheel-pit and stone lined leat.

There are other buildings in reuse, including one that may have been the steam powered mill. (3)

RHOSYDD SH664461

Small hilltop surface workings from the 1830s, developed underground in the 1850s until, with 14 levels and 170 chambers, it became one of the largest underground quarries outside Blaenau Ffestiniog itself, producing in 1883 5616 tons with 192 men. Its first mill, steam driven, was small and was shortly afterwards supplemented by a larger, water-driven mill lower down to the north. In the early 1860s a half mile long tunnel was cut below the then lowest workings to provide access, and to obviate pumping. Here at Level 9 water-powered mills eventually had at least 30 saws, around the same number of dressing machines, and at least one planer, driven by underfloor shafting and with at least attempts to remove mill waste by underfloor tunnels. Subsequent working on the 5 levels below this main tunnel had to be uphauled and pumped.

Steam was initially widely used but, later, maximum use was made of water-power for pumping, hauling, electric generation, air compression as well as mill power. Being elevated (1700' above sea level) and with a poor catchment, this meant using an extensive leat system with several reservoirs, to collect and store the water. Besides the surface reservoirs, several worked-out chambers were used for water storage.

One underground water balance was particularly ingenious; the balance tank running in its own tunnel above the drainage adit to raise loads up to it from below. Latterly, some use was made of oil engines.

The remoteness of the site meant that many of the men used the notoriously uncomfortable barrack blocks; others and their families lived in company housing in Cwm Orthin.

At first transport was difficult, product being sent by pack horse via Moelwyn and Cwm Maesgwm; later some use was made of Cwm Orthin, but this was beset by way-leave problems. After 1864 the finely engineered tramway to the head of Cwm Croesor and the splendid incline down to the Croesor Tramway was used. With a workforce down to 30 making a mere 500 tons p.a. production ceased c1930, but the site was not totally abandoned until post WW2.

Remains From the two pits to the south (the surface near the eastern one showing signs of a 1900 collapse) the dressing sheds, other buildings, inclines, adits, shafts and so on follow a chronological order northwards. In the western Twll is a winder. Immediately northward is 2 Level adit and remnants of the early steam mill and workshops. Beyond, at 3 level, is the square outline of the second mill, above which can be seen the depression for the flat rods that carried motion from this mill to a pump in the eastern Twll. There is also the pit of a haulage wheel. Further on is 4 adit and ruins of the original c1860 barracks, workshop and lavatory.

Inclines lead down to the big mill area at 9 level, there being no adits for levels 5 to 8. Like the other mills, the two contiguous mills here have now almost vanished. From one of the two wheel-pits the culvert that led away the tail-race under the working area is traceable. There are numerous other buildings, some with exceptionally nice windows and other detail. The 'street' of two-storied barracks progressively erected 1860-1890 is notable.

Near the 9 adit is the pit for the pitchback wheel (and some fragments of that wheel), which powered the endless rope haulage system, which pulled wagons along the adit. Recent excavation has revealed that the mechanism for this haulage was far from simple. There are also parts of trucks, including a gripper truck that towed the journeys of trams. Underground, at the far end of the adit, is the sheave for this system.

Since the workings are now flooded up to floor 9, only the head of 9-14 incline is visible; but the tunnel up from floor 9, in which ran the water balance tank which powered it, is clear (this system was later superseded by Pelton wheel power). Adjacent is the 5-9 mass balanced incline. In the eastern workings is the similar 3-6 incline. Both these inclines have, (late 1990s) headsheaves, tables and balance trucks intact. In the western workings, which were damaged by a collapse in 1900, are the degraded traces, with some artifacts of another incline down from above. Underground there is much trackwork, piping, bridges and other artifacts.

Amongst the prominent surface remains is a big structure alongside the track down to Cwm Orthin, which is an unfinished wheel-pit. Near the foot of this track, adjacent to the Conglog mill (Region 9), is the row of six Rhosydd cottages and not far away, in trees, Plas Cwm Orthin, the manager's house. Part way down that valley is the ruined Rhosydd chapel.

In the vicinity of the site, particularly to the north, are a number of reservoirs and lakes with leat systems partly traceable (a collapsed timber dam is notable).

The old track via Moelwyn can be traced and the later route via Cwm Orthin is obvious.

The most spectacular relic is the magnificent incline down to the Croesor Tramway, and the well engineered tramway to its head. Lack of space at the top of the incline meant that the drum-house is sited some 50′ above, the brake having been controlled by wires. The brakeman's shelter and control wheel platform are to be seen.

At the time of writing planning permission exists to reopen this quarry, so at some time much of the remains may be either obliterated or inaccessible. Fortunately some artifacts have been removed for safekeeping. In any case, the underground workings are now unstable and **entry is most inadvisable**.

Fortunately the whole quarry was thoroughly surveyed and published in 1974 (republished 1993) as *Rhosydd Slate Quarry by M.J.T. Lewis & J.H. Denton. (43)*

BLAENAU FFESTINIOG
Region 9
Including quarries using Ffestiniog Rly (and its feeder tramways),
Ffestiniog & Blaenau Rly, L&NWR Blaenau Branch
and GWR Bala to Blaenau Branch.

General

This compact region of abundant Ordovician slate was worked by some of the largest and most efficient units in the industry, producing in the latter part of the 19th century about one third of the entire Welsh output. Blaenau Ffestiniog, with its satellite villages of Manod and Tanygrisiau, was founded on a bare hillside, becoming a booming community of almost 12,000, not counting the lodgers who slept in almost every stable and outhouse, with virtually every employed person engaged in some aspect of slate working. Towering, encircling, waste tips dominate the town, which shows in the detail of its varied older buildings some fine examples of the slatemen's craft, to which the 'Slate Workers' window in the parish church is an unique tribute. Several quarries had family dwellings on site, the self-contained Rhiwbach settlement being particularly interesting.

Although output is a fraction of its peak, two companies continue to work four quarries, and source from other quarries both good rock and waste for processing and hard-core. Three of the quarries use modern untopping methods, but one continues in the traditional underground manner.

Llechwedd as well as being a working quarry, which almost carried on alone during the mid 20th century nadir, has an outstanding visitor centre. Besides providing demonstrations and underground tours, a number of buildings have been conserved and numerous artifacts displayed.

Transport

This area is synonymous with the Ffestiniog Railway and all quarries had access to it. Prior to its 1836 opening, slate was taken to quays on the Dwyryd, downstream of Maentwrog, by cart, the backs of animals or even of men. From there it was taken in a fleet of small boats for offshore

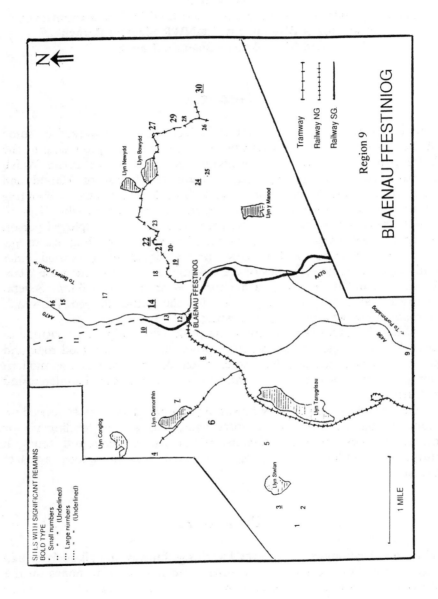

SITES WITH SIGNIFICANT REMAINS
BOLD TYPE
· Small numbers
·· " " (Underlined)
·· Large numbers
··· " " (Underlined)

Tramway

Railway NG

Railway SG

Region 9

BLAENAU FFESTINIOG

1 MILE

trans-shipment on to sea-going craft. Many of these quays, on either side of the river, are extant.

The Ffestiniog Railway itself is too well known to require description; it was reached by some quarries via direct connection, others by two main feeder tramways.

The Cwm Orthin tramway of 1850, is traceable from the mills area of that quarry via two inclines (Tan y Muriau & Village) and a fine embankment and cutting to Tanygrisiau, where it joined the railway. In 1874 it was extended to Conglog, the formation of which substantially follows the present valley track.

The Rhiwbach tramroad of 1863, except for one washed out bridge, forms a continuous track from the top of the Rhiwbach quarry incline, past Bwlch y Slaters, Blaen y Cwm and Cwt y Bugail quarries, to the head of No 3 incline above Maenofferen quarry. From Maenofferen, No 2 incline (which is still in working order) drops down to Bowydd quarry. A level run takes it to the head of No 1 incline which descends to where it joined the Ffestiniog Railway at the present town car park. Horses pulled between the inclines but, in its last days, a rail tractor operated from the top of No 2 to Rhiwbach.

There are also the spectacular quarry-connection inclines, such as the multi-pitched Moelwyn and Graig Ddu runs, and the single pitch, partly in tunnel, Wrysgan. The Llechwedd and Oakeley inclines are decayed, but the Diffwys incline is now a public path.

From 1879 Llechwedd also used the L&NWR Llandudno Junction-Blaenau branch loading at the Pant yr Afon yard and, from 1934, Oakeley also loaded there. Product could either stay on the railway or be shipped at Deganwy on the Conwy estuary where, at SH782788, there are still relics of the slate wharves. In the latter case, 2'G. quarry waggons were entrained pic-a-back. This line is, of course, still in use.

The G.W.R. Bala-Blaenau branch of 1883 carried little slate traffic, largely continuing the function of the 1868 2'G Ffestiniog & Blaenau Railway as a feeder for the Ffestiniog Railway. Apart from some traffic picked up at Llan Ffestiniog, it mainly carried Graig Ddu output. This line which, north of Llan Ffestiniog, substantially used the Ffestiniog & Blaenau Railway formation was joined end on to the ex-L&NWR, ex-LMS line at Blaenau in the 1960s, and closed south of Trawsfynydd. The abandoned route runs along a spectacular rock ledge until, after the fine Cwm Prysor viaduct, it was incorporated into the main road. From there it may be followed until its trackbed is drowned in the Tryweryn (Llyn Celyn) reservoir, below which its route to Bala is plain.

1. SH658442 etc. Bwlch Stwlan *
2. SH661439 Cloddfa Sion Llwyd *
3. SH661442 Moelwyn ** (R)
4. SH668467 Conglog ** (R)
5. SH671446 Chwarel Twm Ffeltiwr
6. SH678456 Wrysgan *** (R)
7. SH681459 Cwm Orthin * (R)
8. SH689462 Nyth y Gigfran ** (R)
9. SH690421 Rhyd-y-sarn (Mill) *
10. SH690466 Oakeley **W (R)
11. SH693483 Ffridd-y-bwlch
12. SH697467 Glan-y-don (Tip & Mill) (R)
13. SH697469 Pantyrafon (Sidings) *W (R)
14. SH700470 Llechwedd ****WV (R)
15. SH701482 Cloddfa Cribau *
16. SH701484 Clogwyn Llwyd *
17. SH704473 Olwyn-goch (Pumping shaft)
18. SH707468 Foty (R)
19. SH708462 Bowydd **W (R)
20. SH709454 Pant-yr-ynn (Mill)
21. SH712463 Diffwys (Casson) ***W (R)
22. SH715467 Maenofferen ****W (R)
23. SH718467 Hysfa
24. SH724454 Graig Ddu **W (R)
25. SH725452 Manod ('Old' Manod) *
26. SH732455 Bwlch y Slaters ('New' Manod) *W (R)
27. SH734469 Cwt y Bugail *** (R)
28. SH735463 Blaen-y-cwm *** (R)
29. SH740462 Rhiwbach **** (R)

BLAEN-Y-CWM (Incl. Ffridd or Pen-y-ffridd) SH735463 etc.
Pit/Underground. Four distinct workings, the earliest dating from at least 1813. Much developed during the 1870s when the presently extant mill was built, with 5 saws and 5 dressers. Its water-wheel was backed up by the steam engine which powered the incline connection to the Rhiwbach Tramway. Although geographically extensive, its sporadic annual tonnages frequently failed to reach three figures.

Prior to the use of the tramway to Blaenau Ffestiniog, output was carried via Cwm Machno to Trefriw, and later via Cwm Teigl to the Dwyryd. Closed WW1.
Remains The main feature is the mill which has a very large wheel

housing at one end, with access provided by cantilevered steps, and a fine tail-race tunnel. At the opposite end is an engine house and coal store, and nearby are remnants of the portable engine boiler and firebox which replaced the original boiler. There are rope apertures in, and pulley support pillars near, the engine house for the incline haulage.

The mill waste chutes along one side are nicely constructed of slate, and they feed into an unusually deep rubbish wagon run, which is bridged at intervals by slate slabs. There are several buildings, weigh-houses etc. and some artifacts including the upper sheave of the exit incline. This incline was extended down towards an underground working, where there are some small buildings, and an adit with rail *in situ* leading to some chambering. Although there are rope markings indicating use, this extension was apparently never completed.

Near the mill is a lavatory block built over a large pit, undoubtedly the wheel-pit of an earlier mill. There are several other buildings, weigh-houses etc. in this area, and a little way off to the south, a powder-house. Above the site was a small reservoir formed by pounding behind the Rhiwbach Tramway formation.

The most obvious working area is immediately to the south of the mill. This is a pit accessed by an adit, and was formed by untopping old underground workings. The formation of a balanced incline leads down into the pit to form a through route to the mill from the Bwlch Carreg y Frân quarry, when it was re-worked by Blaen-y-cwm. Here are vestiges of dressing sheds and an early mill. The small pit working to the south of the tramway was accessed by a short tunnel (now blocked).

Further to the south, and immediately east of the Bwlch y Slaters branch of the Rhiwbach tramway, is a further pit; these were the early Ffridd workings. Adjacent are remnants of dressing sheds and a curious circular structure, possibly a caban. (28)

BOWYDD *(Chwarel Lord Newborough, Percival's)* SH708462

A late 18th century working substantially developed from the 1820s. By 1825 it had an (originally 2'2"G) rail layout (that was locomotive worked from 1878). An early user of both hand and circular saws and of Mathew's dressers.

Amalgamated from the big Foty & Bowydd quarry in the 1870s, producing in 1882, 12,092 tons with 344 men, which built up at the end of the 19th century to over 17,000 tons p.a. and 500 men.

Ultimately there were three mills plus a writing slate factory, using water in tandem with a total of 50 saw tables and 50 dressing machines. The three big mills, on massively terraced waste, were lettered downward

A, B & C. They had central wheel pits driving through underfloor line shafting, with the track for the waste wagons inside rather than outside the buildings. There was also a second water-powered (later steam) writing slate factory in the town.

Limited electric power was available from 1899 from Yale's Dolwen station, later supplemented by a supply from Maentwrog which enabled diamond saws to be used, but water-power was still employed for the C-B & B-A water balances, a 3 track water haulage incline and a hydrostat pump. In 1925 two oil engines aggregating 250hp were installed in an effort to reduce their power bills.

As with all the quarries in this area, material was at first carried for shipment near Maentwrog; it was not until 1854 that an incline made direct connection with the Ffestiniog Railway, which was a few years later supplanted by the use of the No1 incline of the Rhiwbach Tramway. By 1880, most material was going out by a connection made part way down the Diffwys incline.

Rockfalls prevented full advantage being taken of the early 1900s mini-boom so, although it fared better than the once mighty Diffwys, the 20th century was a time of struggle, beset by flooding and falls. Run as an outlier of Oakeley for 30 years from 1933, mainly untopping old chambers, this being continued from the 1980s under Llechwedd ownership.

Remains Owing to untopping operations on the quarrying site, and to landscaping operations lower down, much was lost during the 1980s.

There is an extensive network of tramway formations, some with track. A tunnel leads to a slab-floored terrace with a haulage rope guard rail, which is an entrance to the machine-bored Cooke level to Maenofferen. The big Tuxford haulage incline is just discernable alongside 1930s untopping.

A nice feature is 'Quarry Bank', the ruined manager's house alongside the Rhiwbach No 2 incline. At about this level are several other buildings, including the remnants of the two-storey writing slate factory. There are also a number of other buildings such as offices, loco sheds and weigh-houses, as well as several inclines. There is much substantial revetment work to retain terracing and to hold back rubbish from adits and working areas.

The original 1854 incline has been lost in subsequent work, but the connection to the Rhiwbach Tramway near the foot of No 2 incline is obvious. In spite of clearance, the route from the lowest mill level to join the Diffwys incline is traceable. The Rhiwbach route to the head of No 1 incline down to Blaenau is well engineered, with cuttings and embankments. The No 1 incline itself is in good condition, but the rock-cut remote drum-house has largely collapsed. The lower end of the Diffwys incline, below the Bowydd connection, has been surfaced as a path.

At the top of the site, the old Foty pit is flooded and serves as a water source. (9)

BWLCH STWLAN SH658442
Trial level.
Remains Collapsed adit. (1)

BWLCH Y SLATERS (Bwlch Manod, Manod) SH732455
Open workings near the summit, dated from the c1780s, but the main underground development with a steam mill came with the 1866 connection to the Rhiwbach tramway.

The rock was harder to win than in most places in the region, which may account for the variable tonnages which sometimes fell below 100 p.a. There was a vigorous expansion in 1903 when a new site was opened at 730548 linked by an incline, and in some years around 2000 tons was turned out.

The original route out was via Cwm Teigl, the same route being reverted to when the tramway charges were increased in the 1920s. The road was improved to service the section of the quarry which was used for Art Storage during WW2. After de-requisition in the 1980s, the scale of working was dramatically increased.
Remains The site, which now incorporates Graig Ddu, is much disturbed by untopping work and by the cutting of roads; the 1900s incline for instance, has been virtually obliterated.

The mills area has several interesting buildings, including a fine office. The present mill dates from 1985, and its modern equipment includes an automatic dressing machine, a profiler, and a line for the flow production of flooring/cladding slabs. As a working operation, access is not normally possible.

The route of the connection to the Rhiwbach tramway, including the reversing loop, is traceable. (26)

CHWAREL TWM FFELTIWR SH671446
Small, underground, mid 19th century.
Remains Gridded adit and possibly a second adit (run in); traces of a dressing shed. Also an abortive trial (gridded adit) at 677451 has been associated with this operation. (5)

CLODDFA CRIBAU SH701482

Group of 3 or 4 underground trials. Mid 19th century.
Remains One adit open but flooded; another has vestiges of a dressing shed. (15)

CLODDFA SION LLWYD SH661439

Early working, possibly a precursor of the main Moelwyn working.
Remains Run in adits; dressing shed remnants. (2)

CLOGWYN LLWYD SH701484

Late 19th century trials.
Remains One of the two adits is open (60 yds.). A vertical shaft from this is possibly 1920s work. No sign of slate or of mineralisation. (16)

CONGLOG (Glan Ffestiniog) SH668467

A compact and delightfully situated quarry operating from 1874 to 1909, much of the time on a part time basis. From adits high up (1425' above sea level) at the head of Cwm Orthin, a short incline brought material to a small water-powered mill. Finished product was removed by tramway via Cwm Orthin quarry. In its later days it was operated by two Rhosydd workers in their spare time.
Remains Behind the drum-house, which has a curious extension, the workings are chambered up from below. There is an adit below which leads to chambering; there are trucks and rail but the lowest adit has collapsed. A leat partly runs alongside the Rhosydd track. The mill has been substantially adapted for agricultural use, but the wheel-pit and launder pillars are extant.

The cottages alongside the mill, the nearby house, and the chapel part way down the valley were Rhosydd property. The tramway is readily traceable along the present track. (4)

CWM ORTHIN (New Welsh Slate Incl., Tai'r Muriau) SH681459

A substantial underground enterprise that was notorious for bad working conditions. Commenced c1810 as an open quarry, it was worked sporadically until the early 1860s when, following tramway connection to the Ffestiniog Railway, there was extensive underground development.

Originally, chambering was above the water table with material being brought out by adits to mills at lake level. As work progressed downward, pumping and haulage were called for, at first steam, later electrically powered. Output in 1882 was 10,376 tons, with over 500 men employed. The 3 mills (one steam, 2 water-powered) contained up to about 50 saws and 50 dressing machines. After a serious collapse in 1884, production was much reduced. In 1900 it was incorporated into Oakeley quarry, and all surface works and the use of the Cwm Orthin tramway were abandoned. In 1925 there was a big development project, for which a fine powder house and other buildings were erected but, like a further 1930s scheme, this was not proceeded with. Work underground continued until Oakeley closed in 1970.

It was worked afterwards on a very small scale using a saw in one of the chambers, transport underground being by Land Rover. In the 1980s, outside capital enabled work to be scaled up and a mill rebuilt, but the backers failed. Re-opened by a local company in 1995, work ceased again in 1997.

Remains Due to vigorous working much has been lost from this working site, particularly the fine powder house and the main incline.

Near the lake are traces of the Lake mill which, in its later days, was steam powered. There are ruins of several other buildings, including the tree-screened manager's house.

Near the southern end of the lake, with its obvious rubbish tippings, its the main barracks block (the early end built of country rock has fallen, but the later end, built of slate off-cuts, stands), and the ruinous 'Tiberias' chapel. The short Lake incline down to main mills level also carried Conglog traffic. Near the foot of this incline a new mill was built in the 1980s on the site of the 1855 Cross mill.

The site of the Lower or London mill, and much of its associated river channelling, has been cleared and converted into a miniature park. A slate-built shelter covers the deep pit housing the Pelton wheel which drove the mill line-shafting by chain. This wheel has been restored to working order and now drives a 4Kw generator by flat-belts.

On the hill above the site, leats can be traced and one can see where the ground has sunk as a result of the underground collapse. Also to be seen are the cast iron markers defining the surface boundary between Oakeley and Cwm Orthin property.

The exit tramway is a delightful feature. (7)

CWT Y BUGAIL SH734469

A remote, partly underground, quarry which was an enlargement of the old Bugail working opened in the 1820s. Constrained by lack of transport (there was a proposal in 1853 to build a tramway down to Penmachno), it was able to develop during the 1860s with the opening of the Rhiwbach tramway, producing 1,662 tons in 1882, and later perhaps twice as much.

Material was uphauled from two pit/underground workings to be reduced in a mill equipped with at least 20 saw tables and dressing machines.

Water supply was minimal, and was only used for saw cooling and for a waterbalanced incline. Steam powered the uphaulage inclines and the mill, replaced in the mill by an oil engine in latter years. The quarry was worked on a reduced scale until the 1960s.

Remains The principal feature is the mill, clearly much too large for the output of this quarry, constructed in three sections with a separate engine room. This building survived almost intact into the 1980s, but is now very much collapsed. It contains several wooden dressing machine bases. The barracks block and office is behind it and there are several other buildings including, unusually for this region, a number of dressing sheds. There are traces of the waterbalanced incline which brought material up from subsidiary workings lower down the hill. At the foot of this are vestiges of an older smaller mill.

Owing to a slight adverse gradient, trucks of finished product had to be cable hauled to the Rhiwbach tramway; the mounting for the sheave can be seen near the junction. A little distance off, near the tramway main line, are the ruins of the family houses.

The principal workings are reached by a cutting and a curved tunnel. There is a deep pit in two parts from which several adits lead to chambers.

There are various artifacts on site, including remnants of a crane, a pump and track underground. Notable is a steam winder, boiler and a weighing machine at the head of an incline. Primarily for rubbish disposal, it may also have powered some kind of ropeway. (27)

DIFFWYS (Diphwys Casson, Incl. Henwaith, Penffridd, Twll Newydd) SH712463

The first organised quarry in the district, opened in the 1760s by Methusalem Jones of Nantlle who is said to have dug in this locality as a result of a dream. It covers a big area, as much was originally shallow pit worked, although some underground working may have been done as early as 1812. A pioneer user (1805?) of hand cranked circular saws.

At first, sledgeways and packhorses were used to take material for shipment on the Dwyryd, eased in 1801 by a cart road to Manod village. An early user of internal tramways (originally 3'4½" gauge plateways), and of internal inclines; 9 were in use at one time. Later 2'2" gauge was used, the 3'4½" being retained for the trwncs. This gauge difference may have accounted for their reluctance to use the Ffestiniog Railway, a reluctance demonstrated in 1846 by building the water-powered Pant-yr-ynn mill alongside their exit road. This was not their first mill; a small water-powered mill (later enlarged and converted to steam as No 4 mill) slightly predated it, making it one of the earliest steam mills in the region. Their No 6 steam mill of 1859 is claimed to have been the first integrated mill, but it may have been predated by the mill at Minllyn (Region 14). Trimming was by massive Mathews dressers.

They eventually connected with the Ffestiniog Railway in 1860 via the Bowydd incline (later to become No1 Incline of the Rhiwbach Tramway), but continued to cart for loading on the Dwyryd until the completion of their own direct incline to the railway in 1863.

The earliest, open, workings (Hen Waith) were at the top of the site with work more or less progressing downhill with the first tentative underground working. Serious underground extraction started much lower down, and this was followed by work at (Drum Boeth) higher up, close to the original diggings.

By 1826 its 6000 ton output totally dominated the Blaenau scene, but within 2 years, competition from Holland's and the Welsh Slate Company (both later part of Oakeley) halved their sales. It was not until the late 1870s, with a workforce of over 300 and 3 steam mills, that the mid 1820s outputs were exceeded.

These outputs declined dramatically in the 1880s even though a fresh underground working, New Quarry, was opened in 1882 to the east of the site. When the plant was sold in 1892, of the 42 saws on offer, less than a dozen seem to have been serviceable. One of the two planers was broken and the dressers included the long outmoded Mathew's guillotine type. It enjoyed a short revival around the turn of the century.

Reopened in 1920 after war-time closure, its 23 saws and 19 dressers were powered by two 15hp electric motors. Two 30hp motors hauled, there was a 38hp compressor and a 25hp pump in the New Quarry, but the 50 men could only make a few hundred tons p.a. and, after mounting losses, work ceased in 1927. Bought by Oakeley in 1935 as a dumping ground for Bowydd, they did work it; untopping continuing up to about 1955 and from 1972 it was recommenced by Llechwedd.

Remains The site is now somewhat confused by the modern untopping work and the roads that have been constructed. Also, near the lowest part of the site, there is some intermingling with the Bowydd site, as this undertaking tipped to the south-east of Diffwys using a tramway that bridged the main Diffwys incline.

At the top of the site are some of the earliest buildings, weigh-houses etc. constructed of massive blocks of country rock in the traditional

Meirionnydd manner. There are also several ponds, an interesting stone embanked leat, and some tramway formations with the old 'wide' gauge slate sleepers. The original Hen Waith workings have been obliterated by the progression of the later Drum Boeth operations.

Nearby are the separate New Quarry workings with adits and some buildings, and a tramway that leads, via two inclines and a narrow terrace, through a tunnel (collapsed) to the upper mill. Near the lower of the two inclines is a fine flight of steps.

In the upper part of the quarry is a particularly intersting drum-house, a conversion of a conventional self acting unit into a single acting, powered table incline. The standard drum was shortened and supported by a third wall. A small working platform was sited alongside the end of the shortened drum, up under the eaves, to provide a housing for the electric motor and a cramped space for the driver, who controlled a screw-type brake. This platform was reached by slate slab steps, cantilevered out of the back wall.

Lower down the site near the No 6 mill is a similar drum-house powering a haulage incline. It is a suite of buildings, comprising a weigh-house and office, as well as the drum-house holding a shortened drum. The control/motor platform in this case was reached by a conventional external stairway. The brake is an adaption of standard brake gear but, since the lever had to be. shortened, it is heavily weighted to assist application. There are still some rails on the crimp.

The No 6 mill walls are in fair condition. The rubbish track alongside still has rail on the ground and a rubbish wagon in position. There are parts of Mathews dressers.

There are several other interesting drum-houses; the one immediately below the upper mill is singularly massive. Another, which has a fine flight of steps nearby, has been converted into an office type building. At the lower levels, the original mill and other buildings have been buried by waste from recent work.

There are many other buildings and artifacts on this site, and the untopping operations, and collapses, reveal chambers and inclines (some with rail *in situ*).

Landscaping in the mid 1980s obliterated much of the main incline, but the drum-house is extant, incorporating a weighbridge (on the opposite side to the brakeman's cabin) and the drum with a central brake using automotive type linings. This incline also, by mid run hitching, served Bowydd, after its use by Diffwys was abandoned. The old 1800s road is still a road for much of its length, and the upper part forms a natural access to the site. A number of the cottages in this area were built and owned by the quarry. (21)

FFRIDD-Y-BWLCH SH693483

Underground, mid 19th century.
Remains Obviously disused by the 1870s as it is overlain by the debris
from the L&NWR tunnel air shaft. One adit is open; another may have
been buried, but there are some vestiges of walling. At 692482 is a trial,
with collapsed adit; almost certainly non-productive. (11)

GLAN-Y-DON (Pen-y-bont) SH697467

Site of a tip and mill reached from the Welsh Slate Co's quarry by a
viaduct.
Remains Viaduct pillars. (12)

GRAIG DDU SH724454

A remote and elevated 1840s development adjoining the 1800s Manod
workings, notable for the ingenious use of limited water supplies. At the
workings which, uniquely for Blaenau, did not go underground until the
1920s, there were three mills. Their over 20 saws (including 3 Hunters),
at least 20 dressing machines and 5 planers, were driven by a water
wheel backed up by a 15hp steam engine.

One of the last quarries to boat product down the Dwyryd, this
arduous journey was obviated in 1865 by a magnificent four pitch incline
to the Ffestiniog & Blaenau Railway.

At the foot of the upper pitch a further three-mill complex was built,
with 12 saws and 11 dressers, driven by a part-buried water wheel
supplied by an underground tunnel. Some water came from ponds to the
north but most came from Llyn y Manod pumped by flat-rods from a
water wheel. A 16hp steam engine provided back up.

After the GWR supplanted the F & B, quarry wagons were carried
from Tan y Manod station to Blaenau on transporters, for transfer either
to the Ffestiniog Railway or onto GWR trucks.

Some men lived in the bleak barracks at the top of the site, but most,
terrifyingly, rode down the incline in 'Wild Cars'.

Output in 1882 was over 3000 tons with 110 men, but although sales
dived the following year, their end of century peak was around double
this. Employment was 86 prior to WW2 closure, but post-war work was
on a very small scale and in the 1980s untopping, in conjunction with
the Bwlch y Slaters site, commenced.
Remains Continuing opencast working has obliterated most of the
quarrying site with its pit and inclines, two tunnels, mills and other
buildings. The vast pit exposes some of the chambering below. Obviously
as a working area it should not be entered. The undisturbed workings to
the south are part of the Manod or 'Old Manod' quarry.

The most obvious feature is the cascade of inclines. The highest leads down to what was the lower mills area (Lefel Dŵr Oer), where there is now little more than some building vestiges, the base of the 1925 gas engine, and the ponds. The pumping-wheel pit and leats are to the south.

Part way down the shorter second incline are vestiges of a small hydro-generator house.

The magnificent third incline down to road level has some wrecked wagons alongside it, including some placarded G.W.R.

The final incline, to the west of the road, down to the railway is less clear but its line is traceable. Both the old cart road from the workings to Llan Ffestiniog and an access track to Dŵr Oer are clear features. (24)

HYSFA SH718467
Short lived working, c1815.
Remains Possible excavation at edge of Diffwys. (23)

LLECHWEDD (Greaves, include. Tal y Weinydd) SH700470
This mainly underground quarry, opened in 1846 by Greaves & Shelton, rapidly becoming one of the largest in the region, and with their 50 tons per man-year and 9-1 waste to make ratio, one of the most efficient in the industry. Also a leader in methodology, Greaves pattern saws and dressers becoming the industry standard. Highly mechanised mills were established from 1852 on several levels, with chambering eventually on 16 floors with 20 miles of tunnels.

As with its immediate neighbours, water was comparatively plentiful and was extensively used for mill driving, pumping and haulage, both by water balance and direct cranking, there being a number of powered inclines, mostly underground, and several gravity ones on the surface. In 1882 24,723 tons were produced by 553 men, this tonnage and payroll increasing in the 1890s.

Steam was introduced in the 1850s for haulage, and later for locos. Some electricity was generated by a dynamo in a mill in 1890, followed by a full-scale hydro station in 1904. There was much innovation in the 1930s, keeping over 400 men in work under Col. Martyn Williams-Ellis' leadership, including electric traction and the unique adaption of a Blondin for tipping and to assist in the pioneering untopping methods of extraction.

An early user of the Ffestiniog Railway, although direct incline connection was not made until 1852. Later this incline, which remained in use until 1964, also reached the main line railway at Pant yr Afon.

Remains As a working quarry it is not normally possible to view much of the site, where opencast untopping of chambers to work the pillars has obliterated many features. Wiresawing is used, all movement is by lorry, and reduction is concentrated in the rebuilt and re-equipped No.7 mill. Several inclines survive, such as the main exit incline passing under the main road, and numerous buildings, including the drum-house of the big 'Inclein Bôn' which was successively water, steam and electrically wound.

In the Visitor section, centred around the original No1 mill, there is a fine exhibition and demonstration display with machines and artifacts, many extremely rare. Besides houses, other buildings and rolling stock, there is a working blacksmith's shop and a complete haulage incline. Tours by rail and by incline to interpretive areas underground are provided.

At the entrance to the site, Plas Weunydd (once the owner's house) is now the main office. Behind there is a barracks and houses, some of which are in use, and above the site there are extensive leats fed from Llyn Newydd and Llyn Bowydd. (14)

MAENOFFEREN (Incl. David Jones') SH715467

A substantial and still active underground quarry occupying a compact site at over 1300' above sea level. Originally opened c1810 but was not notably successful until developed under Greaves' ownership in the 1850s. Independent from the 1860s, it continued to flourish; output in 1882 was 8360 tons with 238 men, growing in the '90s to over 14,000 tons p.a. with more than 400 men employed. Two mills, originally water driven, contained almost 50 saws and dressers. Locomotive power was extensively used from c1900.

Following some use of electricity at the turn of the century, a hydro-electric station, which still operates, was built in 1918. It provided mill power and superseded steam and water-balance uphaulage.

Between the wars, progressive management made its 7000 ton output and over 300 men the third largest in Blaenau. Post WW2 was a struggle; some open working was done to attract men averse to going underground. The Greaves company re-acquired the site in 1975 and continues to work it. Other than Aberllefenni (Region 13), it is now the sole totally underground quarry. In the 1980s it pioneered the use of wire saws and, in compliance with modern legislation, electric fan ventilation is used.

Some use was made of the Diffwys incline, prior to the construction of the Rhiwbach tramway which ran through the site. Thereafter, the No1 & 2 inclines of this tramway were used until 1920, when a new incline through Foty and Bowydd by-passed No1. After Rhiwbach quarry was acquired in 1928, this incline was abandoned and the Rhiwbach line again used until 1962. Use was made of the No2 incline until July 1976, the last self-acting incline in the Industry.

Remains As a working quarry, access is restricted. Block is brought up to the re-equipped mill from Cooke's level by two underground electric inclines, both controlled by the original brine-bath resistors, the sole modernisation being the replacement of the old wooden tubs by plastic bins.

There are a number of buildings in the mills area and many artifacts. The newer roof slating at the middle of the mill denotes the location of the water-wheel. There is a curious 'kinked flue' to one old engine house and adjacent, on the long abandoned David Jones part of the site, there is a machine bored adit, a relic of an unsuccessful 1870s use of a Hunter twin-head boring machine. Of interest is the 'cut and cover' tunnel for a line to where tipping was done on the old Foty site. The No2 Incline and its remote drum-house is in excellent condition with machinery virtually complete, and with trucks and other items near its foot. The tramway through Bowydd property to the No1 incline is clear, and the incline formation itself is intact. It has a compact remote-type drum-house set into the rock. The No3 incline, up from the site, leads onto the level main section of the Rhiwbach tramway and has a fine drum-house. Alongside the first section of this line is the notable, slate lined and slate covered, Bowydd leat with its piped extension to feed the power station. (22)

MANOD (Old Manod) SH725452

An open working dating from the very early 1800s. In spite of being almost 1800' above sea level, it was worked with a dearth of shelter of any kind.

Remains The main workings immediately adjoining Graig Ddu have shallow excavations, rubbish runs, and some traces of buildings. The subsidiary North Pole digging (729458) has been partly covered by modern working, but the little South Pole quarry (726452) is undisturbed.

The old track around Mynydd Manod, by which material went down to the river Dwyryd at Maentwrog, is traceable. (25)

MOELWYN SH661442

A grandly situated, but largely unsuccessful, undertaking. It was originally opened in the 1820s from several small levels on the bleak eastern face of Moelwyn Bach, some 1700' above sea level. In the 1860s it was developed underground on the southern flank of Moelwyn Mawr. There was a mill some distance away at 668444 with 6 saw benches and 7 dressing machines, driven by a 40' x 4' wheel fed from Llyn Stwlan. There were 3 barrack buildings and it is believed that, around the 1860s, whole families lived at this bleak location, with children walking to school at Tanygrisiau.

Active in the 1870s and again in the 1890s, but closed about 1900. Material was originally removed by packhorse down Cwm Maesgwm by a track built in 1826 but, after about 1860, the quarry was connected to the Ffestiniog Railway via the spectacular incline system.

Remains At the original working to the south, there are barracks; some other building remains, and also a possible incline. From the 1860s development, immediately above the lake there are two adits (gridded) and some traces of buildings. The upper two pitches of the incline system were partly lost when Llyn Stwlan was enlarged in 1960 for the pumped storage scheme. This scheme largely destroyed the mills area, but some slight vestiges are extant. The four pitches down past the generating station to the old Ffestiniog Railway line are still a magnificent landscape feature. (3)

NYTH Y GIGFRAN (Glan-y-pwll, Gloddfa Twm Ifan James) SH689462

A small, and most improbably sited, undertaking. Dating from about 1820, adits were driven from a natural ledge in the cliff face. A later adit was driven some 30' below, reached by a rock-cut platform.

From the late 1860s material was lowered by a part timber, part stone, incline to the Ffestiniog Railway at Glan-y-pwll.

The quarry was closed c1870 following a boundary dispute with Oakeley, who incorporated it into their workings in 1920.

Remains There are two adits, the upper stoped out to bank, and the lower giving onto a precipitous stone platform. Nearby are some small buildings and some nice rock cut steps; there is also a possible smithy. The lower adit leads to flooded chambers. The tunnel connection with Oakeley is open.

The stone part of the incline formation is a prominent feature, and cutting and bolt holes indicate where the wooden extension ran.

There is no trace of a powered mill, although there is anecdotal evidence of at least an attempt to take a boiler up the incline. There are sawn ends on site, possibly produced by a hand-cranked saw. It is believed that use was made of a sawing mill, near the north end of the Ffestiniog Railway, Moelwyn tunnel, built by Mathews quarry (later part of Oakeley) prior to their having a steam mill on site.

165

On the cliff face alongside the site are traces of a Rock Cannon. At Glan-y-pwll, at the foot of the incline near the site of the railway siding, are some quarry dwellings still in occupation. (8)

OAKELEY SH690466

This was an amalgamation of three quarries: Lower, Middle & Upper. In 1818 Samuel Holland at the behest of his father, a Liverpool slate merchant, took a lease on some diggings at Rhiwbryfdir farm. In 1825, he sold the by then successful enterprise to the Welsh Slate Co.

In 1827, Holland began a new opening at Gesail, on the hillside behind. It developed into a substantial undertaking, working underground from 1840 with a large steam mill from c1860. A bold feature was the 1000 yard long, gas lit 'Horse Tunnel' which gave connection to the mill from chambers and open workings behind. One of the first users of the Ffestiniog Railway (1839), the extensive tramway system was connected by an incline with its head inside the tunnel. By the mid 1870s, output was around 14,000 tons with over 500 men employed.

By 1830, the land between the two quarries, had been taken by Nathaniel Mathew, trading as the Rhiwbryfdir Company; this middle quarry (Gloddfa Ganol) being invariably known as Mathew's. Working underground from about 1840, they were pioneer users of dressing machines (the Mathew's Trimmer of 1852), and early users of steam for both mill power and for haulage. A number of gravity and powered inclines were used, as well as water balances. Product went down by incline to the Ffestiniog Railway at Dinas. By the mid 1870s, their output was over 10,000 tons p.a. with well over 300 men.

In 1878 the leases on both Holland's upper quarry and Mathew's middle quarry having expired, landowner W.E. Oakeley took them in hand himself.

In the meantime at Lord Palmerston's quarry (as the Welsh Slate Company's lower working was known) there had, after a shaky start, been fifty years of spectacular progress. There were extensive underground workings serviced by a variety of inclines and lifts, with a network of surface tramways which had been connected by incline to the Ffestiniog Railway in 1838. Sand sawing having been tentatively introduced by Holland in the 1820s, a number of mills were built including, circa 1840, the first steam mill in the district. By the mid 1870s, their payroll had reached almost four figures, and their annual output neared 50,000 tons.

This success was only achieved by reckless underground working, resulting in collapses that culminated in the great falls of 1882/3 almost wrecking the quarry, and damaging the two Oakeley owned quarries above it. Following legal action, W.E. Oakeley took over and amalgamated it with the middle and upper quarries under the name Oakeley Quarries.

The damage to the quarries, and the poor trade of the 1880s, meant that the combined unit never matched the output or the profitability of its components. However, having absorbed both Nyth y Gigfran and Cwm Orthin (which the ruined Welsh Slate Co. had tried to run in the 1890s), the Oakeley enterprise, with its eventual 60,000 tons and 1700 men, became the third largest in the industry.

Workings extending from sea level to 1500' on 30 floors, lettered down to R and numbered up to 16 (some letters and numbers were omitted or merged). There were said to be 50 miles of track underground, besides the loco-worked surface tramways. There were 9 mills (plus the 3 at Cwmorthin) with almost 200 saw-tables.

A few water-wheels and a vertical water balance were retained, but water shortage necessitated using almost twenty steam engines for the mills, pumping, and the underground uphaulages, including one of 6 tracks. Electricity started to displace steam after the opening of the Cwm Dyli hydro-station in 1906.

Rubbish disposal was a constant problem; some was backfilled, some was dumped in the old Holland workings; eventually a new tip was made to the east of the railway, reached by a viaduct, later forming the site for the Pen-y-bont mill.

Fresh inclines gave direct access to the Ffestiniog Railway, and later to the main line railway also. As well as some 30 cottages, there was a hospital on site.

With Bowydd and Diffwys, their payroll topped 1000 right up to WW2 (about two thirds of the Blaenau total), and they fared comparatively well immediately post-war, but men and markets were lost in the 1960s. Closed in 1970 but reopened by local entrepreneurs as two separate but associated undertakings, Gloddfa Ganol and Ffestiniog Quarry, they were sold and reunited as Oakeley in 1997.

Remains Owing to vigorous untopping work, the site is constantly changing and artifacts are vanishing almost on a weekly basis. As a working quarry, access is not normally possible.

What was the lower, Welsh Slate Co. site has become a deep pit, with roads and tipping obscuring artifacts. To the south are some old buildings in reuse, and some modern sheds. To the north is the old Bonc Shafft mill and other buildings; there are vestiges of a steam powered tipping incline, and traces of the vertical water balance. Nearby is the modern pulverising plant, producing powder which is taken to south Wales for the manufacture of moulded slates.

The large area higher up, the old No5 level, has a number of buildings from the Middle Quarry at its northern end, including some cottages, as well as the modern mill. Ruins of some other buildings above are extant.

At the southern end of this level is the prominent drum-house of the 1906 incline, with steps leading up from the town. Behind this was the main Upper Quarry working area, where a number of Holland's buildings remain including the ruins of his first steam mill and a variety of other structures such as barracks, dwellings, lavatories, loco sheds etc. The Horse Tunnel runs through the workings from here, but Holland's early inclines which fed it from the far end have been mostly quarried away. The earliest workings at the top of the quarry are, for the time being, undisturbed with several open workings, accessed by short tunnels, each with its own tramway formation and weigh-house leading to tipping areas. A tunnel leads to a sort of balcony where rubbish was tipped down the cliff face. There is also a powder house and some buildings possibly dating from the original Holland days. There is a tunnel through to the Nyth y Gigfran workings, with some chambering off it.

The Pen-y-bont (Glan-y-don) tip, mill and incline have been cleared, but the pillars of the viaduct which gave access to it over the main-line railway still stand, and the incline down can be seen. This incline also served as the main route down to the Ffestiniog Railway, but the old Welsh Slate Co's incline which it replaced has been buried. The two pitch middle quarry incline is still visible, but the old incline which it replaced has long since gone. A proposal to exploit the tips on a major scale will undoubtedly further degrade this site. (10)

OLWYN GOCH SH704473

Not a quarry but the site of a large water-wheel which, via rods in a 200' deep shaft, pumped water from levels B & C of Llechwedd to level 2 and also hauled from level B to level 2.

Remains Filled in pit; spoil from original construction and spillways. (17)

PANTYRAFON SH697469

Terminus of the Dinas branch of the Ffestiniog Railway, and foot of Llechwedd incline. Subsequently the L&NWR loading point for Llechwedd and Oakeley.

Remains Sheds, a crane and trackwork. Also the Llechwedd hydro-power house, which still generates with the original 1904 Pelton wheels and generators. (13)

PANT-YR-YNN SH709454

The 1845 mill for Diffwys Casson; subsequently a woollen factory.
Remains Building still in use with disused water-wheel alongside. (20)

RHIWBACH SH740462

An 18th century digging seriously developed from the 1840s. The initial working, immediately south of what became the main complex, was developed partly underground. Pits were also worked a little distance further south again. In the 1860s, having built the Rhiwbach tramway, the pit working to the east was considerably extended underground, ultimately going down 8 floors. The mill engine, besides powering the exit incline up to the tramway, wound up from underground. It may have also, for a short time, wound a vertical shaft and, certainly, powered a short incline up from a second mill. Just below the main mill a virtual 'village' of houses, barracks, a shop and a schoolroom/chapel was established.

Output reached a peak of almost 8000 tons by 1869, although within a few years it fell back to less than half this. Well before the end of the century its fortunes became mixed, and the costs of maintaining a big layout, complete with steam locos, were undoubtedly subsidised by revenues from other quarries using the tramway.

From the 1890s, all but the two lowest levels were dewatered by a 600 yard long tunnel that emerged at 745475.

By 1935, with tonnage down to 1000, electricity displaced steam. Beset by manning problems, closure came in 1952; the two men still barracking (in a temporary building) being the last in the industry to do so.

Material was originally carried via Cwm Machno for shipment at Trefriw, stock being held at Betws-y-coed owing to high wharfage charges at Trefriw but, from the 1830s until the opening of the Rhiwbach Tramway in 1862, product was carted to Maentwrog for shipment on the Dwyryd. The original tramway proposal had been for a route down to Cwm Machno, but the convenience of using the Ffestiniog Railway outweighed the length of track required to reach it. Thoughts of this route were revived at the turn of the century, using the drainage tunnel. The tramway continued in use until closure.

Remains The massive sheave mounting incorporating a banksman's cabin at the head of the incline provides a fine viewpoint of the quarry, undoubtedly a welcome sight to housewives who had walked the tramway after their Saturday shopping in Blaenau. At the foot of the incline, with wooden sleepers attached to slate slabs still in place and support wheels for the return rope, some in their wooden mountings, is the big stack. Alongside it is the house for the 20hp engine and its fuel store, with the later electricity building between. Behind are the ruins of the upper mill which had 18 saws and 18 dressing machines. A shallow tunnel runs under the floor of the mill, with apertures clearly intended for the disposal of sawing waste. The choked state of the tunnel suggests that the presumed water scour used to clear it was not too effective. Alongside this mill are some stanchions for the rope which hauled the main incline.

There are vestiges of a number of other buildings, but prominent is a big group that were part dwellings, part barracks. Alongside is a building clearly identifiable as the schoolroom/chapel. Facing these are traces of the manager's house, unusual in being so close to the workers dwellings and to the operating site. There are carefully decorated lintels etc. incorporated into these buildings, and the sweep of road to this domestic site is lined on one side by a most interesting 'post & rail' fence entirely made of slate. Nearby, there are two rows of lavatories.

Immediately south of the incline are the 'old' workings. There are several adits off these leading to some underground chambering. At a lower level are traces of the 'new' mill, which had 6 saws and 7 dressing machines driven by a 7hp engine. The incline up from this mill, hauled by a rope that passed through the rafters of the upper mill, is now buried.

The so called 'new' workings are a little way off to the south. These comprised two pits, one being later partly dammed as a reservoir. There are ruins of the house for the 12hp engine which uphauled from these workings, and off to the east is the pit of the wheel which pumped them, the flat rod trench being obvious. There are some traces of several other buildings, and a rock cannon.

The main underground workings to the east begin in a large pit which was worked in the open down to floor D, the incline continuing underground. The opening is now gated, so it is no longer possible to descend to floor H to reach the drainage tunnel, which has rail track in place. There is evidence of 'pillar robbing' and 'cupboarding', and test bores can be seen emerging from the roofs. There are also a number of bore-cores on the surface.

Floor 1 is flooded. There was a proposal during the early 1920s boom to cut a second tunnel and develop floor J, but levels would have prevented it being lower than I. (29)

RHYD-Y-SARN SH690421
Not a quarry but nevertheless notable as it is believed that, before 1802, slate was sawn here in a water-powered timber sawmill. Site also of early

circular sawing experiments by Diffwys quarry, powered by horse whim. *Remains* Wheel-pit and leat; present building is a later woollen mill. (9)

FOTY (Hafoty Cwm Bowydd) SH707468

Pit working, operated from c1810; probably used horse-whim haulage, the first mill being built in 1850. Amalgamated with Bowydd in the 1870s. Never had any direct rail access, material being brought out via Bowydd.

Remains Main pit flooded; site much used as a tip area, so little if any original Foty work can be identified. (18)

WRYSGAN SH678456

Underground on a small, elevated (1390' above sea level), and inaccessible site. Opened in the 1830s, the first mill was built in 1854 and a second at a lower level in 1865, having a total of 18 saws including at least one Hunter, 20 dressers and 2 planers.

In 1850 a balanced incline down to Cwm Orthin obviated the precipitous zigzag descent by pack animals. This was replaced in 1872 by a spectacular incline approached by a deep cutting, with its upper part in a tunnel, which gave direct connection to the Ffestiniog Railway some 600' below. The gradient on the lower section proved too slight to properly self-act, so a steam engine had to be installed to raise the empties.

The tiny Llyn y Wrysgan proving too small to keep the water-wheels supplied, a steam engine was installed c1890 in the lower mill; another drove the underground incline serving the levels then being opened below lower mill level.

Output built up by fits and starts to 3000 tons in 1904 with over 100 men working on 8 levels, but declined markedly afterwards. With steam proving costly and negotiations to rent the disused Cwm Orthin Cross Mill having failed, in 1890 a 50hp producer gas engine was installed for mill drive, with uphaulage from the lower levels by a water balance alongside the original exit incline. Later, this incline was powered by an old car engine. Steam proved continually troublesome on the exit incline, mainly due to an inadequate boiler. Following electrification in the early 1920s, this incline was powered by 'borrowing' the electric motor from the mill, and coupling it to the haulage drum each time a journey of empty wagons needed to be raised. Finally a lorry engine was used. Somewhat unusually, fan ventilation was used at one time.

Manning was down to thirty in late 1930s, tapering to a dozen before the 1950s closure.

Remains The obvious feature is the big incline. The access cutting, tunnel, and upper part of the formation are in good condition but it was severed in the 1950s by the Stwlan dam road, partly obliterating the lower end. The old drum-house has collapsed, but much of the drum gear is on site as well as part of the steam haulage engine, and the remains of the lorry chassis used as the final power source.

The main mill, like the other buildings, are much degraded, but there is an interesting tail-race under the mill site. There are only traces of the gravity incline on the Cwm Orthin side, but the pack-horse track at its foot, the landing platform (Cei Mulod), and some runs of steps are all in good condition. The later haulage incline is visible with some parts of its motor-car engine.

The upper incline from the highest adit is in fair condition, and at these higher levels are the ruins of some of the early dressing sheds, and the upper mill barracks. The stone embanked reservoir, with its double dam, trapping water in a saddle above the site is a nice feature.

Apart from the one at main mills level, all 5 adits are open and at the top of the site, workings break out. There are relics of the underground ropeway which was used in the final small-scale working. The roof is unstable and falls are continuing, so entering is **most unwise**. There are several outlying trials to the south-west, and another alongside the main incline. (6)

NORTH-WEST MEIRIONNYDD
Region 10
Including quarries using Ffestiniog & Blaenau Rly, GWR Bala to Blaenau Branch, Cambrian Rlys.

General

The quarries in the north of the region, working outliers of the Blaenau Ffestiniog veins, formed a cluster centred on Llan Ffestiniog. Several are ancient much predating the development of Blaenau but few were of any size. Some were active during the early 1900s slate shortage but, apart from one brief 1980s re-opening, there has been little extraction post WW1.

To the south, a few outcrops give a glimpse of the vast resources of Cambrian slate that lies deep under the Rhinogydd. At only two places were they really exploitable, Braich-ddu and Llanfair, where the villages of Gellilydan and Llanfair, respectively formed quarrying communities. Apart from Braich-ddu, which has been used as a source of block, all work has long ceased. Llanfair quarry is open to the public with interesting artifacts on display.

Transport

Most quarries being very small, transport arrangements were generally confined at best to a cart track or, in a few instances, a tramway to the nearest road. Indeed most produced almost exclusively for a local market.

Llanfair shipped at Pen-sarn; Braich-ddu and Cae'n-y-coed used the river Dwyryd.

From the 1860s some quarries in the Ffestiniog area expanded, carting output to the Ffestiniog & Blaenau Railway, by which time Llanfair could use the Cambrian Railway. From 1883 when the GWR line from Bala absorbed the F & B, Braich-ddu could load at Maentwrog Road.

As described in Region 9 the F&B/GWR is open from Blaenau to Trawsfynydd and the rest is mostly traceable. The Cambrian Railway is still open.

Geographically within this area, on either side of the Dwyryd downstream from Maentwrog, are the slate quays mainly used by the Blaenau quarries.

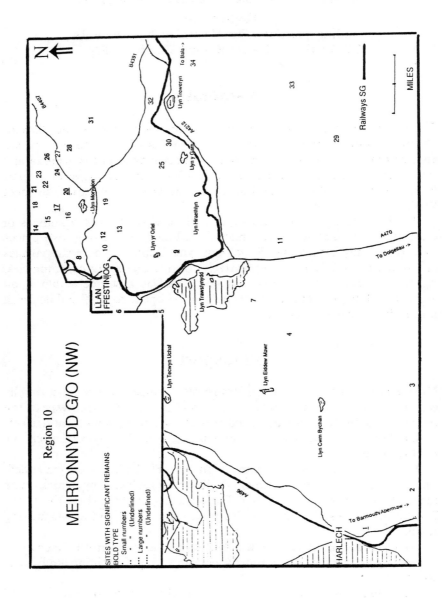

Region 10

MEIRIONNYDD G/O (NW)

SITES WITH SIGNIFICANT REMAINS
BOLD TYPE
· Small numbers
·· " (Underlined)
··· Large numbers
···· " " (Underlined)

N

HARLECH

LLAN FFESTINIOG

Llyn Tecwyn Uchaf

Llyn Eisddew Mawr

Llyn Cwm Bychan

Llyn Trawsfynydd

Llyn yr Oddl

Llyn Morwynion

Llyn Hiraethlyn

Llyn y Garn

Llyn Trewerryn

To Bala ->

To Barmouth/Abermaw ->

To Dolgellau ->

A470

A4212

A496

B4391

B4407

Railways SG

MILES

1. SH580288 Llanfair **V
2. SH590266 Coedyllechau *
3. SH649268 Graig Uchaf
4. SH681320 Moelygwartheg
5. SH681399 Brongelli
6. SH681408 Cae'n-y-coed *
7. SH684336 Cefn-clawdd
8. SH713421 Y Cefn
9. SH718384 Braich-ddu **
10. SH719412 Bronyrerw
11. SH728328 Gelli-gain
12. SH728414 Bryn-llech *
13. SH729402 Hafod Fawr
14. SH730445 Chwarel Llew Twrog *
15. SH731436 Sarnhelen
16. SH732314 Bedd Porus
17. SH732423 Bryn-glas **
18. SH732448 Clogwyngarw
19. SH735411 Cwm Cynfal
20. SH735431 Drum **
21. SH736446 Cwm Teigl *
22. SH739434 Y Garnedd
23. SH742444 Afon Gamallt
24. SH744428 Foel Gron *
25. SH750384 Moelycroesau
26. SH751433 Nantypistyll Gwyn *
27. SH754416 Moel Llechwedd Gwyn
28. SH754424 Croes y Ddwy Afon *
29. SH757304 Taicynhaeaf
30. SH763388 Conglog
31. SH776414 Serw *
32. SH786396 Cloddfa Llechwedd Deiliog
33. SH791324 Afon Cain
34. SH806376 Cefn-glas

AFON CAIN SH791324
Putative site.
Remains Possible excavation. (33)

AFON GAMALLT SH742444
Tiny underground working.

Remains Collapsed adit, no buildings, waste suggests some production. (33)

BEDD PORUS SH732314
Putative site.
Remains Nothing found. (16)

BRAICH-DDU (Hendre-ddu) SH718384
An ancient shallow working which exploited one of the regions's few outcrops of good Cambrian slate. Its 1850s circular and sand saws were augmented in 1863 by a 4' diameter *Hunter saw*.

Some of the mainly slab product of 5/600 tons p.a. went by boat down the Dwyryd; this being, from 1868, the last quarry to use this route. Output tapered off in the 1870s, but during a flurry of activity c1890, a tramway to the GWR was started but only the section on the site itself was completed. Occasionally used as a source of rock for much of the 20th century.

Several houses in Gellilydan are floored with its slab and it provided cladding for the Tanygrisiau power station in the 1960s.

Remains The site is somewhat disturbed by later operations, but there are the ruins of a mill with wheel-pit and a later engine mounting, a barracks and some other buildings, including traces of an earlier mill. A feature is the tramway causeway, with a bridge made of the massive slabs which this quarry could produce. (9)

BRONGELLI SH681399
Unlikely to be slate.
Remains Possible excavation. (5)

BRONYRERW SH719412
Small underground working with 2 tandem adits around 1875-1900.
Remains Collapsed adits, considerable rubbish runs. (10)

BRYN-GLAS SH732423
A small underground working with a steam mill, active in the early 1900s with 3 men. Subsequently an upper level connected to the mill by a tramway and incline; seems to have only been briefly worked. In the final 1960s phase, a fresh access was made to the lower workings, material being brought out by a temporary ropeway.

Remains Ruins of the mill, some other buildings and the tramway and incline from the upper adit. The upper tunnel, which appears to have been driven from one of the several tiny earlier surface workings, comes to a blind end with attempts at chambering only close to the entrance, near which are the remains of an 'A' frame. There is some chambering in the more extensive lower working, and evidence of an abandoned attempt to roof up to the upper level. There are remains of the 1950s ropeway and cradle used to bring block out from underground.

There is a small reservoir and leat to supply the boiler. The access track defines a short-lived tramway to the Ffestiniog-Bala road. (17)

BRYN LLECH SH728414

Underground, may have produced slab as well as roofing slate, circa 1870s.

Remains Circular-sawn ends in the waste but the one surviving building seems too small for even a hand-cranked saw. Vestiges of a forge. The tip and access track is partly encroached on by forestry road widening.

Underground, a tunnel, partly worked out to bank, leads to chambering. Later downward working in this tunnel left the inner workings isolated. (12)

CAE'N-Y-COED (Llechrwd) SH681408

Small working in a river gorge, dating from at least the mid-18th century, material was taken by tramway to a water-powered mill. Probably the first user of boats on the Dwyryd, and a possible source of a very early hand-sawn gravestone at Llan Ffestiniog (William Davies 1775).

Remains Launder pillars in the quarrying area, tramway formation and incline (much degraded) to a mill building with wheel-pit, which was subsequently used as woollen mill giving rise to farm name of Ffatri. (6)

CEFN-CLAWDD SH684336

A small pit working accessed by an adit that also drained it.

Remains Pit and Adit, rubbish run and possible working area to south of the road. No buildings. (7)

CEFN-GLAS SH806376

Putative site.

Remains Some digging in forestry. (34)

CHWAREL LLEW TWROG SH730445

Small underground, worked in 20th century, reputedly by one man.

Remains Tiny dressing shelter, using a rock outcrop as a third wall. The paucity of rubbish belies the 150 yards length of the tunnel. It ends in 2 branches with some limited roofing shafts cut. There is some bar rail *in situ* set directly into tenoned sleepers. (14)

CLODDFA LLECHWEDD DEILIOG SH786396
Tiny roadside working. Sporadically worked during latter half of the 19th century.
Remains Virtually none. (32)

CLOGWYNGARW SH732448
Trial.
Remains Excavation. (18)

COEDYLLECHAU SH590266
Hillside quarry on two levels with an incline down to a mill.
Remains Site much disturbed by later stone quarrying. There is a fine mill building with a nice graduated slate roof and other buildings in re-use. The incline has been quarried away. (2)

CONGLOG SH763388
Putative site of slate working.
Remains Possibly stone working only. Site was a source of material for the construction of Cwm Prysor viaduct. The temporary tramway for this purpose is traceable. (30)

CROES Y DDWY AFON SH754424
Underground, worked at intervals with up to 70 men from the 1870s to 1932, material hauled out by incline to a water-powered mill. Finished product carted to Llan Ffestiniog. Revived in 1987 as an open pit by workers displaced following the Blaenau Ffestiniog strike the previous year. Later vigorously untopped by outside investors, who failed in the early 1990s.
Remains Virtually all the underground workings on 2 levels and the surface structures were destroyed by the late 1980s excavations. There is now just a flooded pit, a settling tank, weighbridge pit and some other vestiges of the re-working. The old dam (breached) and leats are extant. (28)

CWM CYNFAL SH735411
Very small, underground circa 1900.
Remains Adit (open) alongside a stream. Trimmings suggest some product. (19)

CWM TEIGL (Alaw Manod) SH736446
Underground, worked in the 1880s with a water-powered mill. Revived

briefly during the slate shortage of the early 1900s.

Remains Small mill which housed 2 saw tables, wheel-pit, launder pillars and a neat slate lined leat, leading down from a small reservoir on the hill above. The adit is collapsed and, a few yards along the access track, there is a collapsed trial adit with an interesting vaulted half-underground shelter. (21)

DRUM SH735431

Pits/underground, worked at intervals from at least 1840, with the availability of rail loading at Llan Ffestiniog spurring its 1860s development. Peak output was probably in 1872 when about 30 men produced 532 tons, but typically it was much less. Apparently used hand cranked circular saws. Closed in the 1880s. Revived c1904 when a 2-saw water-powered mill was built and 6 men employed, but closed in 1906. An early 1990s revival proposal was abandoned due to the backers' failure.

Remains At the upper level, dressing sheds etc. and a building that housed the haulage winch. Ruined drum-house is at the head of the well engineered incline, at the foot of which is the mill. From one pit an incline descends underground into water, but chambers are accessible from the southern pit. Some distance away are 3 collapsed adits with tramway formations, tips and weigh-houses and, on one level, a curious building. The original access track to the site is well defined, it appears to have been levelled as a tramway but there is no evidence that rails were ever laid. (20)

FOEL GRON (Pen-y-llyn) SH744428

Open quarry, commenced around 1850, later some underground extraction. No water was available at the site, so when a water-powered mill was erected it was at SH747423, alongside the main road and connected to the working by a tramway. Employing about 20 men in the 1870s, by 1883 this was down to 4. Closed 1890s, but revived for a few years in the early 1900s with about 8 men.

Remains Later working, first for stone and then for bulk fill, has obliterated the site, leaving some of the underground chambers exposed.

The tramway is defined by the present approach road. The mill, originally breast wheel driven, later oil engined, was destroyed in the 1980s during landscaping work. A small structure and wheel-pit alongside the approach road may have been an abortive early mill. (24)

GELLI-GAIN SH728328
Putative site.
Remains Possible excavation. (11)

GRAIG UCHAF SH649268
Tiny open pit working.
Remains Excavation. (3)

HAFOD-FAWR SH729402
Small early-19th century open quarry.
Remains Afforested. (13)

LLANFAIR SH580288
A moderate sized, almost totally underground, working that was much developed around the 1860s. It exploited an excellent band of Cambrian series rock, going down five levels. It was the only quarry to work this particular occurrence owing to the cost of downward underground working, which may have accounted for its closure after only a few years. Re-opened at the turn of the century, it closed again during WW1. Between the wars machinery was installed for the crushing of stone and for the production of tiles, about 20 men being employed. Used as an explosive store in WW2 it was opened as a visitor centre in the 1960s.

Product was loaded onto the Cambrian Railway, (to whom they may have supplied ballast) but earlier had been shipped from Pen-sarn wharf on Afon Artro, little use being made of their product in the locality.
Remains Several chambers are open to the public and some of the buildings have been reused in this connection. There are some buildings at the nearby Pen-sarn wharf. (1)

MOEL LLECHWEDD GWYN SH754416
Very small scale working c1870.
Remains Almost nothing. (27)

MOELYCROESAU SH750384
Tiny open pit.
Remains Only the pit. (25)

MOELYGWARTHEG SH681320
Small unmechanised underground working.
Remains Two collapsed adits and a dressing area. There is a tiny dug out stone lined shelter, with storage niches, which was possible the sole

shelter on this bleak, remote site. There being no trace of an access track, it is probable that slates were taken away on the backs of the men who produced them. (4)

NANTYPISTYLL GWYN SH751433
Extremely small.
Remains Small pit (flooded), holding-down bolts leaded into rock suggest a winch mounting near traces of a dressing shed. The waste run is narrow, shallow and several hundred metres long, clearly intended to eventually form the bed of a tramway to the road. (26)

SARNHELEN SH731436
Underground, trial only?
Remains Adit leading to a small flooded chamber. (15)

SERW (Migneint, Nant Derbyniad) SH776414
A small remote pit working, probably dating from the early 1800s. Product carted, to the Ffestiniog-Bala road, along a trackway.
Remains Flooded pit, dressing shed and a three part building, smithy, office and stable, typical of small early 19th century quarries. Traces of what may have been a tiny barracks. There are abutments redolent of a chain incline which could have been horse or man powered. No evidence that internal movement was other than by barrows. The access road, though well engineered in places, has largely vanished into boggy ground. (31)

TAI CYNHAEAF SH757304
Tiny vernacular quarry.
Remains Pit only. (29)

Y CEFN (Cefn Bodlosgad) SH713421
Series of shallow pit workings, of very early date.
Remains Site now occupied by a golf course. (8)

Y GARNEDD SH739434
Trifling trial.
Remains Several scratchings. Actual adit (run in) is possibly an earlier metal trial. (22)

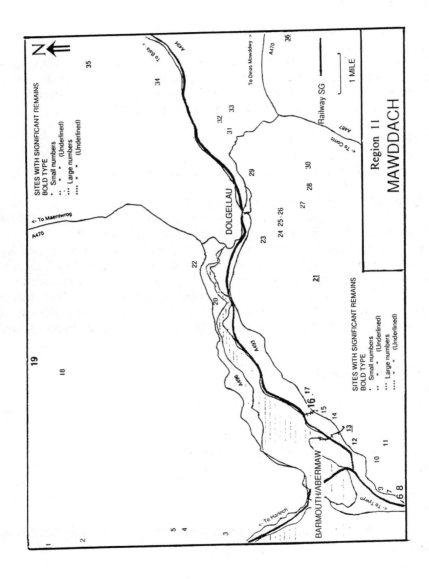

SITES WITH SIGNIFICANT REMAINS
BOLD TYPE
• Small numbers
: " " (Underlined)
:: Large numbers
···· " " (Underlined)

N

19

18

35

34

A494

To Bala →

← To Maentwrog
A470

DOLGELLAU

32

33

31

22

29

To Dinas Mawddwy →

A470

36

27 28 30

24 25 26

23

21

← To Corris
A487

Railway SG

1 MILE

Region 11
MAWDDACH

A493

A496

17
·16·
15
14
13
12
11
10

BARMOUTH/ABERMAW

← To Harlech

To Tywyn →

9
7
6 8

5
4

3

2

1

SITES WITH SIGNIFICANT REMAINS
BOLD TYPE
• Small numbers
: " " (Underlined)
:: Large numbers
···· " " (Underlined)

182

MAWDDACH
Region 11
Including quarries using Cambrian Railways.

General

Most quarries in this region were small and dispersed, attempting to exploit marginal and isolated occurrences of Cambrian slate, during the 1860/70 bonanza. Many were too improbably located to have any hope of success, but a cluster on the south side of the Mawddach estuary, within reach of water or, later, the railway, were developed and mechanised giving rise to slate communities in villages such as Arthog and Y Friog (Fairbourne).

Even these relatively advantageously located quarries suffered from poor rock and geological problems, thus little activity survived into the 20th century, with almost nothing other than the bulk working of tips surviving after WW1.

Transport

There were no quarries large enough to support ambitious transport arrangements. Arthog and Tyddyn Sieffre each had tramways to a wharf; the rest reached shipping points the best way they could which, in the case of Cefn-gam and Gloddfa Gwanas, involved building elaborate tracks. Barmouth ships were heavily engaged in the slate trade, and the port handled trans-shipments from river boats.

When the railways came in the 1860s, Arthog and Tyddyn Sieffre diverted their tramways to them, but most still had lengthy cartages. It was only to Henddol/Golwern that the railways brought opportunity for serious development. Hence neither the Cambrian Coast main line, nor the branch which made end-on junction with the GWR at Dolgellau, had much slate significance.

The coastal line is still open but the Barmouth Junction-Dolgellau line closed in 1965; it is traceable throughout its length, except near Dolgellau where its route is occupied by the by-pass.

1. SH593252 Pant-gwyn *
2. SH596242 Byrdir
3. SH603191 Ffriddolchfa

4. SH605205 Egryn *
5. SH605206 Hendreeirian *
6. SH619122 Hen-ddôl ***
7. SH620122 Panteinion *
8. SH621122 Golwern ***
9. SH621126 Friog
10. SH626129 Brynneuadd
11. SH627124 Cyfannedd *
12. SH627133 Bryn-gwyn *
13. SH630135 Tyddyn Sieffre ** (R)
14. SH639141 Tap-tŵr
15. SH645145 Tanydarren
16. SH650151 Arthog *** (R)
17. SH652152 Ty'n-y-coed *
18. SH678245 Cwm Mynach
19. SH680256 Cefn-gam ***
20. SH702184 Ffridd Isaf
21. SH704149 Penrhyn-gwyn **
22. SH709198 Tŷ-nant
23. SH717171 Rhiw Rhedyn Cochion
24. SH718161 Tanygader
25. SH720160 Bryn-rhug
26. SH728160 Bryn-mawr
27. SH732152 Pantyronen
28. SH738151 Idris
29. SH741175 Fron-serth
30. SH745151 Gau-graig
31. SH749181 Groes-lwyd
32. SH755175 Coed Ffriddarw
33. SH756174 Pant Cra
34. SH777195 Garth
35. SH784233 Cae'r Defaid *
36. SH798160 Gloddfa Gwanas **

ARTHOG SH650151

Terraced hillside quarry opened in the mid 18th century, operating on several levels connected by inclines, the lowest level being developed into a pit accessed by an adit. A tramway took material across the main road, through a short tunnel, to a trackway down to a small jetty. This was replaced by an incline and tramway which, when the railway opened in 1868, was extended to a siding, and at the same time a mill was built.

Closed the following year, but briefly re-opened with just 3 or 4 men in the early 1900s serving local needs.

Remains On the terraces there are some much decayed vestiges of dressing sheds, drum-houses, weigh-houses etc. and the formation of the tramway which enabled Ty'n-y-coed quarry to be used for rubbish dumping.

At ground level recent bulk working has destroyed the area near the foot of incline, but the exceptionally fine dry stone tramroad embankment to the mill is extant and a smithy, (possibly a pre-existing house), stands. The mill area is now a caravan park, the (dated) mill is in nice condition and the short tunnel is open. The stone incline formation down to the railway is in excellent condition. (16)

BYRDIR (Byrllysg) SH596242
Small underground working.
Remains Run in adit. (2)

BRYN-GWYN SH627133
Hillside/underground worked on 3 levels.
Remains Run in adit on lowest level. Weigh-house on level 2. (12)

BRYN-MAWR SH728160
Probably only a trial.
Remains Excavation. (26)

BRYNNEUADD SH626129
Underground trials and open pit.
Remains Excavations. (10)

BRYN-RHUG SH720160
Some work done here.
Remains Excavation, possible building. (25)

CAE'R DEFAID (Rhobell, Tŷ Ucha) SH784233
An underground working from which vast amounts of country rock, but little slate, seem to have emerged.
Remains Two adits; the upper one chambered out to a bank show little sign of profitable activity; the lower one (driven c1911 by the Inigo Jones company of Groeslon, (Region 3) which leads to some limited chambering, does seem to have produced some slab. There are ruins of a

small building, but no obvious mill. Some short tramway formations and an access track to the road. (35)

CEFN-GAM SH680256

A series of shallow pits worked at intervals over a long period, producing tough flexible roofing slate of good colour, handicapped by inaccessibility. In spite of limited catchment, both a mill and an uphaulage were water-powered.

An attempt (c1880) was made to avoid this uphaulage by accessing the workings via a tunnel, but this project was not completed. Finally, there was some very small scale hand re-working.

Finished product was taken down to the river by a well engineered road.

Remains A number of buildings on site, including dressing sheds, a workshop/office and a mill with launder pillars adjacent. There is an interesting slot in the mill structure for the haulage rope wound by the mill wheel. To the south is the exit of the tunnel from the pit, with tipping suggesting that some slate was dressed here. In the main pit are the shelters used in the final phase.

There is a further building, possibly a barracks, and a fine manager's house. This latter has a nice underground food store, and the garden still shows evidence of careful cultivation.

Except near the quarry itself, the access road is in good condition, the lower section subsequently serving the Diffwys metal mine. (19)

COED FFRIDDARW (Tyddyn Garret) SH755175

Probably only crude block produced.
Remains Excavation only. (32)

CWM MYNACH SH678245

Very small pit working alongside track to Cefn-gam.
Remains Tiny quarry face. (18)

CYFANNEDD SH627124

Underground. Was, from around the 1840s, a metal mine. Worked for slate 1870/80.
Remains The old ore cobbing floor re-used for slate dressing, with a stock of small slates. Lower down the hill are a crusher house and other metal-mining relics.

The adit and shafts are open, and underground there is rail *in situ*. In the vestigial chambering, some blocks await carriage to the surface. (11)

EGRYN SH605205
Small hillside quarry, material carted to the road at Egryn Abbey.
Remains Two small buildings and a possible powder house. (4)

FFRIDD ISAF SH702184
Probably a trial.
Remains Excavation. (20)

FFRIDDOLCHFA (Plas Canol) SH603191
Very small hillside quarry.
Remains Excavation. (3)

FRIOG SH621126
Small, underground.
Remains Tips, run in adit. (9)

FRON-SERTH SH741175
Trial?
Remains Excavation only. (29)

GARTH SH777195
Reputed trial.
Remains Possible excavation. (34)

GAU GRAIG SH745151?
Anecdotal report of slab having been brought from this summit early
19th century.
Remains None identified. (30)

GLODDFA GWANAS SH798160
Small open workings, producing a poorish slate. Remotely situated on
either side of a 2000 ft peak; sporadically operated over several periods
from before 1840. Initial development was to the west of the summit,
with subsequent working from the east, producing both slab and roofing
slate. Sawing by a hand-cranked circular saw.

Material taken away by a short incline to a most extravagantly
engineered cart road, which was later extended right to the quarry. This
road seems to have been preceded by one, or possibly two, pack-animal
tracks.
Remains To the west a tiny saw mill; an office/forge and a dwelling; the
incline formation, partly tipped over; and a collapsed tunnel to the pit.

To the north a small barracks or second mill? To the east, at a lower level, some dressing sheds, and another collapsed tunnel which has been worked for product. The two tunnels are the only places where there is any sign of (hand) drilling, so one assumes that explosives were not used for quarrying. Other than on the incline, there is no evidence of any rail ever having been laid. The road is a spectacular feature. (36)

GOLWERN (Goleuwern) SH621122

Hillside quarry/pit, early 1860s, carting to Penrhyn Point (where the southern end of the viaduct would be located), for boating to Barmouth. From 1868 used a siding at the then Barmouth Ferry (later Fairbourne) station, a tramway to which was planned but never built. In 1871 an incline to the road replaced a steep track. The 1882 output was a mere 50 tons with just 4 men.

Taken over by Henddôl in the 1890s, but little extraction can have been done after 1901 when the lowest of the pit-access tunnels was blocked to form a reservoir for an abortive hydro-electric scheme to supply Fairbourne. Machinery on site, apparently oil engine driven, probably dealt with Henddôl material.

Remains On the highest, earliest, level are dressing sheds and a weigh-house with the wagon platform still *in situ*. There is a nice flight of steps down to the next level, built on a disused incline. At this level are further buildings and an underfloor horizontal sheave, with three little tunnels which carried, respectively, the two ropes and the brake rod, thus enabling a rubbish run track to pass between the sheave and the crimp of the incline. Nearby there is a stone slab covered culvert of unknown purpose.

On the next level down is a further rake of dressing sheds, and a tunnel which divides to enter the pit at two points. The flooded pit makes an attractive lagoon. On this level is some unusual light gauge track; the remains of four Amos & Francis patent dressing machines made by De Winton & Co; and the remains of a saw table, although there is no trace of any building nearby to house them. From this level, the long incline goes down to the road. The drum-house has collapsed, but the fragments of the drum are lying in an uncompleted wheel-pit. There is a further working level below this; at the head of the original access track is a rake of dressing sheds and the lowest, now blocked, adit.

There are at least three fine stone archways on this site. At road level are some remnants of the power house. (8)

GROES-LWYD SH749181
Probably only a trial.
Remains Excavation. (31)

HENDDÔL SH619122
Open/underground, dating from 1865, it shared Golwern's siding from 1868. Closed during the early 1870s, it was employing 28 men in 1883 but only produced 410 tons. By the 1890s, combined with Golwern, over 80 men were employed. After this output declined, finally closing in 1928.
Remains At the higher levels are 2 nice weigh-houses, with fireplaces, for which the steeply sloping ground provides deep mechanism pits. On the next level down is a most crude miniature drum for a primitive incline to the level below, possibly from late re-working. There are a number of dressing sheds and some well constructed buildings. From the lowest level a tunnel (open) provides access and drainage for the workings. Some chambering is accessible where there are rails *in situ*, including a Hughes bar rail. An intermediate level (2 floors up), gated, leads to some further chambering.
   The lowest incline seems to have originally gone right down to road level but later appears to have joined the Golwern incline, presumably with some interchange arrangement. At road level, bulk working has caused much disturbance. (6)

HENDREEIRIAN SH605206
Small, unmechanised pit working, producing a green slate.
Remains Tunnel to the pit, some traces of small buildings. (5)

IDRIS SH738151
Underground, was idle by 1848 when it was offered for sale as having 'water available'; probably not worked since then.
Remains Run in adit, quantity of waste. (28)

PANT CRA SH756174
Possible site.
Remains Some excavation. (33)

PANTEINION SH620122
Small open quarry straddling the boundary between Golwern and Hen-ddôl, apparently predating both.
Remains Quarrying face, with Hen-ddôl underground workings breaking out. Combined dressing shed and weighbridge. (7)

PANT-GWYN (Llyn Einion) SH593252
Small underground working.
Remains Flooded tunnel and collapsed workings, rubbish runs and possible building traces. Other adjacent tunnelling probably metal trials. (1)

PANTYRONEN SH732152
Small open working.
Remains Excavation, access track. The unusual circular structure is a WW2 farm *Silage hopper* built by Italian POWs from materials gleaned from the site. (27)

PENRHYN-GWYN (Crown) SH704149
Originally a small, unmechanised open quarry; developed mid 18th century on several levels underground, with a water-powered mill.

Despite the large volumes of waste, production was only a few hundred tons p.a., which by 1883 had dropped to 54 tons, their planing machines having been sold off in 1875. Output was carted down to the nearby road. Closed 1899.

Remains Topmost level, old open working. Next level down, old working deepened into a pit with an incline, possibly water-powered, bringing material up from chambers below. There are some rubbish runs; two buildings with fireplaces, and trackway downhill.

The third level down has a collapsed adit, a forge, and other buildings including a barracks, a drum-house and, some distance off, a powder house.

Fourth level down has a rake of dressing sheds, a weigh-house and, alongside the river, a well engineered but partly collapsed tramway to a run-in adit.

On the lowest working level; another weigh-house, a further rake of dressing sheds, and a tramway to an adit with recent metal arching and door, which leads to some chambering.

At foot of incline is a large mill building, formed by twice extending a pre-existing structure. (The second extension was apparently never completed). The sparse mill-waste includes circular-sawn ends. At a lower level, and not immediately adjacent, is a wheel-pit (40' x 2'?), which apparently drove the mill by belt. The leat for this wheel is clearly visible. Nearby is an office type building and a dwelling. (21).

RHIW RHEDYN COCHION SH717171
Not slate?
Remains Excavation only. (23)

TANYDARREN SH645145
Almost certainly only a trial c1900s.
Remains Flooded adit 200m long with small chamber. Now forms a garden feature. (15)

TANYGADER SH718161
Trial.
Remains Possible excavation. (24)

TAP-TŴR SH639141
Trial (Slate?)
Remains Traces of excavation. Also another at 644142, probably seeking metal. (14)

TYDDYN SIEFFRE SH630135
Open workings which reached a mill by a tunnel and a short incline. A further incline led down to a tramway to a shipping point at 633148, with a later branch to the railway near Morfa Mawddach station. Closed by 1901.
Remains The mills area is largely cleared but near the entrance to the now blocked tunnel are some buildings in agricultural re-use. The house of the quarry name is still in occupation, and some of the houses on the main road clearly had quarry associations.

The tramway crossed the road near the war memorial, and its formations to the neat river-quay and to the railway is readily traceable, part of the former re-used as a road. (13)

TŶ-NANT SH709198
Tiny open quarry.
Remains Excavation only. (22)

TY'N-Y-COED SH652152
A small, early working, later used as a dump for Arthog waste.
Remains Very little, as so much material has been dumped in the old pits. Notable however is a drystone tunnel some 50 yards long, built to prevent the Arthog material blocking an occupation road. Further tip removals are causing degradation of the site. (17)

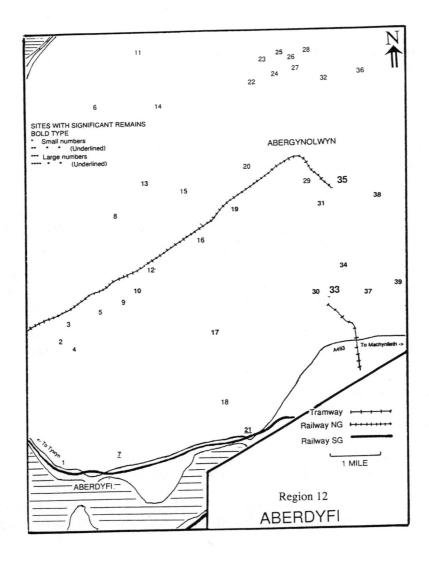

N

11

23 25 28
26
24 27 32 36
22

6 14

SITES WITH SIGNIFICANT REMAINS
BOLD TYPE
• Small numbers
▪▪ " " (Underlined)
▪▪▪ Large numbers
▪▪▪▪ " " (Underlined)

ABERGYNOLWYN

20

13 29 35
15 38
19 31
8
16

34

12
10 30 33 37 39
9
5
3 17
2
4

A493 To Machynlleth ->

18

Tramway ├──┼──┼──┤
21 Railway NG ├┼┼┼┼┼┼┼┤
Railway SG ━━━━━━

<- To Tywyn 7
1
⌞____⌟
1 MILE

ABERDYFI

Region 12

ABERDYFI

192

ABERDYFI
Region 12
Including quarries using Talyllyn Railway and Cambrian Railways

General

Most of the quarries in this region were seeking scattered outcrops during the mid 19th century stampede for slate. They worked, or tried to work, the Ordovician veins that run in a swathe from Tywyn and Aberdyfi to northern Maldwyn (Montgomeryshire). These veins represent the southern exposure of the Harlech Dome anticline which had their northern, richer counterparts at Blaenau Ffestiniog. Much of the rock they found was of questionable quality, and the only quarry to really successfully exploit the rich but elusive Narrow Vein was Bryneglwys, which contributed to it totally dominating the region's output.

This quarry built over seventy houses in Abergynolwyn, creating the sole substantial slate community in the region, which is an outstanding example of a quarry-generated settlement.

Transport

Two quarries had tramways to navigable water. The Fron-goch line was a very short link to a stone pier on the adjacent shore of the Dyfi estuary. The 1½ mile Cwm Ebol line dropped by an incline to cross the Dyfi flood plain to a shipping point.

There was some shipment at places such as Tywyn but most carted to Aberdyfi, providing that port with an appreciable slate trade. It had been predicted that the opening of the Cambrian Coast line would bring Aberdyfi increased traffic, as indeed it did, largely thanks to Bryneglwys's Talyllyn Railway terminating at exchange sidings at Tywyn. However, since goods loaded on rail increasingly tended to stay on rail, the railway ultimately hastened the port's decline.

The 10 mile 2'3" gauge Talyllyn Railway of 1866, was the first narrow gauge railway to be exclusively steam hauled, and is still very much in business as is the ex-Cambrian main line. The two quarry tramways are readily traceable.

1. SN600962 Yr Horon
2. SN600998 Fronheulog

3. SH603005 Tŷ Mawr
4. SN604994 Caethle
5. SH614010 Cwm Cynfal
6. SH614073 Cwm Ych
7. SN620964 Allt-goch **
8. SH621040 Ffridd Cocyn
9. SH623013 Braich-y-rhiw
10. SH625017 Rhydyronnen *
11. SH626092 Peniarth
12. SH630029 Pandy
13. SH630055 Perfeddnant *
14. SH634070 Garth Fach
15. SH643048 Nantymynach
16. SH645038 Ffridd Llwynhynydd
17. SN650998 Dysyrnant *
18. SN652972 Pant Eidal
19. SH653043 Dôl-goch * (R)
20. SH664062 Tainewyddion
21. SN664972 Fron-goch ** (R)
22. SH666084 Castell y Bere
23. SH669094 Gernos
24. SH670087 Llechwedd
25. SH671097 Pennant *
26. SH675095 Ty'n-y-fach
27. SH676091 etc. Cerrig y Felin
28. SH678098 Gwastadfryn
29. SH679055 etc. Foel Fawr
30. SH682012 Rhaeadr *
31. SH684045 Tarren Hendre *
32. SH685088 Nantyreira
33. SH689017 Cwm Ebol *** (R)
34. SH693024 Afon Alice *
35. SH695054 Bryneglwys *** (R)
36. SH700089 Maesypandy
37. SH706014 Pen-y-bryn *
38. SH708043 Cwm Breichiau *
39. SH709019 Gyllellog *

AFON ALICE (Allt Rhos Fach) SH693024
Tiny underground working, opened around 1860, revived early 1900s, probably had one water-powered saw.

Remains Run in adits; ruins of a mill; tramway to a cart loading point with rail in place; rubbish runs with sawn ends. (34)

ALLT-GOCH SN620964

A small underground working redeveloped in the 1870s boom, closed by 1882. Material carted to Aberdyfi.
Remains Much of site wooded or disturbed, a C.G.I. building occupies the presumed mill site. The main adit leads to some chambering. Another lower adit leads to a shaft down from main adit, there was an upper adit but this seems to be lost in forestry. (7)

BRAICH-Y-RHIW SH623013

Small hillside quarry on two levels, material may have been carted to the Talyllyn Railway.
Remains Excavation only. (9)

BRYNEGLWYS SH695054

The largest quarry in mid-Wales, developed underground in the 1840s from two small open workings of Bryneglwys and Cantrybedd. Prior to the installation of a water-wheel, the saws in the small mill were hand-cranked.

Taken over in 1864 by Lancashire men, who were diversifying out of the cotton trade due to a shortage of supplies during the American Civil War, it was vigorously expanded. Their most notable investment was the building of the Talyllyn Railway, which replaced packhorseing to Pennal, or sledging down to the valley for carting to Aberdyfi. Besides serving the quarry itself, an incline branch to Abergynolwyn accessed tracks running to the rows of quarry houses, for the delivery of coal and the removal of earth closet waste.

Much use was made of water for hauling, pumping, and for mill drives; the latter with steam back up, and later also for air compression. It had an extensive network of tramways and inclines.

As well as families living on site, many men barracked, including, owing to the steep climb, older Abergynolwyn men. There were two barrack buildings, both two storied, the ground floor of one being a carpenter's shop, the other a family dwelling and messroom. Most unusually, some men lodged with the manager.

Output around 1880 reached 8000 tons p.a. and manning neared 300, which had halved by 1890, recovering somewhat up to the early 1900s; closed in 1910. An immediate reopening briefly touched 4000 tons during the post WW1 boom, but thereafter declined to final closure in 1952. It is doubtful if, even at its peak, it ever showed a profit.

Remains Regrettably, virtually all buildings have been demolished on this heavily afforested site, but much is traceable on the surface. The underground workings are **most unsafe**.

The first relics to be seen on approaching, by the quarry road, are the old broad vein workings and the tramway formation to the top of the Beudynewydd incline, which led down to the lower mill area. Below the road is an adit connected by tramway to a point part way down that incline. Just beyond where the access road crosses the Llaeron stream are, on the left, the remnants of the 1920s compressor/generator house and the drum-house for the water-wheel winding gear. Associated with this is a very fine slate lined leat and launder pillars. Behind is a two pitch incline formation down from the upper, narrow vein, adits. To the right are vestiges of the manager's house and other buildings.

Further on, near the collapsed opening of the Daylight Tunnel, so called because it ran to an open pit, were the old and new mills. The former was a several times extended hotchpotch, driven by turbines with a steam back up, and incorporating workshops and a smithy. The short-lived new mill was smaller and neater. Beyond is a tramway formation which descended *via* two inclines from adits above to the south-west, and beyond, traces of another incline. Nearby were the barracks and, some distance off, the magazine. Behind the rubbish tips above an adit are the remains of the elaborate housing for the twin water-wheels which powered the double chain incline (later a normal ramp incline) up from the main narrow vein workings. Besides the wheel-pits and drum housings there are rope tunnels and several maintenance and access passages.

Behind this is the now dry, small boundary reservoir, and much higher is the breached dam of the big Llaeron reservoir. There are a number of trials and detached workings around the main site.

In the lower mill area, at the foot of the Beudynewydd incline, is the extensive level area of the storage yard and here are traces of the exceptionally long 1880s turbine powered mill; like the other mills it was an integrated mill with dressers, as well as saws; at one time there were more than 30 of each on site in addition to several planers. The long tunnel which drained all but the lowest workings, emerges at this level.

The tramway formation is readily traceable past Cantrybedd cottages to the head of Cantrybedd incline. The drum-house being set well back from the crimp, the brake was controlled by a long rod. A spectacular but much overgrown formation leads to the Alltwyllt incline, with its drum-house high on a rock shelf, to make end on connection to the Talyllyn Railway, and is now incorporated into a designated walk.

The drum-house of the village incline straddled the Talyllyn Railway mid-way between the present Nant Gwernol and Abergynolwyn stations. Unfortunately only the drum of this unique structure, through which the crimp of the village incline passed at right angles to the railway, is now extant. The incline is traceable down to Abergynolwyn village where, near its foot, was a water-powered writing slate factory. (35)

CAETHLE SN604994
A small open working, material carted to Tywyn.
Remains Almost none. Site now a caravan park. (4)

CASTELL Y BERE SH666084
Ancient working?
Remains Possible traces. (22)

CERRIG Y FELIN SH676091 & 678094
Trials.
Remains Some surface disturbance. (27)

CWM BREICHIAU SH708043
Underground c1872. Poor slate, little useful product.
Remains 2 or 3 dressing sheds, nothing identifiable as a mill, although there are circular-sawn ends. An adit leads to limited chambering, a second adit 250 yards downstream is now lost. (38)

CWM CYNFAL SH614010
Tiny open quarry; little, if any, useful product.
Remains Only the pit itself. (5)

CWM EBOL (Rhos Fach) SH689017
Open working, started circa 1860, with water-powered mill(s) to saw its mainly slab product. Cartage to the river Dyfi was replaced by a tramway c1868. Output in 1883 of 260 tons with 9 men, but may have been more earlier.
Remains There are ruins of an upper mill, which had an unusual double roof and a low level water-wheel, later replaced by a Pelton wheel, fragments of which are on site along with traces of its underground feed pipe. To the east are vestiges of a steep incline which brought block to this mill from early workings. A later route along the top of the dam reaches the mill by a shallow incline. The final route is on the level via a cutting. The now dry reservoir has a farm building which must have been

under water at one time.

The present path, which was the original exit route, was clearly railed as far as a remote-type drum-house and a steep incline with slate sleepers, which leads to the abutments of a bridge at the start of the exit tramway.

Up valley from the foot of this incline are the ruins of another mill which had an unusually high roof and a walled wheel-pit alongside it. The layout and purpose of this second mill is unclear. A rough path joins the two mills, which may have been intended as an incline. Internal tracks were 2'3", apparently the later gauge of the tramway.

There are a number of trial adits further up the valley.

The tramway is easily traceable to the river at 702996. There is the formation of an incline at 695009, near which is a small quartz mine. Spillage shows that the tramway was also used to carry this product to the main road near Pennal. (33)

CWM YCH SH614073
Possible trial.
Remains Traces of ground disturbance. (6)

DÔL-GOCH SH653043
Not to be confused with the ballast quarry and siding some distance up line. Briefly re-worked by men laid off from Bryneglwys in 1910.
Remains Virtually only a small face and possible run-in adit. (19)

DYSYRNANT SN650998
Extremely small underground operation worked in the 1850s. Material carted to the road at 668998.
Remains Spoil, collapsed adits. (17)

FOEL FAWR SH679055 & 681057
Putative trials.
Remains Lost in forestry. (29)

FFRIDD COCYN SH621040
Possibly slate.
Remains Excavation only. (8)

FFRIDD LLWYNHYNYDD SH645038
Very small, possibly only a trial.
Remains Excavation only. (16)

FRON-GOCH SN664972

Underground. Although small it had a steam powered mill and its own shipping jetty. Originally an open working with a track to the beach, this route was cut by the 1866/67 railway construction, and one assumes that the tramway was in use by this time. Much money was spent during the early 1870s, including the building of the steam mill, but it closed following a disastrous winter frost of 1883/84. Later, some trials for copper were made here.

Remains There is much on this compact site. The tiny mill with brick chimney, cottages, and a delightful chapel-like structure with cast iron window frames. The slate-waste jetty is still usable. The tunnel, which leads to a pit, is blocked by a fall. (21)

FRONHEULOG SN600998

Very small open working.

Remains Excavation only. (2)

GARTH FACH SH634070

Almost certainly not slate.

Remains Excavation only. (14)

GERNOS SH669094

Trial?

Remains Slight excavation. (23)

GWASTADFRYN SH678098

Possible trial.

Remains In forestry. (28)

GYLLELLOG SH709019

Pit dating from 1870s/80s; largely unproductive.

Remains Pit with adit access, dressing shed, abutments of bridge across stream. (39)

LLECHWEDD SH670087

Possible trial.

Remains Ground disturbance. (24)

MAESYPANDY SH700089

Trial.

Remains In forestry, possible signs of disturbance. (36)

NANTYREIRA SH685088
A very small pit working; possibly only a trial.
Remains Excavation only. (32)

NANTYMYNACH SH643048
Trial.
Remains Traces of excavation. (15)

PANDY SH630029
Very small hillside quarry, possibly only producing block.
Remains Quarrying area. The adjacent building was fulling mill. (12)

PANT EIDAL SN652972
Small open working.
Remains Site occupied by chalet development, but much slate on site. (18)

PENIARTH SH626092
Also at 625089 & 624084, tiny scratchings with the possibility of carting down the Dysynni valley by existing roads.
Remains Excavations and rubbish with a trace of one small building near main site. (11)

PENNANT SH671097
Small hillside quarry, possibly only a trial.
Remains Excavation only. (25)

PEN-Y-BRYN (Coed Rhonwydd) SH706014
A small working, material being taken down a short incline to the road, where there may have been a mill. Later, material was removed on the level by a tunnel. Active around 1880, but may have worked much earlier. Material carted to Pennal.
Remains Two pits connected by a tunnel, with a further exit tunnel, collapsed to surface. Vestiges of dressing sheds and what may have been an incline. There are extensive rubbish runs on two levels; on the upper one is a building which may have been a magazine. There may have been other buildings obliterated by the forestry road and yard. (37)

PERFEDDNANT SH630055
A small hillside working, deepened into a pit accessed by a short tunnel.

All handworking, slate conveyed to the main road by a cart track.
Remains Pit and tunnel. (13)

RHAEADR (Talgarth) SH682012

A tiny underground working lodged in a small gorge, apparently used water-power for sawing. Operated 1865-1905 with an average of six men. Output taken away by cart.

Remains Just upstream of a collapsed adit is a small building, which possibly held a water-powered saw. Slight vestige of a second building, and a rubbish run with some rail in place. There is also a massive square stone structure of unknown purpose. A number of circular-sawn ends are on the ground. Above the site are two breached dams in tandem. (30)

RHYDYRONNEN SH625017

Small underground working, probably operating in the late 1860s, revived 1910 by men made idle by Bryneglwys's temporary closure. Material may have been carted to Talyllyn Railway.

Remains Nothing on the surface. The lower adit is collapsed, the upper adit is open but blocked inside by falls. There is a 'Jwmpah' jammed in a shot hole. (10)

TAINEWYDDION SH664062

Trial only?
Remains In forestry. (20)

TARREN HENDRE SH684045

Tiny digging on a very steep slope.
Remains Excavation, with collapsed adit roofing up to it from lower down the hillside, trimming waste suggests some production. Rail appears to have been used at least in the lower adit. There may have been associated trials at 681048 (site of forestry hut), 686049 (subsequently source of hardcore) and 684047 (lost in planting). (31)

TŶMAWR SH603005

Small open working. Local use only?
Remains Shallow excavation. (3)

TY'NYFACH SH675095

Tiny hillside quarry, possibly very early, for local use only.
Remains Excavation. (26)

YR HORON SH600962

Two small hillside workings, mainly working shales for building, may have produced roofing slate at an early date.

Remains Pits. (1)

CORRIS

Region 13
Including quarries using Corris, Machynlleth & River Dyfi Tramroad,Corris Railway, Cambrian Railways.

General

Slate has been worked at Aberllefenni for at least 500 years. At Corris itself, land was let for quarrying by John Edwards of Machynlleth in the late 18th century, but serious exploitation did not commence there until the 1830s when his son John Edwards II, later Sir John, caused the present main road to be built. He, and more particularly his daughter Mary, Marchioness of Londonderry, exercised a decisive influence on Corris and the Dulas valley for the rest of the 19th century.

Trade in the region's roofing slate, not always of the best quality, failed to fully recover from the late 1870s slump. However Braich Goch's narrow vein slab enabled it to survive a further hundred years, and Aberllefenni's even better product is still being turned out.

Apart from Corris itself; Aberllefenni, Corris Uchaf and Ceinws are all settlements created by the quarries, the former two in particular having many interesting quarry-built dwellings. Also notable is the tiny self-contained hamlet at Ratgoed. In addition, the ancient market town of Machynlleth became a centre for slate trading.

Transport

Originally, product was carted to the then important river port of Derwenlas (SN719991) Although this difficult journey was eased by the 1830s Dulas valley road, it was not until the 1859 opening of the horse-drawn, 2'3"g Corris, Machynlleth & River Dyfi Tramway from Aberllefenni to Derwenlas that anything like economic transport was available. Since the capacity of the three quays at Tan-y-ffordd, Cei Ellis and Cei Ward, was limited, it was not until 1862, when loadings onto the Cambrian Railways could be made at Machynlleth (either for shipment at Aberdyfi or for further rail distribution inland, that the tramway became fully effective.

In 1879 the tramway to the south of the town having fallen into disuse, the Machynlleth - Aberllefenni section was steamed as the Corris Railway. Although this provided the quarries with transport competitive

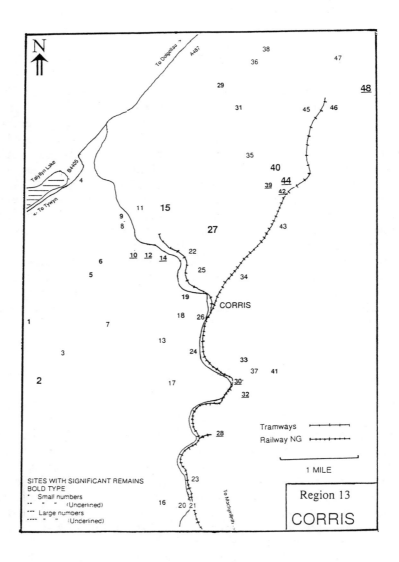

N

To Dolgellau
A487

38
36
47
29
48
31
45 46
35
40
39 44
42
To Tywyn
Talyllyn Lake
B4405
4
11 15
9
8
27
10 12 14
22
6
25
5
34
19
CORRIS
18 26
1
7
13
24
3
33
37 41
2
17
30'
32
28
23
16 20 21
To Machynlleth

Tramways
Railway NG

1 MILE

SITES WITH SIGNIFICANT REMAINS
BOLD TYPE
*   Small numbers
··   "   "   (Underlined)
···   Large numbers
···· "   "   (Underlined)

Region 13

CORRIS

204

with that of the major regions, it came after the end of the great mid 19th century boom, which meant that both quarries and railway never attained their full potential.

At Aberllefenni, the elevated terminus, with its fine cantilevered step access is prominent. After following the road, the trackbed goes through fields to Corris, where there is a fine bridge and the station buildings now house a small museum. From here to the engine shed at Maes-poeth about half a mile distant, the track has been relaid by the Corris Railway Society who intend to extend to Pantperthog. From Maes-poeth to about half a mile short of Machynlleth, the trackbed can be almost continuously traced alongside the main road. There are several 'bus shelter' stations and one fine house, still in occupation. The route leaves the roadside just north of Machynlleth, cutting across fields to Machynlleth station, via the remains of the Dyfi bridge, whose collapse precipitated closure of the line in 1948. Alongside Machynlleth station, new buildings occupy the site of the terminus. The bricked up arch, where the main road passes under the railway, denotes the path of the original tramway, which can be traced to Derwenlas. Since railway construction altered the course of the river, little is now identifiable there, other than a building once known as the Tan-y-ffordd inn.

The main feeder branch, the Corris Uchaf tramway, forms a footpath down the western bank of the river to Corris, where it passes close alongside the main road in a gully between the road and houses, accommodation bridges still being in use. Its trackbed then forms the Braich Goch hotel car park, from where it ran alongside the road to make a junction with the Corris Railway at Maes-poeth. It was intended to extend this line from Corris Uchaf to Glyn Iago. Near that quarry the formation forms part of a forestry road, the part-built incline down to Corris Uchaf is traceable.

Longer, but carrying much less traffic, was the Ratgoed tramway. Most of its trackbed from Ratgoed to Aberllefenni is now track or road. Having bridged the Cwm Llefenni road (once the main route to Dolgellau), it ran along the top of the mill dam to make end on junction with the main line.

1. SH719072 Glyn Iago *
2. SH721058 (723057) Darren ***
3. SH725064 Hafoty
4. SH729104 Dôl-ffanog
5. SH730082 (733084) Mynydd Ty'n y Ceunant *
6. SH732088 Cwm Dylluan *

7. SH733070 Tarran Cadian
8. SH735092 Tap Ddu
9. SH735099 Penygarreg *
10. SH738087 Tŷ'n-y-berth **
11. SH738097 Ty'nyllechwedd
12. SH744088 Ty'nyceunant ** (R)
13. SH745066 Goedwig West
14. SH745086 Gaewern ** (R)
15. SH746093 Abercwmeiddaw *** (R)
16. SH747030 Coed-y-ffridd *
17. SH748054 Pantperthog
18. SH748073 Bryn-llwyd Uchaf
19. SH748078 Braich-goch * (R)
20. SH749029 Afon Dulas
21. SH750029 Dolydderwen
22. SH750085 Afon Deri
23. SH751038 Glan Dulas
24. SH752063 Goedwig
25. SH752082 Abercorris (Trial)
26. SH753071 Bryn Llwyd
27. SH754089 Abercorris *** (R)
28. SH757045 Llwyn-gwern ** (R)
29. SH757121 (759125) Fron-fraith *
30. SH759059 Esgairgeiliog (mill) ** (R)
31. SH759115 Hen-gae *
32. SH760054 Rhiw'rgwreiddyn **
33. SH760064 Era * (R)
34. SH760081 Pandy
35. SH761103 Cwm-yr-hen-gae
36. SH761128 Foty y Waun
37. SH762060 Ceinws Bach
38. SH763132 Mynydd y Waun
39. SH765101 Hen Gloddfa **W (R)
40. SH765108 Cambergi ***
41. SH766062 Cwm Gloddfa *
42. SH766099 Ceunant Du **W (R)
43. SH768091 Matthews Mill (R)
44. SH768103 Aberllefenni ****W (R)
45. SH775114 Ffynnon Badarn
46. SH779116 (etc.) Cymerau * (R)
47. SH781126 (etc.) Dolgoed
48. SH787119 Ratgoed **** (R)

ABERCORRIS (Cwmodin) SH754089

Developed underground in the 1860s but, in spite of being on good narrow vein rock, inaccessibility contributed to its relatively limited success. Output at the turn of the century of around 1000 tons p.a., with about 40 men being about its maximum.

Material was lowered by incline to a water-powered mill, some 600' below. Later, a larger oil-engine driven mill with 4 saws, a planer, and a dressing machine, was built alongside it.

Originally reached by cart track, later by connection, via an incline to the Corris Uchaf tramway. Finally closed c1950.

Remains The early pit work is overgrown; both tunnels to these pits, and the underground adit at incline-head level, have been lost; but one at a level above is open, leading to some chambering, with a shaft for lowering material to the level below. The main incline has a remote type drum-house, with a banksman's shelter on the crimp. Some rail and rope is on the ground; alongside is a small reservoir. Only traces remain of the original mill, and the galvanised roof of the later mill has collapsed. Nearby is a small ruined building and a mess hut.

At a lower level, there are an office and dwellings in fair condition. Incline connection down to the Corris Uchaf tramway is traceable; the abutments of the bridge over Afon Deri is near the present footbridge. (27)

ABERCORRIS SH752082

Tiny trial.
Remains Short adit. (25)

ABERCWMEIDDAW SH746093

Probably begun in the 1840s with underground extraction; later worked as an open working, with finally some attempt to revert underground. In 1882, 188 men produced 4173 tons, making it briefly one of the 'big three' of the region, but tonnage declined sharply towards the end of the century.

Material was at first lowered by an incline to a mill which had 6 saws, 2 dressers and a planer. As the open working developed material was brought out on the level, drawn by the only steam locomotive in the region. The working having deepened into a pit, a tunnel was bored that emerged at a point below the mill. Rubbish was run out on a shelved tramway, bridging the public road to a new tipping area. Block was hauled up to the mill, originally by water balance, later by a drive off the mill wheel; finally, both mill and incline had their own steam engines.

Finished product went down a short incline and over a river bridge to the Corris Uchaf tramway. Some underground development was made from within the tunnel. Sporadic working continued up to WW2.

Remains The constricted nature of the site required high retaining walls to contain tipping and these are notable. At the quarry itself, the prominent feature is the 'Corris Binocular' twin tunnels, machine bored in the 1860s during probably abortive attempts to extend underground. The right-hand bore is only about 10 metres long, the left-hand about 80 metres. Above, rail dangles from another machine boring.

From the south-western corner of the pit, a strike tunnel for underground working runs for some 120m to a fall. The 250m drainage/access tunnel, starts from the same point, with slate sleepers *in situ*.

The original tramroad formation at mill level passes a building, (now in reuse) which was intended to be a mill, but was probably never used as such. Alongside is an engine house with chimney and a store; opposite them is a lavatory served by the nearby leat, which ran from a reservoir a little way up valley.

The mill area, which stands on a massive platform of waste, is now almost entirely cleared. Below this mill area, adjacent to the tunnel mouth, is the pit for the 45' wheel with part of the gearing and line shaft, which was some 15 feet below mill floor level. The uphaulage incline, serving the access tunnel is alongside and it is clear how the wheel was enlarged to provide extra power. There is a structure above the wheel-pit to hold the haulage drum with internal stairs to allow for maintenance. On the far side of the old upper tramway is the base for the return sheave.

The exit incline ran between high retaining walls, but these and the massive revetments and fine cantilevered steps, were lost in 1990 by landscaping. There is also a nice revetted platform for the rubbish tramway from the tunnel. Above the mills area there are signs of the early, high-level working with traces of an incline down. The line of the exit tramway and bridge to the Corris Uchaf tramway is obvious. (15)

ABERLLEFENNI (Foel Grochan) SH768103
Underground, a working quarry yielding a very high quality slab.

Developed mid 19th century as an extension of the two quarries on the opposite sides of the valley, which were also on the narrow vein. After some tentative open work, 8 tunnels were driven through the mountain at intervals from near the hilltop to the valley floor; worked successively down, they enabled almost the whole of the almost vertical vein to be extracted underground; the incline which served them being shortened as work progressed.

In spite of much back filling in the chambers, rubbish disposal from the lower levels became a problem; waste had to be piled up on the valley floor, and water balanced inclines used to reach the top of them.

The first mill was near the foot of the incline but in the 1860s a large mill, also water-powered, was built at Aberllefenni village, near the terminus of the Corris Railway and connected by a tramway.

In the latter decades of the 19th century, annual tonnages (including Ceunant Ddu and Hen Gloddfa) frequently exceeded 4000 and in 1895 peaked at over 5000, with employment averaging more than 150. Steam power never used but electricity from a hydro plant on Nant Llwydiarth was available from the 1920s.

Remains As a working unit, the privacy of the site must be respected, and certainly **no attempt should be made to enter any adit**.

The two water balances, one near the main adit and one at the far side of the valley, are relatively complete and now the only known survivors of a device once commonplace in the industry.

The main *trwnc* incline, which originally reached all the upper adits, shortened in single-acting form to serve just level 7, is in fair condition. At its foot is the recently re-aligned entrance to level 8, near which are an old office and the present compressor house. Between them and the building which housed the 1890s water-powered compressor, fed from what had been the Cambergi reservoir further up the valley, are the foundations and wheel-pit of the original mill.

Most of the tunnels went right through the hill and at 773106 are winches and a crane, where some material was extracted and precariously carted to the mill.

Underground, the unique downward working produced spectacular chambers, some almost 600' in vertical extent. Most are abandoned and choked with rubbish. One is being (late 1990s) worked, some 100' below adit level. Blocks are extracted by chainsawing and wiresawing, resulting in a minimum of waste. Blocks are lifted to adit level by a crane and taken out by a loco, for conveyance to the mill by bucket-tractor.

The reservoir which used to power the present mill is a nice feature with its slate leats and sluices (it still provides water for cooling and washing). There is a fine chapel-like building with a bell, that was once the office. The mill, which still has traces of the original central water-wheel driving 20 saw-tables, has been re-equipped with modern machines, including several diamond saws and, in a separate building, a unique multiple frame saw. Some older machines and notable old lifting equipment is still in place. There are still some traces of rail of the tramway which, until the 1970s, connected the working to this mill.

Most of the older houses in the village were built by the quarry. (44)

AFON DERI SH750085
Early pit/underground working.
Remains Collapsed adit, rubbish runs, ruins of a hut. Possible incline alongside. (22)

AFON DULAS SH749029
Underground trial, possibly as late as 1920.
Remains Trace of adit. (20)

BRAICH GOCH SH748078
Development commenced as an offshoot of Gaewern in the 1830s, with a small mill. Independent from the 1840s and following the opening of the Corris Uchaf tramway, vigorously expanded in the 1860s, with ultimately 8 floors underground. A new mill alongside the tramway eventually had 42 saws, 19 dressing machines and 3 planers. Water was used for pumping and for mill drive, the latter replaced successively by steam and then electricity.

Re-combined with Gaewern in 1880, by the 1890s tonnage well exceeded 6000, much of it slab in large sizes, with employment reaching 250, making it the largest in the region. Latterly, underground haulage was by marine donkey winches driven by compressed air.

Closed in 1906, but revived several times on a reduced scale, finally closed in 1971 when, uniquely, it was still enamelling on site. Became a *Theme Cavern* in 1994.
Remains Shortly after closure the southern part of the site was landscaped, obliterating the mills area and all traces of the external inclines which joined the upper levels. On the northerly part, there are vestiges of workings and of the tramway from Gaewern.

The tourist centre and present main road is on made ground, leaving the old road as an access route; houses on the line of this road are some of the last survivors of the extensive dwellings owned by the quarry.

Underground there was extensive chambering working the rich narrow vein. The lowest adit was No.6, emerging under the road at mills level, it is now the entrance to *King Arthur's Caverns*. No.5 adit, immediately above, like No.6 accessed a strike tunnel which ran left and right to the chambers, it was connected to the mill by a bridge over the road. To the north is the adit to Vanes level which runs to chambers underneath the southernmost Gaewern workings. The last to be worked, they contain winches and other artifacts. Until an underground incline was built in the 1950s down to Level 6, material was trammed out of this adit to a surface incline. Virtually all underground work to the south of the adits was blocked during landscaping, and 7 and 8 levels have long been flooded up. All the abandoned underground areas are subject to roof falls and **should not be entered**. (19)

BRYN LLWYD SH753071
Tiny underground working, early 1900s.
Remains Ground disturbance alongside Dulas Valley hotel. (26)

BRYN LLWYD UCHAF SH748073
Investigative trial on Braich Goch property.
Remains Adit, and short tunnel. (18)

CAMBERGI (Wenallt) SH765108
Hillside terraces spectacularly developed in 1875 on 7 levels, with an incline down to valley floor where there was a water-powered mill. Generally working on the south side, with tipping on north side. Closed in 1877 before the planned extension of the Aberllefenni tramroad could be built. Some trifling work done in the early 1880s.
Remains A spectacular 4 pitch incline, now much degraded, is a main feature, with several ruined drum-houses, (2 and 3, being remote type). Dressing sheds are on various levels. Some additional working on two levels above the top of incline.

The mill on the valley floor contained 9 saw tables and a planer driven by belts from a shaft, in a large underfloor tunnel, that was driven by a 30' wheel behind and below the mill. There is a leat from a reservoir some distance up valley, and a particularly fine tunnel taking the tail-race to the river. Nearby, a dwelling has been made from the remains of the 'Blue cottages'. A little distance off are their allotment gardens, each with an earth closet.

Higher up the valley is the reservoir which was grandly rebuilt by Aberllefenni quarry to supply its water-powered compressor. Some of the pipework is traceable. (40)

CEINWS BACH SH762060
Possibility of tiny early scratching.
Remains Some slate traces. (37)

CEUNANT DDU SH766099

This may be the site of the earliest of the Aberllefenni workings, dating from at least the 15th century and still nominally in business. Mainly open, but with some underground at the highest and lowest of the 6 levels.

When the first incline was installed, it brought material down from a working area (level 3?) down to another working area on level 5, with a further incline coming down to ground level 6.

Another working area at level 4 was connected by incline and tramway to the contiguous Hen Gloddfa quarry. There was some late underground working on level 6.

Remains The site is much degraded. The upper levels (1 and 2) have some underground work exposed and vestiges of inclines. At level 3 there are traces of buildings and of the tramway connection to Hen Gloddfa, with which it was always jointly worked. Level 4 is largely wrecked; below on level 5 are traces of dressing sheds and the most notable feature, which is the drum-house of the incline down to level 6. The drum is entirely of wood and is a magnificent example of an, undoubtedly local, wheelwright's skill.

At level 6 is a nicely portalled adit which descends in a slant. Running past this adit is the cart track by which material was originally carted to the, then, main road through Aberllefenni village. (42)

COED-Y-FFRIDD SH747030

Tiny pit working.
Remains Pit with access tunnel. (16)

CWM DYLLUAN SH732088

A small working in 2 pits, closed by 1876; it suffered from lack of transport facilities which would have been solved had the projected extension of the Corris Uchaf tramway been built.
Remains Site mostly in forestry. There is a long incline, partly stone-built, with unusually massive remote drum-house quite out of scale with the trifling digging. Two pits, rubbish runs and some small structures. (6)

CWM GLODDFA (Cwmodyn, Cambria Wynne) SH766062

A small open, unmechanised, digging in a constricted little valley. Material removed via a short incline, by cart. Probably idle by 1890.
Remains Some rubbish runs and several collapsed adits that seem to have been unsuccessful trials. There is a curious drum-house with an outcrop of rock forming one wall, with the brakeman's platform cut into

a ledge. The trackbed of an intended tramway to Esgairgeiliog mill is obvious. (41)

CWM-YR-HEN-GAE SH761103
Probably only a trial.
Remains Collapsed adit. (35)

CYMERAU (Troed yr Esgair) SH779116, 777111, 777106
Commenced c1860 in conjunction with Ratgoed, the original southernmost site was underground, with its 5 chambers pumped and hauled by water-wheel. Adjacent was a Pelton wheel driven mill, (electrified 1936). The northernmost site dating from c1880 was a series of adits, connected by an incline to the Ratgoed tramway. The middle site seems to have been less successful. Producing around 700 tons p.a. with about 30 men, The Ratgoed Tramway connected the diggings as well as conveying output to the Corris line at Aberllefenni. Worked up to WW2.
Remains At the southern site where the Ratgoed tramway crossed the river are traces of the mill. Nearby is the pit for the wheel which hauled and pumped the adjacent, now flooded, slant. Cottages associated with the quarry are still occupied. Up valley at both upper sites, there are adits some of which are open to chambering and at the northernmost, vestiges of an incline. The circular-sawn ends on the tip of the middle site are from late re-working with a portable saw. Alongside the Ratgoed tramway route are traces of a powder house. The reservoir and pipework are extant. (46)

DARREN (Tarran y Gesail) SH721058 & 723057
Pit/underground working that was an 1850s attempt to develop underground on an ancient site, (Drainllwydion) which, located on a packhorse route, had provided a handy source for local use over very many years. An unpowered mill and other buildings were erected but the high iron content in the slate hampered sales. A further attempt was made at a lower level in the hope that better product would result, but this too was unsuccessful.

Subsequently there was some small scale working on the opposite side of the hill but, quality apart, the lack of water for power and the remote location made this site a very doubtful proposition.
Remains Pit, and at the end of the cutting to the collapsed adit which accessed it, a nice suite of buildings. These include an office, stocking shed and a tiny mill which contains fragments of a hand operated saw

table. There is a big stockyard area and this, with a large area of the adjacent ground, is covered with many thousands of finished slates; most are broken or decayed, but at least 10,000 remain almost intact, as well as a number of headstone and billiards table blanks. At a lower adit is another small mill with remnants of machinery which may be part of the same, or another, hand cranked saw-table. Lack of waste suggests that little work was done here.

Around the southern shoulder of the hill are several collapsed adits and a small dressing shed. There is some finished product on the ground, of rather better quality than that near the main working. Unusually, for such a remote site, there are no barracks or other dwellings. (2)

DOLFFANOG (Talyllyn Lake) SH729104
Tiny working in a valley cleft, c1860s.
Remains Site disturbance has virtually obliterated it. Possible tramway formation to the road, nearby building may be connected. (4)

DOLGOED SH781126, 782212, 782123
Tiny workings from mid 19th century.
Remains The first site is just ground disturbance, the others collapsed adits, one with possible traces of a dressing shed. (47)

DOLYDDERWEN SH750029
Tiny hillside quarry.
Remains Excavation alongside road. (21)

ERA (Colorado) SH760064
Open working, started in 1870s, employing about 50 men producing around 600 tons p.a. Material was trammed to the water-powered mill at Esgairgeiliog. During WW1 closure, the tramway was extended for forestry use. Some work in the early 1920s.
Remains Almost nothing on the quarry site itself, other than the incline formation and a tramway to the mill. (33)

ESGAIRGEILIOG MILL (Ceinws) SH759059
A conversion of a Grist mill c1875, intended to saw, plane and enamel for Cwm Gloddfa, but actually used for Era, ceased in the 1920s.
Remains Only the walls of the original building stand but the later extension, which is in re-use, is a fine example of a slate mill. Remains of the bridge of Corris Railway branch. (30)

FFYNNON BADARN SH775114

Tiny hillside trial for which a branch of the Ratgoed tramway was planned.
Remains Excavation. (45)

FOTY Y WAUN (Y Waun, Waunllefenni) SH761128

Tiny open quarry c1870, revived on a small scale c1930.
Remains Rubbish runs, vestiges of dressing shed, access track. (36)

FRON-FRAITH SH757121 & 759125

Some underground work at 759125 c1865. Probably work at both sites in the inter-war years.
Remains At 759125 2 adits lead to some chambering. Shed with cgi roof. At 757121 traces of one or possibly two collapsed adits and a curious square building, with some sawn ends. (29)

GAEWERN SH745086

Slate was worked here in the 18th century. The opening of the 1830s road spurred the combination of several diggings, two of which were already underground. After originally using hand-cranked circular saws, by 1850 it had a water-powered mill with 5 saws and 3 planers. Following the opening of the Upper Corris tramway, product reached it by a tunnel under the road, a second mill being built alongside the tramway. Water may have also been used for hauling and/or pumping. Something of a hotchpotch underground as levels from two earlier workings did not coincide. This, and successive dodgy ownerships, meant that the fine narrow vein rock was never fully exploited.

In 1880 when activity had dived from its 1500 ton and 80 men peak, Braich Goch took over, building a surface tramway to enable reduction to be done in Braich Goch mill.
Remains The site has been much disturbed by road widening and bulk working. There are several adits and traces of tramway and incline formations. The one extant drum-house has become much degraded in recent years. There are traces of the drum-house for the incline which went underground to the tunnel which ran under the road; nearby are traces of the original mill. There is a slate covered leat leading to it from the dried-out upper reservoir. The Lower reservoir to the south still holds water. All trace of the works adjacent to the tramway have been obliterated by road widening. Some adits are open and chambering is accessible but **dangerous**. (14)

GLANDULAS SH751038
Very small quarry.
Remains Quarrying face. (23)

GLYN IAGO (Y Glyn) SH719072
Underground, worked 1899-1905 with up to 12 men.
Remains A small pit with chambering breaking up from below, but the adit to this is run in. There is record of a barracks, but no buildings have been located. (1)

GOEDWIG SH752063
Underground trial.
Remains Possible traces of collapsed adit. (24)

GOEDWIG WEST SH745066
Underground trial.
Remains Trace of adit. (13)

HAFOTY (Tap-llwyd) SH725064
Underground trial c1860.
Remains Run-in adit. (3)

HEN-GAE SH759115
Small, underground, from at least 1875, probably idle by 1900.
Remains One or possibly two, collapsed adits. Structures at Hen-gae farm contain slab material and are undoubtedly connected with the quarry. (31)

HEN GLODDFA (Hen Chwarel) SH765101
Although on the surface contiguous with Ceunant Du, its mainly underground narrow vein workings were separated by an intrusion. Unlike Foelgrochan, whose 7 level layout it resembled, it yielded good roofing slate.

Active up to the mid 20th century and still nominally open, it originally had a small water-powered mill on level 4, which also served Ceunant Du and also had the use of the original Aberllefenni mill at Foel Grochan via a tramway across the valley floor. It also used one of the rubbish water balances. Later working went down below level 7 and above level 1.

Remains At the highest level is a dressing floor with an extensive stock of slate, also some rail and trucks. A dry stone anchor block suggests that this area may have been reached by ropeway. There is an uncompleted drum-house and trwnc incline and the never installed Cast Iron axle, a brakedrum, 2 spiders and a ring spider, as well as the winch used to raise them. Behind is the abortive 1970s shaft, reached by a road and intended to re-develop these workings.

At level 1 below are old open workings and a reservoir. Level 2 is much disturbed but has an adit, a vertical shaft and a tramroad running to an interesting remote type drum-house with extended brake lever. Notable is the fine slate troughing which supplied level 4 mill. At level 3 there are vestiges of buildings and an embanked tramroad running to another trwnc incline, also possibly never completed.

On level 4, which is at the foot of the uncompleted trwnc incline from the topmost level, is an adit with rail *in situ*, the ruins of the mill and traces of rubbish runs and an incline down. An embanked track runs south east to a most curious banksman's cabin set into the rock controlling a drum-house which truncated a steep incline down from level 2.

Level 5 has some building remains and a connection to the above mentioned incline. Level 6, largely built up on waste, has an adit. Below, on level 7, is a portalled adit. (39)

LLWYN-GWERN (Glandulas) SH757045

Worked from at least the early 19th century and well developed by the 1850s. Except at the end of the 19th century when tonnages briefly exceeded 2000 p.a., output was modest.

Block was brought down from the original hillside quarry by an incline, to a 30 foot water-wheel (later steam, afterwards oil) powered mill containing over a dozen saws, and several planers and sanding machines.

As the working deepened, a cutting and tunnel enabled block to be trammed out on the level. Since overburden and the position of the reservoir limited the advance of the working face, the working was further deepened into a pit, with some chambering off of it. To further this development a tunnel was bored from the foot of the exit incline, under the mill area to a point below the quarry. Although rail was laid, it is unlikely that material was ever trammed through it, and it served merely as a drain. In the 1900s, due to site constraints, a steam powered aerial ropeway was installed to take rubbish to a tip high on the hillside. Later, this was powered by electricity generated by a producer gas engine.

An incline from the mill enabled loading onto a branch of the Corris Railway.

Some working went on until the early 1950s.

Remains The mills area is now in re-use by the National Centre for Alternative Technology who have restored several buildings. There is some rail *in situ* and there are several quarry artifacts on the ground. Within the quarry are loading platforms, a derrick, the base for a later haulage winch, and there is some chambering on either side.

Above the access tunnel is the lower mounting for the ropeway. At a higher level are rubbish runs from small subsidiary workings and, above again, the upper mounting of the ropeway with tipped waste and a building.

The reservoir is still in use as a water source. The drainage tunnel emerges near the foot of the present passenger water balance. The car park occupies the loading area for the Corris Railway branch; the abutments of the railway bridge across Afon Dulas stand, and the high embanked approach causeway to it is a notable feature. (28)

MATTHEWS MILL *(Y Magnus)* SH768091
Works for enamelling and sawing slate, c1850-1931.

Remains The site has been cleared except for some waste and fragments of artifacts. Bryn Derw house is on the site of the weigh-house. The short spur off the Corris Railway is obvious, as is an abutment of the moveable slideway used previously to reach the railway. (43)

MYNYDD TY'N Y CEUNANT *(Fronfelin)* SH730082 & 733084
Possible trials.
Remains In forestry. (5)

MYNYDD Y WAUN SH763132
Trial.
Remains Collapsed adit in forestry. (38)

PANDY *(Fronfelin)* SH760081
One or possibly two highly optimistic attempts to reach non-existent slate.
Remains Wheel-pit and some stonework of never completed surface structures. Excavation at 758074 may have been a proving cut for this project. (34)

PANTPERTHOG SH748054
Trial.
Remains Run-in adit. (17)

PENYGARREG SH735099

Small underground working from late 19th century. Re-worked in the 1920s.

Remains Collapsed adit, traces of a dressing shed. (9)

RATGOED (Alltgoed, R'Alltgoed) SH787119

Mainly underground; opened in the early 19th century, having three mills operating at various times. Lack of planning led to complicated working and movement of material. Early extraction was at valley floor level, the main workings being on eight levels on the almost pinched out narrow vein high on the hillside.

Annual tonnage, mainly slab, rarely exceeding 700, with a manning of 25-30. Enamelled products were offered but it is not clear where the process was carried out. After a chequered history, closed 1946.

Finished product was taken on the Ratgoed tramway to Aberllefenni, which was the only link apart from field paths, to the quarry settlement.

Remains At highest levels, 1 and 2, above the forestry road, are two small adits, possibly late trials. Below the road is a large pit, divided into three parts and accessed by a tunnel at level 3 and a cutting at level 5. Chambers break through from below. A short incline, which had horizontal sheaves, leads down to level 6 where there is a mill that was Pelton wheel or turbine driven, with some evidence of overhead shafting. This seems to have been the second mill to have been erected. Nearby are vestiges of dressing sheds and other buildings, one possibly a barracks.

Another incline with underfloor sheaves, and a flight of steps alongside, goes down to level 7. Here, there is a collapsed adit with an isolated tramway, so if useful make came out, it may have been removed by the ropeway which is believed to have been used somewhere on this site.

At level 8 is Middle mill, apparently the third to be built; its ruins contain the base of an oil engine with a stairway leading down to what was seemingly a Pelton wheel-pit. There are building foundations at this level and several rubbish runs emanating from an adit some 200 yards long, with rail *in situ*, cut through country rock. There are no workings but it has 3 vertical shafts dropping from the chambering above.

This level was fed by two inclines, both trwnc type, with remote type drum-houses. The drum of the one down from level 5 is in two separate parts with unusual brake gear between the halves. The one down from level 6 is curious in that the drum was shortened at some time.

From this level 8 a long incline goes down to the valley floor. The drum gear, also remote type, is unusual as the brake has a shaft to couple up a second brake, and there is a spare band on the ground; but there does not seem to have been space for a second brake drum. The remote brake lever was abandoned and replaced by a direct operating lever with a very crude wooden pin-down pillar. Part way down is a powder house and near its foot are buildings; the northerly one seems to have been an old water mill adapted, possibly, as a workshop. The southerly one could have been a dwelling or barracks.

There is also another incline down from level 7 which probably became redundant at an early date. Again of the trwnc type, it clearly had a horizontal sheave and part way down is another powder house.

Ongoing forestry felling is unfortunately destroying many of the structures.

There are several ruined buildings at valley floor level, including the original mill, with some evidence of underfloor shafting and, embedded in the ground, the table of a saw-bench.

Close above this are some small workings, including an open adit, and a possible short incline.

There are the ruins of a row of four cottages, the one nearest the track being a shop, as well as a chapel, manse and a manager's house. Ratgoed Hall, the owner's residence, is still in occupation. In front of the Hall is a most ornate stable block.

High above the site are traces of a reservoir. (48)

RHIW'R GWREIDDYN (Jeremiah) SH760054

Open quarry c1818. Material was originally brought down to a water-powered mill by inclines but, as the workings deepened, it was hauled out on the level, mill waste being tipped on the far side of the public road.

Later a further opening was made a few yards to the north. The block was excellent for enamelling and it is possible that some was done on site. After a mixed career, when up to about 70 men were employed, it finally closed in the 1930s after being an outlier of Braich Goch. Reused post WW2 as a factory.

Remains Little on the quarry site itself other than a weighbridge and a redundant drum-house converted into a lean-to shelter. A fine range of mill buildings remain, some in reuse, one altered and extended in brick. A small reservoir has piping leading to the housing for the turbine which replaced the original wheel, with the covered channel which carried the tail-race under the stocking area.

On the newer northern workings, little but the pits themselves remain. The present road is on the line of the tramway which joined the two workings and led to a bridge across the old road to the tipping area. The bridge abutments are extant. The present road also traces the line of a launder which brought water from Ceinws and a planned tramway to Esgairgeiliog mill. (32)

TAP-DU SH735092
Trial c1874.
Remains Pit and waste run. (8)

TARRAN CADIAN SH733070
Some trifling work c1903.
Remains In forestry. (7)

TY'N-Y-BERTH (Hillsborough) SH738087
Underground development in the early 1850s possibly from an earlier pit working, in anticipation of rail transport being available. Material was brought down by incline to a water-powered mill which, although designed for 10 machines, may have had only 2 saws and 2 planers. Following numerous doubtful promotions and failure to obtain tramway connection, it finally closed in the 1890s.
Remains In forestry, but several of the six adits in tandem down the vein, some small building ruins, traces of a reservoir, and the incline formation are discernable.

The mill has been rebuilt as dwellings; nearby is the fine office building. The Hillsborough cottages, on the main road, are still occupied. (10)

TY'N Y CEUNANT SH744088
Early 19th century working with an incline to the main road, on the other side of which was a small mill that was subsequently used as a chapel. Although on the narrow vein, difficult geology and speculation precluded its further development. Could have been connected to the Corris Uchaf tramway, but there is no evidence of this. Closed 1878.
Remains Two pit workings with adit access, one open. Incline formation from lower adit to main road. The old mill is very ruinous. (12)

TY'N Y LLECHWEDD SH738097
Anecdotal evidence of an early trial.
Remains None identified. (11)

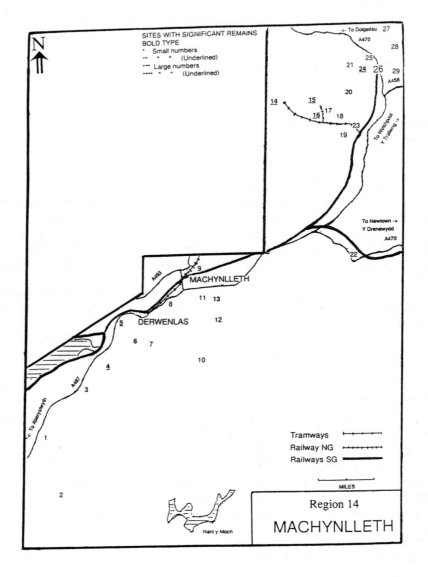

SITES WITH SIGNIFICANT REMAINS
BOLD TYPE
• Small numbers
•• " " (Underlined)
••• Large numbers
•••• " " (Underlined)

N

MACHYNLLETH

DERWENLAS

Tramways
Railway NG
Railways SG

MILES

Region 14

MACHYNLLETH

Nant y Moch

MACHYNLLETH
Region 14
Including quarries using the Mawddwy Railway
& Hendre Ddu tramway.

General

In this region apart from the widespread scatter of tiny local workings and optimistic diggings during the 1860s/70s boom, real productive activity was mainly in two areas. The larger exploited the easterly, continuation of the Corris veins in the upper Dyfi valley, bringing a measure of industrialisation to Dinas Mawddwy and Aberangell.

On the lower Dyfi a small dispersed group flourished during the late 1890s mini-boom, briefly augmenting hamlets such as Glandyfi.

All were predominately producers of slab. There was little activity post WW1.

Transport

Traditionally almost all the region's trade went down river from Derwenlas and prior to the Cambrian Railways' arrival in 1862, most slate leaving the region would have been carted there for shipment.

The railway shortened cartage distances for some producers, and enabled them to use either the better port facilities at Aberdyfi, or to distribute inland by rail.

Matter dramatically changed for Minllyn at least, in 1867 with the opening of the Mawddwy Railway, a private railway, operated as a branch of the Cambrian Railways. Closed in 1951, it was exceptional in being a Standard Gauge line laid primarily for slate quarry traffic.

Shortly after the Mawddwy line opened, the 2'6"g Hendre Ddu tramway was laid down giving Hendre Ddu, and other quarries in the Angell valley the opportunity to load onto the Mawddwy line at Aberangell. A little over 3 miles long, with branches doubling this, it was originally horse-drawn, later having lash-up petrol locos. Until its 1930s replacement by a road it was the sole means of transit along the valley. It also carried timber traffic, particularly during both wars, and part was laid or relaid specifically for this traffic.

Except near Aberangell where the formation crosses fields, its trackbed is defined by the present road.

The Mawddwy Railway trackbed is obvious right from its Cemaes Road junction to Dinas Mawddwy where the terminus station is now a cafe, and the engine shed a workshop.

The Cambrian Railways main line, which enabled development along the south side of the Dyfi estuary, is of course still in use.

1. SN666921 Cletwr
2. SN677885 Cwm Leri
3. SN692947 Tý'n-y-garth *
4. SN698961 Glandyfi **
5. SN716993 Morben **
6. SN717977 Llyfnant *
7. SN724976 Coed Cefnmaesmawr
8. SH738002 Graig yr Ogof
9. SH746014 Machynlleth Station
10. SN755963 Cwm Rhaeadr
11. SH755005 Parc
12. SN763992 Coed Pant-bach
13. SH763000 Pont-faen *
14. SH799125 Hendre Ddu ** (R)
15. SH818127 Maesygamfa ** (R)
16. SH822117 Gartheiniog ** (R)
17. SH825119 Talymieryn *
18. SH828107 Esgairangell
19. SH830095 Coed y Chwarel (R)
20. SH832125 Cwm Du *
21. SH836138 Bwlchsiglen
22. SH844031 Wynnstay Castle
23. SH845102 Clipiau
24. SH846136 Cae Abaty ** (R)
25. SH849144 Nant Minllyn
26. SH852139 Minllyn *** (R)
27. SH853157 Nant Dôl-hir
28. SH855148 Targwrmoel
29. SH872134 Pen-y-graig

BWLCHSIGLEN SH836138
This is the site of the 'Red Dragon mine', but slate is reputed to have been worked here or nearby.
Remains Nothing found connected with slate. (21)

CAE ABATY SH846136

A small pit working, with material being uphauled by a crane and taken by a short self-acting incline to a dressing area. Originally product was carted down Nant Blaen-y-cwm but later hauled over a shoulder of Foel Dinas by tramway to Minllyn quarry mill.

Remains There are several small buildings on site but no evidence of any mill. Artifacts include the remains of a derrick and the incline drum.

The tramway to Minllyn seems to have been light track laid directly on the ground, leaving little trace. Consisting of an uphaulage incline up from the quarry and a gravity incline down to Minllyn, there is dispute as to how the former was powered. At its head are vestiges of a building, gear fragments and remnants of a turntable, but no drum-house or engine. It has been suggested that it was hand wound possibly with gravity assistance; i.e. loaded wagons pulled up from the quarry would be partially counterbalanced by wagons descending to Minllyn, with empties *vice-versa*. (24)

CLETWR SN666921

Very small underground working, probably produced little.

Remains Traces of run-in adit in forestry. (1)

CLIPIAU SH845102

Trial?

Remains Possible ground disturbance. (23)

COED CEFNMAESMAWR SN724976

Tiny vernacular quarry.

Remains Excavation. (7)

COED PANT-BACH SN763992

Possible trials.

Remains In forestry, traces of one adit. (12)

COED Y CHWAREL SH830095

A small open slab quarry. Probably closed by the end of 19th century; may have used a branch of the Hendre Ddu tramway.

Remains Site lost in forestry. (19)

CWM DU SH832125

Small unsuccessful working from the 1880s.

Remains At the upper level, a small open trial; lower down is an opening which has been roofed up to from an adit (blocked). At this adit are ruins of a slab-roofed hut and a dressing shed. (20)

CWM LERI (Felinfach) SN677885
Very small hillside quarry c1890, operated in conjunction with Glandyfi. Some reworking in the 1930s, (including crushing for aggregates?)
Remains Excavation, machine remnants and bases. (2)

CWM RHAEADR SN755963
Very small, operated from 1866 to the early 1880s, possibly slab only.
Remains Almost nothing, site disturbed by a forestry road. (10)

ESGAIRANGELL SH828107
Tiny hillside working, rough slab only?
Remains Small excavation. (18)

GARTHEINIOG (Coed y Ffridd, Hendre Meredydd) SH822117
Intermittently active 1870s-1930s, possibly on the site of an earlier working. It had a water-powered mill with 6 saws and 3 planers. The first connection to the mill was via a tunnel and incline, later, as the pit deepened, a second tunnel brought block out on the level. Output 1883, 250 tons, 9 men. Connected to the Hendre Ddu tramroad.
Remains Large pit working into overhangs. In forestry there are vestiges of the tramway and incline connecting the upper adit to the mill. A tramway formation can be traced from the lower adit past some machine bases to the mill. This originally open sided building, now in reuse, has line shaft brackets. Behind is pipework for a turbine or Pelton wheel. Enamelling was said to have been done on site but no evidence of this has been found. The link to the Hendre Ddu tramway has been lost in road construction. The nearby house, like the machine bases, is from later forestry activity. (16)

GLANDYFI (Cardigan Slate Works, Cymerau, Dynyn) SN698961
Open working yielding mainly slab; developed c1880 with the greatest activity probably in the early 1890s when 12/18 men produced 2/300 tons p.a. From 1904 to 1909, operated by an Aberystwyth slate enamelling firm. Output carted to Glandyfi station.
Remains Quarrying area with trial adit. A nice mill building had saws, a planer and lathe; originally water-wheel but later steam powered, it is in re-use. There are extensive rubbish runs and the ruins of a bridge which carried a tramway to the road. (4)

GRAIG YR OGOF SH738002

Very small open working, possibly only building block produced.
Remains Quarry face, no trace of reputed tramway to Derwenlas. (8)

HENDRE DDU SH799125

Underground, opened c1870 with up to 16 saws, 10 planers and a Jenny Lind polisher, in a 50 hp. water turbine powered mill. Steam engine backup was planned but, as outputs were disappointing (878 tons, 31 men, 1883), the engine and some of the machines may not have been installed. A barracks, 6 cottages and a manager's house were built. A 10 ton steam crane was used presumably to lift block at the initial open workings. Product went out via the Hendre Ddu tramway. Back to back with, and working the same narrow vein as, Ratgoed (Region 13), its better layout meant that it was a much more efficient operation than that quarry. Surviving until the 1930s (with around 17 men and lorry transport), it was the last producer in the region.
Remains Site, now much afforested, was on 4 levels. The compact mill area is cleared except for a fine 2 storey building in re-use, and the foundations of a number of other structures. There are three adits; the lowest, at mill level, has some chambering. Above there is a second adit, which is flooded. Above is a third adit which leads to some chambering and to open workings. Above are the early open workings. At each adit level, there are massive spoil heaps and tramroad formations leading to an incline down to the mill. There is a trial adjacent to the head of the incline. The main exit incline down to join the Hendre Ddu tramroad is traceable. At the top of the site, one reservoir holds water, a second is dry. (14)

LLYFNANT SN717977

Small unmechanised underground working, active early in the 1870s; material carted down valley.
Remains Little, apart from the adit itself. Possible ruins of one small building. Some rail on the ground. There is a small underground trial at 718975 and an open working at 723975; both were possibly associated with this site. (6)

MACHYNLLETH STATION SH746014

Reputed site.
Remains Loco shed and goods depot of Cambrian Railway occupied site of old quarry, which may have produced slate for local use. (9)

MAESYGAMFA SH818127

Modest pit working but with a quite elaborate mill etc., producing ornamental blocks. Originally, material was brought down by incline to the mill but, as the working deepened, blocks were run out on the level via a short tunnel. Opened 1881 and employed 20 men in late 1890s, but mostly far fewer. An incline connected with a branch of the Hendre Ddu tramway.

Remains The only site in the valley to have substantial surface remains. Ruins of a mill (stone used to re-build Maesygamfa farm?). There is clear evidence of leatwork to feed a breastshot mill wheel. There are several other ruinous buildings including a barracks, and a drum-house of substantial block construction that had a horizontal sheave, and may have been single acting trwnc. Unusually, there seems to have been an unhoused weighbridge. In the pit, reached by a short tunnel, is evidence of the use of a channelling machine. There are parts for ornamental fireplaces in the mills area indicating that, besides saws, the mill had a planer. There are some slate sleepers on the tramway formation between the mill area and the head of the exit incline, where there is a building in agricultural reuse. The route from the foot of the incline to the Hendre Ddu tramway followed the eastern bank of the river, and there are rollers, rail etc in evidence. (15)

MINLLYN SH852139

An extensive site that was established before 1840, producing mainly slab. After initial open quarrying, all extraction was underground at one main and several subsidiary workings. In spite of its extent and having a standard gauge rail link, output was modest other than for a few years following reopening and re-equipping in 1872, when annual tonnages briefly approached 3000 and manning exceeded 100. The 1894 total of 550 tons and 20 men was more typical.

The first mill with 3 saws and 3 planers was in use by 1845. It is believed that it also had slate dressing machines and if so, it was the first Integrated mill, predating the earliest at Blaenau Ffestiniog by several years. It was first powered by a water-wheel and later by a Pelton Wheel with steam back up. An incline lowered material to valley floor level, with a further short incline to the Mawddwy Railway.

Its 1870s expansion included a large mill at valley floor level described as having 40 machines, including at least 8 planers which reduced material both from the main workings and subsidiary tunnelling. Closed in 1925, when machinery was down to 3 saws and 2 planers.

All the tramways on site were of 2'4¼" ('half standard') gauge; an unusual dimension also used in the Glyn Valley. (Region 15).

Remains On the upper mills area is the very ruinous mill with a contiguous compressor house, workshops, weigh-houses, other buildings and traces of an extensive tramway network. The chimney is standing, and in the adjacent boiler-house wall is the flue damper. The feed pipe for the turbine is *in situ*. There is a run of crude pillars for compressed air piping. The formations of the long incline which brought material from Cae Abaty, and two shorter ones from the early open workings, drop to this point. The main adit is reached via a fine stone lined tramway tunnel. Above this, near the head of a short incline, is a crane base.

Underground there are extensive, but seemingly almost random, passages and chambering that are flooded up to adit level. There are several winches and much chain etc., as well as rail track. Near a flooded up working is a boiler, other remnants of a steam crane, and parts of what may have been pump gear. The engine, one assumes, pumped and wound. There is much evidence of pillar robbing and also of the use of channelling machines. The workings can also be entered by a sloping air shaft.

From the mills area, a tramway leads past some other buildings, small workings and an air shaft, to the head of the main incline down to the lower mill. On this incline there are, partially lost in forestry, tramways to other adits of underground workings clearly unconnected to the main chambering. One adit is open, leading to a large chamber on the floor of which are the support chains and timbers of a bridge which has fallen from high above.

There are a number of large but unsuccessful excavations to the south.

The quite magnificent Lower Mill is in reuse, as are most of the railway buildings. (26)

MORBEN SN716993

Small hillside quarry active around 1900, attempting to exploit a very narrow vein.

Remains Working face with vestiges of an investigative tunnel, and an incline to the road with drum-house ruins. Two buildings, one an office and the other a powder house. This wooden-lined, two room powder house is the most complete example known.

Although clearly a slab operation, no traces either of a mill or of sawn ends have been located. (5)

NANT DÔL-HIR SH853157
Tiny trial.
Remains Blocked adit. (27)

NANT MINLLYN SH849144
Small underground trial.
Remains Collapsed adit. (25)

PARC SH755005
Trial?
Remains Excavation only. (11)

PEN-Y-GRAIG SH872134
Trial?
Remains Traces of digging. (29)

PONT-FAEN SH763000
Pit, with a mill which had 5 saws and 2 planers.
Remains Flooded pit. The mill area has been entirely cleared and a modern house built. Material was clearly originally moved across the road on the level. It is not clear if there was any later, lower level, access to avoid uphauling and pumping. The rubbish runs, being shallow, are very long. (13)

TALYMIERYN SH825119
Small hillside working.
Remains Pit with tunnel access, whcih contains a number of large slabs. Although connection to the Maesygamfa tramway branch was planned, there seems little evidence that this was ever done. (17)

TARGWRMOEL SH855148
Early open working.
Remains Hillside quarry, now occupied by Water Company installation. (28)

TŶN-Y-GARTH SN692947
Pit working, producing a coarse slab, established 1866, closed mid 1880s.
Remains Two pits, (to N and S of road), the northerly one accessed by a tunnel; there was presumably a now lost tunnel to the southerly one. The nearby house is a later structure. (3)

WYNNSTAY CASTLE SH844031
Small underground quarry.
Remains Two run-in adits in forestry. (22)

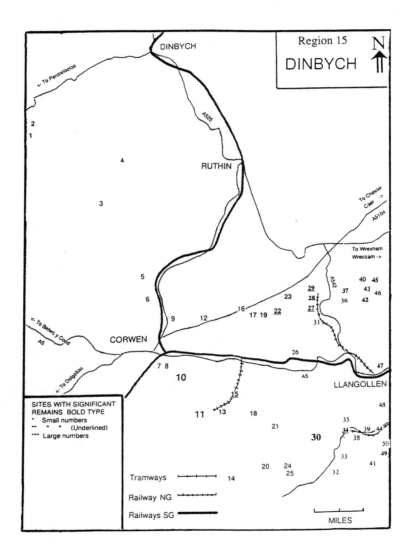

Region 15

DINBYCH

N

SITES WITH SIGNIFICANT
REMAINS BOLD TYPE
* Small numbers
** " " (Underlined)
*** Large numbers

Tramways
Railway NG
Railways SG

MILES

DINBYCH & LLANGOLLEN
Region 15
Including quarries using Deeside Tramway, Oernant Tramway, Glyn Valley Railway and GWR.

General

Slate was produced in this region from at least the 14th century. By the 17th century it was routinely being carted to Shrewsbury and beyond, a traffic which undoubtedly developed out of wool trade connections.

Its landlocked location and the questionable durability of its Silurian rock, particularly in the north, meant that the region never fully shared in the 19th century explosion in demand for roofing slate. However a number of quarries did produce excellent slab, often in very large sizes, and they successfully developed this market.

There were three main areas of activity: Glynceiriog which was also a centre for stone quarrying, where underground working continued up to the 1940s; Corwen, Glyndyfrdwy and other villages in the Dee valley, where slate was worked underground until 1960 and on the Maesyrychen mountain, north of Llangollen, which spawned several small settlements and where production on a small scale continues.

Being geologically different, geographically separated from the other important slate regions, and being close to the north Wales coalfield, some distinctive working methods developed.

Transport

The first alternative to lengthy cart journeys was provided from the early 1800s by the Llangollen and the Montgomeryshire canals, which not only assisted the expansion of the inland trade, but also offered, via Ellesmere Port, the possibility of export.

The Maesyrychen quarries on Bwlch yr Oernant (the Horseshoe Pass), used pack horses until the turnpike road was built in 1811. From 1857, they had direct connection with the canal and later the railway at Pentrefelin (218436), via the 3'g, 3 mile, Oernant Tramway. This is readily traceable from Moel Faen quarry, through Oernant and Clogwyn quarries to the head of an incline, where there are vestiges of a most unusual 2 storey drum-house which enabled the banksman to have a clear view of the run. On the incline are slate sleepers and, from its foot, the line is obvious partially as a lane, partly alongside the main road. The final stretch to the Pentrefelin mill (218436) at the canal is on a fine embankment. Disused by the early 1900s.

At Glynceiriog, the Cambrian and Wynne quarries had incline connections to the 2'4¼"g, 8 mile, horse-drawn Glyn Valley tramway from 1873, which ran mostly alongside roads to the canal at Gledrid (298368), with a branch to a siding on the GWR, the final part making use of a disused colliery tramway formation and wharf. In 1888, the line was steamed and a passenger branch made to Chirk station. Slate use ceased c1930, but granite traffic continuing until 1935. Most of the original is course partly alongside the road, partly across fields. As well as the Chirk diversion at Pontfaen it is readily traceable.

The opening in 1865 of the Llangollen & Corwen Railway (later GWR) enabled the Penarth and Deeside/Moel Fferna quarries to develop. The former was directly connected by an incline, the latter by the fascinating Deeside tramway. Opened around 1870, this must have been one of the last wooden railed tramways in Europe. 2'6"g, and 3 miles long, it was gravity powered, wagons descending singly with a brakeman aboard, empties being brought up in a horse-drawn train each morning. Originally running from Deeside quarry to the main road via the Nant y Pandy mill, it was later extended (with steel track) to Glyndyfrdwy station and to Moel Fferna quarry, remaining in use until the 1940s.

Most of the route is readily traceable. The intermediate incline, immediately above Deeside quarry, still has its horizontal sheave gear, remotely mounted in a block housing. In the vicinity of Nant y Pandy mill there is some wooden rail, some pieces of the iron sheathing and iron tie-rods. Near the main road, the drumhouse of the final incline still stands, but its horizontal sheave gear was removed in the late 1970s. The prevalence in the area of horizontal sheaves, instead of drums, undoubtedly reflects coal mining influence.

The Vale of Clwyd Railway (later L&NWR) may have, from 1858, been used by the tiny workings near Dinbych. Closed in 1965, most of the trackbed is traceable.

The ex-Cambrian main line through Chirk is still open; part of the ex-GWR Dee valley line, closed 1964, has reopened as the Llangollen Railway and the canal, including the unique Pontcysyllte aqueduct, carries pleasure boats.

1. SH977594 Aber *
2. SH978598 Nantglyn *

3. SJ031546 Nilig
4. SJ048478 Clegir
5. SJ065481 Wern-ddu
6. SJ074464 Ty'n-y-rhos
7. SJ081434 Corwen
8. SJ085434 Colomendy
9. SJ088444 Caer Derwen
10. SJ107424 Penarth *** (R)
11. SJ125399 Moel Fferna *** (R)
12. SJ130442 Coed Tirllanerch
13. SJ138404 Deeside * (R)
14. SJ141327 Sarffle *
15. SJ148417 Nant y Pandy Mill ** (R)
16. SJ157453 Cwm Tydi
17. SJ160448 Mynydd Bychan *
18. SJ161398 Ty'n-y-graig *
19. SJ162448 Cymmo *
20. SJ163342 Tŷ-nant
21. SJ165382 Nantyr
22. SJ169453 Rhiw Goch **
23. SJ171478 Westminster *
24. SJ176342 Ty'n-y-rhyd
25. SJ177325 Bwlch Adwy Wynt
26. SJ177446 Rhewl Mill
27. SJ185463 Clogau ** (R) W
28. SJ185469 Oernant * (R)
29. SJ185477 Moel-y-faen ** (R)
30. SJ189378 Cambrian *** (R)
31. SJ193462 Craig-las
32. SJ195326 Fron Ucha
33. SJ199351 Spring Hill
34. SJ199379 Wynne **V (R)
35. SJ199385 Tan-y-foel
36. SJ201468 Pentre-dŵr
37. SJ202473 Craig Wynnstay *
38. SJ207375 Tŷ-draw
39. SJ208378 Hafodgwynfe
40. SJ208476 Ffynnon y Gôg
41. SJ209344 Llechwedd Gwyn
42. SJ210469 Foel *
43. SJ210471 Aber Gwern

44. SJ215382 Pen-y-bryn
45. SJ215478 Pant-glas *
46. SJ216472 Eglwyseg
47. SJ218436 Pentrefelin Mill *
48. SJ229399 Craig y Dduallt
49. SJ234362 Craig yr Orin *
50. SJ239364 Cilnant

ABER SH977594

A small and very primitive, shallow open slab working. Hand saws were apparently used right up to 1920s closure, although mechanical sawing was used at some time. It seems unlikely that rails were ever laid on this site, all movement being by barrow. Slate in the horizontal beds lacked cleavage but came out in convenient 2/3" thick slabs, often with joints nicely at right-angles so a minimum of work was required. From 1858, could load onto the railway at Dinbych.

Remains Shallow pit, partly backfilled with rubbish, having vestiges of a number of tiny buildings, little more than alcoves. To the south-west, in forestry and connected by a track, is the trace of a low dam, downstream of which is a small building with pipe saddles behind it, probably a turbine house. In front is a floor about 15' x 4' consisting of 3 massive slabs 4'8" x 4' divided and edged by slate kerbs. In front of this is an open-fronted working shed. Clearly this was the site of a powered sandsaw, which is confirmed by the sawn ends around it, some of which are curiously bevelled. This area was connected to the quarry site by a cart track. (1)

ABERGWERN SJ210471

Small hillside quarry, carting to road. First half of 19th century.
Remains Access tunnel (blocked), small dressing shed and other buildings, access track. Also a digging at 210469, now in forestry. (43)

BWLCH ADWY WYNT SJ177325

Possibly only building block.
Remains Roadside scratching. (25)

CAER DERWEN SJ088444

Trial.
Remains Excavation. (9)

CAMBRIAN SJ189378

Following some excavation close to the ancient Chwarel Isaf (192378), serious exploitation commenced in 1857 at McEwen's quarry, a pit working a little to the west. In the 1860s there was vigorous development of the old Chwarel Uchaf (186381) with a water-wheel powered mill. Dubbed Martin's quarry and deepened into a pit, a tunnel was bored from it, some third of a mile eastwards, to emerge from the hillside below McEwen's. Rails though it led to an incline to the Glyn Valley tramway. By the mid-1870s a shaft had been sunk down to the tunnel a little to the east of Martin's, and another between it and McEwen's, these shafts being developed into Townsend's and Dennis's quarries respectively.

The late 1870s slump brought work to a halt, but was energetically renewed in the early 1880s. Townsend's was worked down to the tunnel, and McEwen's, having also been further worked downward, to a branch of the tunnel. Thus all four pits had drainage and three could also send out waste and block by steam (later petrol) locomotive haulage. The shallower Dennis was accessed by two tunnels of its own which emerged to the south; one was abandoned early; the later, lower one, was connected by tramway to a new mill near the main tunnel adit.

Underground work was commenced off and under the main tunnel near Townsend's and, via an extension of the main tunnel beyond Martin's, into new ground to the west. These latter workings eventually extended to 4 levels.

Due to lack of space to the east, rubbish from underground was uphauled out of Martin's and Townsend's, and also by a new uphaulage slant from the westerly chambering. Dennis's was later abandoned and used as a reservoir.

Output, except in the early 1870s, occasionally reached 2000 tons p.a. with manning up to 90, but they were the only quarry in region to retain an appreciable roofing slate market, with tonnages continuing undiminished into the late 1930s. Final closure came because most of the 50 men found other work during the lay-off in the hard winter of 1946/47.

Remains The whole site is afforested, and demolition and the highly degradable nature of the material has left few surface buildings. Even much of the very extensive waste has reverted to soil.

To the north-west of the byroad that skirts the top of the site, and adjacent to the reservoir, a rubbish haulage incline, with an engine house and weigh-bridge at its head, emerges from underground chambers. These are flooded up as falls prevent drainage into the main tunnel.

The pit of Martin's is immediately within the loop of the road, which was diverted in 1878 to allow expansion. Almost no trace survives of the water-powered mill, dressing sheds etc. which were to the north-east of this pit, as much ground was quarried away in the 1880s.

In the pit is the much degraded ramp of the uphaulage incline, the frame of a trwnc carriage, and the ruins of an engine-house and coal bin. There are also an air-receiver, cranks and other compressor parts. The tramway formation runs through the pit, with an adit at either end. The north-west adit leads to a fall, sealing off the extensive chambering beyond and above. Immediately inside are the frames of two trwnc-incline carriages, a nearby tank suggests they were water-balanced, presumably to lift rubbish internally. There are parts of a hand-pump and a 2 seater lavatory.

The south-east adit, which is the start of the main drainage tunnel, also leads to chambering. Inside there are two triangular wooden structures that were apparently incline trwnc frames.

Within the convoluted chambering, with evidence of 'cupboarding' and pillar robbing, is a flooded incline down to the lower chambers that were abandoned much before closure. At its head is a substantial engine mounting, possibly air driven. Another chamber contains the mounting and earthenware supply pipes for the Pelton wheel of a compressor, with discarded saw-blades acting as 'washers' for rods bracing the masonry. A further chamber breaks out up into Townsend's quarry. Within this open chamber is a well-preserved *caban* and an air-receiver. This is alongside a mounting for the engine which powered an up-haulage incline. This incline which removed rubbish from the underground workings is mapped as a ramp, but the absence of a formation and the presence of possible anchorages at its head suggest that it was a chain incline.

On the main tunnel there is some heavy rail and proper weighted-lever points, appropriate for locomotive working, but several parts of the workings seem to have been inaccessible to rail track.

Continuing along the main tunnel, one passes a side tunnel concrete-plugged with a valve, which connects to the flooded Dennis's quarry. On from here are some signs of a trench in the tunnel floor, presumably for a feed pipe for a Pelton wheel or turbine in the later mill.

The final pit on the main tunnel is McEwens quarry, on a side-loop of the main tunnel, and it can be seen how the original tunnel serving this pit was utilised as a final part of the main tunnel.

Shortly beyond McEwens the tunnel has been culverted for its final 30 yards, to the adit mouth, by a 3' diameter concrete pipe.

On the surface, Dennis's pit is in two parts; both are flooded, and in one there is a sunken boat. A short tunnel, possibly the remnant of the early rubbish tunnel now well above water level, connects them. The blocked lower tunnel is below water level; amongst the tree-covered waste runs to the south it is possible to see its exit.

At the exit to the main tunnel, there are a few traces of the Pelton wheel powered mill, office, workshops etc.; one more recent structure is possibly built from stone robbed from the old buildings. The head of the incline, with extensive rubbish runs alongside, is obscure, but it is possible to trace it to its connection with the Glyn Valley line in the village. (30)

CILNANT SJ239364
Putative site.
Remains Possible ground disturbance. (50)

CLEGIR SJ048478
A small face working, yielding a very pale coloured slate, operated c1870 to c1880.
Remains Quarrying area and access track. (4)

CLOGAU SJ185463
The rock here is unsuitable for roofing slate, but can yield slab in very large sizes, examples up to 20' x 10' having been made.

Shortly after the quarry's 1844 opening, the Pentrefelin mill was built; block was carted to it by the road which was reached by a short incline and a track. Finished product was sent out by canal.

The Oernant tramway obviated cartage in 1857, and from 1865 dispatch could be made by rail.

Employing up to 100 men in the 1870s, by which time a mill with 4 saws and 2 planers, driven by steam, had been built on site, although much handsawing was still done. Some use of the Pentrefelin works continued for final finishing.

Declining into closure during the 1890s, little if any work was done until 1934, when it reopened on a smaller scale with diesel power. By the mid-1990s activity had again tapered off with mill drive being supplied from an old tractor; it was taken over and re-equipped to produce very large slab.

Remains As a working quarry, access is not normally possible.

At the top of the site, where there are vestiges of the earliest working, is the ruin of a dressing shed with forge attached and a walled stocking area.

Below is the main pit, with a cutting leading to an incline formation down to the mill, with another cutting opposite leading to the rubbish tips. Extraction here is now by wire saw, with rubbish being handled by a digger and loader.

A road now leads to the mill which was rebuilt using part of the original structure. It houses diamond saws and polishers, one of the latter being the largest in the industry. Outside, near the entrance ot an old tunnel to the pit, is a very large diamond frame saw. Adjoining are the back walls of the old big slab dressing sheds and, nearby, is a rake of two storey buildings which formed dwellings, a store and a smith's shop.

The Oernant tramway formation runs through the site and forms the present access road. In front of the mill is the bed of the original exit incline, which became part of the Oernant tramway, and was reused after the tramway closed. (27)

COED TIRLLANERCH SJ130442
Small open working.
Remains Rubbish runs. (12)

COLOMENDY SJ085434
Described as producing 'coarse slate' in the early-20th century, reported as working inside, i.e. underground, 1924.
Remains In forestry, not positively identified. (8)

CORWEN SJ081434
Possibly building stone only. This name was also applied to Penarth quarry.
Remains Some excavations. (7)

CRAIG LAS SJ193462
Tiny, briefly worked during the 1830s.
Remains Excavation. (31)

CRAIG WYNNSTAY SJ202473
Old pit developed in 1886 with 30 men, failing shortly afterwards. Several brief revivals, the last being for a year in 1909 with 3 men.
Remains Pit with blocked tunnel, small building remains, access track. (37)

CRAIG Y DDUALLT SJ229399
Small late-19th century working.
Remains Excavation. (48)

CRAIG YR ORIN (Nant Gwryd) SJ234362
Pit with some underground. Already long established when it was owned by Chirk Castle in the 1790s, and it was recorded as producing 300-600 tons of roofing slates p.a. plus slab. Declined after this and possibly was only sporadically worked. In 1887, 55 tons, 2/3 men. The underground work dates from the 1890s.
Remains Some small buildings, tunnel under the road, traces of a drumhouse and incline, very limited underground chambering, access track. (49)

CWM TYDI SJ157453
Very small; part underground possibly a trial only.
Remains Run in adit, spoil heap. (16)

CYMMO SJ162448
Two small workings on either side of a hilltop, operating before 1850. Claimed to have provided slab for flooring the Crystal Place.
Remains Traces of a dressing shed. (19)

DEESIDE (Glyndyfrdwy) SJ138404
Possibly ancient hillside working developed in 1869, shortly following the opening of the main line railway. Due to the lack of water at the quarry, a substantial water powered mill was sited at Nant y Pandy (148417) which it shared with Moel Fferna, and which was reached by the wooden railed Deeside tramway. The 600 tons produced in 1883 by 34 men was probably fairly typical of its mainly slab output.

Production tapered off in the early 20th century but there was some work done immediately post WW1.
Remains Very little to be seen at the quarry site, apart from some slight vestiges of small buildings. The incline within the working has been almost entirely quarried away. The sheaves of the incline bringing down the tramway from Moel Fferna are still in place.

At Glandyfrdwy, the house now in reuse near the head of the trwnc incline, running under the road to the station, was the quarry office. (13)

EGLWYSEG SJ216472
Tiny working active early 1880s.
Remains In forestry; vestiges of access track. (46)

FFYNNON Y GOG (Pen y Gog) SJ208476
Hillside quarry, mid-19th century.
Remains Almost everything destroyed by forestry and roadworks. (40)

FOEL (Craig y Foel, Pentre Dŵr) SJ210469
Tiny hillside working, operated 1820s-1840s.
Remains Now in forestry, some buildings. (42)

FRON UCHA SJ195326 etc.
Possible trials.
Remains Excavation, also at 195329 (and possibly 190321 Nant Ganol). (32)

HAFOD GWYNFE SJ208378
Small, mid-18th century.
Remains Quarry face. (39)

LLECHWEDD GWYN SJ209344
Small, old, partially underground working.
Remains Excavations run-in adit, traces of 3 dressing sheds, access track. There is a possibly connected trial at 215340. (41)

MOEL FFERNA SJ125399
Almost entirely underground. It opened in the 1870s, eventually working on seven levels, and quickly established a reputation for good slab and efficient working. Tonnage in some exceptional years exceeded 6000, with manning nearing 200.

Until 1911, when a mill was built on site, slab was reduced in the Nant y Pandy mill. The new mill, in a curious mixture of technologies, used a gas engine to power sandsaws. In 1923 an oil engined electric generator enabled them to be pioneers in the use of diamond saws. By 1932 a further 2 such saws were in use, by which time compressed air was used for drilling.

The head of the extension of the Deeside tramway was reached by a trwnc incline. Besides acting as an exit incline it also connected three levels, and was extended as further levels were opened.

Although it remained profitable post WW2, the difficulty of finding men prepared to work in such an inhospitable location forced closure in 1960.

Remains On the upper level there is an adit, and a building of unclear purpose but a plummer block suggests machinery was installed. There is a weigh-bridge, a remote type drum-house which housed horizontal sheave gear, and the remains of one table of the *trwnc* incline.

At an intermediate level are an adit, weigh-house, a double rake of buildings which may have been a barracks, and also two massive pillars which supported the gantry for transferring wagons from 2'g to 2'6"g. The narrower gauge was used underground, with the tramway gauge on the surface.

At the lowest level is a further adit, a large stockyard, weigh-house, offices, powder house and the mill. The construction of the mill is unusual; it has fairly crude walling with a corrugated iron roof and, along one side, a sort of lean-to with sloping walls giving a buttressing effect. This large lean-to seems to have had very restricted access into the main mill itself. At one end of the mill is a massive concrete base for the oil engine.

There are a very large number of collapsed dressing sheds, besides many which have been tipped over.

Underground there is chambering on several levels but, since all adits were sealed on abandonment, access is only possible via an air shaft. On level 4, there is an intact bridge over inaccessible workings below. Above this, levels 5 and 6 and levels 6 and 7 were connected by underground gravity inclines. They both have rollers *in situ*, but no rail. In spite of using sheaves on the surface inclines, those underground had drums, which was a reversal of usual practice. The 5/6 drum is intact on the ground, the 6/7 incline drum is still in its mounting.

On level 6 there is a massive wooden, coalmine type, *cog* supporting the roof of a chamber, reflecting the employment of coal mining men. There are various artifacts, including winch frames and a hand pump. There are several air doors and a ventilation shaft rises to bank from level 7. (11)

MOEL-Y-FAEN SJ185477

Probably dating from the 17th century it was much developed from the 1820s and expanded following connection to the Llangollen canal via the Oernant tramway in 1857. At its 1860s peak, 160 men produced about 5000 tons p.a., possibly all roofing slate, which then represented much of the region's output. Extraction was from an east/west vein, in 6 or 7 separate workings. By the 1870s, work was concentrated into 3 pits accessed by tunnels with some work underground. It is possible that block was sent to Pentrefelin mill, certainly about the time that mill closed, a mill with two saws was built at the foot of the incline down from the eastern working at Moel-y-faen.

Afterwards, fortunes were very mixed and, prior to the 1936 closure, outputs which came mainly from the eastern working were extremely small.

Remains Three main workings deepened into pits, with several smaller hillside workings. The largest (easterly) pit has vestiges of dressing sheds at the highest, original, working level. There were many on site some being clearly intended to deal with large slab. The access cutting has an incline down to it with some slate sleepers on the ground. Nearby are further dressing sheds and a weigh-bridge. Below is a run-in adit, and lower still roughly at pit-bottom level, where rock falls all but obscure the floor, is a further run-in adit.

The upper adit is open at the pit end, where there are two entrances. Inside there is rail on the ground and some attempt at chambering. Part way down the north face of the pit a line of chambering has broken through. These chambers are inaccessible and presumably connect to the lower run-in adit.

The middle pit, partly water filled, has a cutting access with traces of what may have been a winding house for a chain incline.

The western-most pit, partly water filled, is at a slightly lower level and has the foundations of what may have been a steam winding house for an incline which, for whatever reason, replaced tunnel access.

The mill area is much disturbed and little remains, apart from a free-standing smithy hearth and the foundations of several buildings. Some way to the north is a row of cottages, Tai Newyddion, built for workers use. A tiny trial at 192483 may have been associated with this quarry.

The line of the Oernant tramway, with some slate sleepers *in situ*, is clearly traceable. (29)

MYNYDD BYCHAN SH160448

A tiny hillside quarry that mainly produced block.

Remains Ruins of a tiny shed and some trimmings suggest the possibility of roofing slate being made. (17)

NANTGLYN SH978598

Extensive, shallow working for slab, using hand sawing; closed c1950. The slate beds which are similar to, but less regular than the nearby Aber quarry contain a number of inclusions, some almost spherical. These metalliferous inclusions are migrations which are commonly seen as ellipsoid spots on slates.

At one time a tramway to the main road was proposed. From 1858, loadings could be made onto rail at Dinbych.

Remains Very shallow working face. Some signs of small buildings. (2)

NANT Y PANDY MILL (Deeside Slab Works) SJ148417

The mill for Deeside and Moel Fferna quarries. It was sited here c1870 to take advantage of abundant water power. A 40' water wheel powered sandsaws and a planer. Closed c1915, but some small-scale work mainly on stock in hand continued to 1923.

Remains The substantial buildings are extensive and, apart from being roofless, are in fair condition. Besides the mill, with wheelpit and associated launder pillars, are several other structures, including an office, stable, and formations of a tramway network with two bridges. Nearby is a small reservoir and some neat leat-work. (15)

NANTYR SJ165382

A small pit working operating 1870s and 1880s with about 3 men. Had the hoped for extension of the Glyn Valley Tramroad been made, expansion might have taken place. Cambrian quarry attempted a reopening in 1920.

Remains Main pit is now an ornamental pond in a picnic area. (21)

NILIG SJ031546

Small open working.

Remains Excavation only. (3)

OERNANT SJ185469

An open quarry producing roofing slates from at least the 17th century. Plateways may have been used for internal movement. Closed c1870.

Remains The original working is in trees below the main road. The present buildings on the site may be adaptions of quarry buildings.

The later, and larger, working above the main road is much disturbed by bulk fill removal. There is a tiny trial at 189471. (28)

PANT-GLAS SJ215478

Elongated hillside working, material taken to a mill by an incline. Working in 1883 in conjunction with Wynne, when 35 men produced 735 tons. Closed c1886, but reworked briefly in the early 1920s.

Remains Some vestiges of buildings, a drum-house and incline to possible mill building which is now in re-use. Collapsed tunnel, which may have been investigative. (45)

PENARTH (Chwarel Graig, Pen-y-glog) SJ107424

A moderate sized quarry, initially terrace worked, developed underground in the late 1860s, following the opening of the railway to which it was connected by an incline. Its 150 man payroll of 1868 suggests vigorous expansion.

In 1883 only 10 were employed but they creditably produced almost 500 tons. This high productivity suggest a high proportion of slab, and that power sawing of some kind was in use.

Closed in 1890 but reopened five years later, shortly after which a small water powered mill was built near the foot of the incline, with a sandsaw which may have come second-hand from Pentrefelin mill. It was stated in 1903 that all sawing was done in this 'Wharf' mill.

In 1904 a new mill was built at the quarry, driven by a 12hp Blackstone oil engine and in 1909 a Hornsby 40hp producer-gas engine was installed, which is reported to have operated a *force pump* (presumably an air compressor). At about this time, a large reciprocating oil engined shot-saw was installed. A rarity in the Welsh slate industry.

In the years before closure in 1932, only slab (about 1000 tons p.a.) was produced.

Remains There are a number of buildings on site, including many dressing sheds; some, as is typical in the region, were clearly intended for slab. The mill contains remnants of shafting, pulleys etc. and at one end there is a motor room bearing the date 190? There are obvious traces of the sandsaws, with drainage channels and some sawn slab still *in situ*. There are remnants of the open-air horizontal ganged shot-saw with carriage and, alongside it, concrete machine bases. There are a number of artifacts around the site, including pipework for the producer-gas plant, and discarded sand-saw blades.

The old open quarry is at the side of the working area; the extensive terraces are much degraded with almost no trace of the central incline. There are the ruins of further dressing sheds and a quantity of severely weathered slates.

The main incline has an unusual drum-house; it is a shallow construction in the rock above and behind the incline head, which almost totally enclosed the horizontal sheaves which were connected to a brake cabin by a rod. Much of this mechanism is in place, including traces of a remotely controlled crimp sprag. There are traces of what may have been an incline table. Where the incline passed under the main road is now a culvert; nearby are some signs of the 'Wharf' mill.

All the adits are blocked, including one which was internally dammed to provide a water supply for the saws. Near the lower, drainage/rubbish adit is a weigh-house which contains mechanism. Near the old quarry the underground workings break out, and inside there are extensive, though in places apparently haphazard, tunnelling and chambering exploiting two veins. Three of the five levels are accessible and contain several winches and other items, including one wagon. There is rail in the tunnels, and on at least one short incline.

Above the quarry are traces of a small block making operation using country rock. It is believed that in the early years of the century this rock may have been sent to Llanfair quarry (Section 10) for crushing. Some nearby houses were connected with this quarry, but no trace has been found of the workers' cottages that were immediately below the site. (10)

PENTRE-DŴR SJ201468
Relatively large working, disused by the 1870s. The eponymous village was a quarrying settlement.
Remains Degraded tips. (36)

PENTREFELIN MILL SJ218436
A slateworks on the canal wharf. Powered by an 18' x 4', 14hp waterwheel, it dealt with material brought from Clogau and possibly other quarries, by the Oernant tramway. Dating from 1836 it had a Jenny Lind polisher and sandsaws. Re-equipped with 7 (later 8) planers and 3 circular saws in 1856, employing 30 men, it continued in use despite complaints over tipping in the river until 1897; latterly used for stone crushing. It is believed that some enamelling was done.
Remains Buildings (in reuse as a Motor Museum) and canal wharf. A cleared area defines the site of the, railway siding. (47)

PEN-Y-BRYN SJ215382
Slab quarry, disused by late 1890s.
Remains Excavation. The tiny digging at 215380 may have been associated. Not far away at 223373 & 223374 are other diggings, but these probably just yielded building block. (44)

'RHEWL MILL' SJ177446?
This is the possible site of an 1830s/40s slate sawmill used by Craig Las.
Remains Ruins of a woollen mill fed by Afon Cymmo, but no evidence of slate use. (26)

RHIW-GOCH SJ169453
A partly underground working producing slab. Developed from 1847; poor rock and bad communications seem to have scarcely justified the somewhat elaborate buildings erected in the 1890s, and the installation of 2 saws and 2 planers driven by a 12hp steam engine. After a period of

closure, revived in 1909 with 34 men. Operated up to WW2, latterly employing about 5 men, producing well under 100 tons p.a.

Remains The quarrying area is much decayed and the formation of the hand-wound incline is scarcely visible. There are several substantial mill and other buildings of nice architecture, but the layout is not easy to follow. Notable are the marine tanks that were used for engine fuel. (22)

SARFFLE SJ141327
Very small working c1860.
Remains Quarry face rubbish runs, possible building remain. (14)

SPRING HILL SJ199351
Probable site of trial workings in 1920s.
Remains Run-in adit alongside farm road. (33)

TAN-Y-FOEL SJ199385
Open pit latterly owned, but possibly not worked, by Cambrian.
Remains Excavation. The two tiny pits at 196388 may have been associated. (35)

TŶ-DRAW SJ207375
Early pit working.
Remains Excavation traces. (38)

TŶ-NANT SJ163342
Tiny trial.
Remains Excavation. (20)

TY'N-Y-GRAIG SJ161398
Small open working, operated in at least 2 separate periods. Cart road to Glyndyfrdwy.
Remains Dressing sheds and rubbish runs. (18)

TY'N-Y-RHOS SJ074464
A tiny pit.
Remains Virtually none. (6)

TY'N-Y-RHYD SJ176342
Small digging, possibly not slate.
Remains Excavation. (24)

WERN-DDU SJ065481
Stone quarries, possibly early use for slate.
Remains Nothing related to slate. (5)

WESTMINSTER (Craig Newydd) SJ171478
Of several tiny ancient scratchings, e.g. 171473, 176477 & 180475, two small adjacent pits were developed here in the late 1870s, and again at intervals from the 1890s to 1935, with up to 30 men.

Had a steep water balanced incline; later steam wound, with the same engine powering saws (internal-combustion engined later?).
Remains Tips used as a source of hard-core; pit filled in. Vestige of top of haulage incline and some concrete machine bases. (23)

WYNNE SJ199379
Originally a terraced hillside working claiming establishment in 1750; but this may have been the tiny quarry working immediately above the present site, which was one of many at the time, e.g. 188391 & 203390. Opened in its present form in the 1870s there was serious development in the 1880s with a water-powered mill and incline to the Glyn Valley tramway, with underground working by the end of the decade. A steam haulage raised blocks and such waste as could not be backfilled. Later a water balance lifted waste to a tip. After amalgamation with Cambrian in 1891, a Pelton wheel powered both a compressor and a generator.

Prospered during the early 1900s slate shortage, with outputs of around 2000 tons p.a. Closed in 1912, but it reopened in 1923 with an oil engine to drive the compressor and another to back up the mill water wheel. Work ceased in 1928, but the quarry continued to supply water to the village until 1952, and in the 1970s was opened to the public.
Remains Some chambers on the upper 2 of the 3 floors are open to visitors by arrangement. The mill has been superseded by a new building, but traces of the wheelpit remain; as does the exit incline drum-house and the adit for a part cut and cover tunnel; traces of a drum-house for a late gravity incline and, overgrown, the formation of the water-balance incline. An interesting collection of quarrying relics are on view, but the rake of wagons shown are coal drams. The tunnel is blocked. (34)

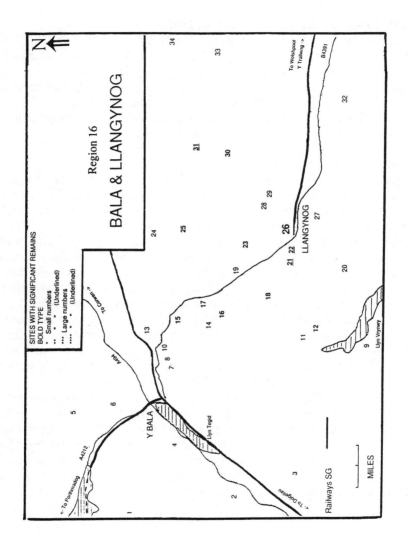

Region 16

BALA & LLANGYNOG

SITES WITH SIGNIFICANT REMAINS
BOLD TYPE
• Small numbers
• " " (Underlined)
••• Large numbers
••• " " (Underlined)

MILES

Railways SG

BALA & LLANGYNOG
Region 16
Including quarries using Tanat Valley Railway and GWR.

General

Much of the quarrying in this region, particularly in the Bala area, was confined to ephemeral vernacular scratchings, with some in the Efyrnwy valley being a little more substantial.

The greatest activity was in the Tanat valley, where there were relatively abundant Ordovician occurrences. These and lead mining made Llangynog a flourishing industrial village, where slate activity survived to WW2.

Transport

For most of the region no transport other than cartage was used or, indeed, needed. When the GWR Ruabon to Y Bermo (Barmouth) line reached Bala in 1868, almost its sole user was Cletwr. Although never directly connected, that quarry was able to expand as a result of rail availability. It would have been possible for the Vyrnwy quarries to have used the Llanymynech-Llanfyllin branch of 1863, but no record has been found of such use.

The quarries of the Tanat valley had, from the 1790s, the opportunity to load onto the canal at Llanymynech, (266211) but long before that Craig Rhiwarth was sending appreciable tonnages to England by cart. From 1861 loadings could be made onto the Cambrian Railways at Porth-y-waen (270240). It was 1904 before the Tanat Valley line opened, too late to be of great slate significance, and only Craig Rhiwarth was directly connected. Had it been built when it was first proposed 40 years earlier, the upper Tanat valley might have become an important slate producing area. The railway closed in 1967, but the whole of its 14 mile length is easily traceable, with a number of structures surviving.

1. SH848362 Ffridd y Gloddfa
2. SH862291 Tŷ Mawr
3. SH875258 Aran *
4. SH897330 Coed Cerrig Llwydion

5.   SH915407 Wern-fawr
6.   SH921371 Ty'n-y-coed
7.   SH944338 Beudy'r Ffridd
8.   SH946341 Gelli-grin
9.   SH959208 Afon Hirddu
10. SH959343 Dolfeirig
11. SH965250 Afon Nadroedd
12. SH969243 Nant Alltforgan *
13. SH973353 Rhiwaedog
14. SH978315 Nant-y-sarn
15. SH985348 Cletwr *
16. SH987328 Afon Cletwr *
17. SH995341 Queens *
18. SJ041271 Glanyrafon *
19. SJ042291 Bwlch-gwyn
20. SJ043230 Clochnant
21. SJ047262 Craig y Gribin **
22. SJ049259 West Llangynog **
23. SJ051289 Llwyn-onn *
24. SJ051346 Carnedd y Ci
25. SJ052336 Cwm Tywyll *
26. SJ053263 Craig Rhiweirth *** (R)
27. SJ057243 Chwarel Ddu
28. SJ060278 Moel Crynddyn
29. SJ066274 Craig Glanhafon
30. SJ074294 Powys *
31. SJ075326 Cwm Maengwynedd **
32. SJ126223 Brithdir
33. SJ176303 Tŷ-gwyn
34. SJ182311 Nant Fach Gynan

AFON CLETWR (Hafod Uchel) SH987328
Small open working.
Remains Flooded excavation; foundations of a dressing shed and another building; possibly a store. Fine access track. (16)

AFON HIRDDU SH959208
Tiny open working *circa* 1830.
Remains Excavation and access track. (9)

AFON NADROEDD SH965250
Underground.
Remains In forestry; adit collapsed. (11)

ARAN SH875258
Very small 18th century open working; later underground.
Remains Open workings into a steeply dipping exposure. Vestiges of shelters; lower down, 2 adits, the larger one open but flooded. The long access track is readily traceable. (3)

BEUDY'R FFRIDD SH944338
Tiny early working.
Remains Excavation only. (7)

BRITHDIR SJ126223
Some slate extraction on the site of pre-existing metal workings. Development planned in 1880. Machinery was bought but, almost certainly, never installed.
Remains Pit; possible rubbish run. (32)

BWLCH-GWYN SJ042291
1880s trial.
Remains Excavation. (19)

CARNEDD Y CI SJ051346
Tiny hillside scratching.
Remains Slight traces of excavation. (24)

CHWAREL DDU SJ057243
Tiny open quarry probably worked around the 1900s.
Remains Small quarry working, vestiges of a dressing shed. Rubbish tipped down now afforested hillside. (27)

CLETWR (Llandderfel) SH985348
Open quarry developed into a deep pit (possibly with underground workings off it), having a tunnel connecting to a mill lower down the hillside. Finished product carted to the main line railway. Although it had 10 saws with a 12hp portable steam engine to back up a waterwheel, its 1882 output of a mere 50 tons with 6 men, was not too untypical.
Remains Site is now largely in forestry. At the edge of the pit is the ruin of a small building and, nearby, another in re-use as a shooting lodge,

both presumably dating from the early open workings. The mills have been levelled but vestiges of a wheel pit and underfloor water channels exist. The access tunnel is blocked (dammed as a water source for Pale house hydroelectric plant). The cartway is partly traceable; a stopped up arch shows where it passed under the main road near the railway. (15)

CLOCHNANT SJ043230
Very small underground.
Remains Two adits, one to a shaft above. Dressing shed. (20)

COED CERRIG LLWYDION SH897330
Putative site.
Remains Possible excavation. (4)

CRAIG GLANHAFON SJ066274 (also 066276)
Small pit/underground workings, worked early 20th century.
Remains Excavations and tips. (29)

CRAIG RHIWEIRTH SJ053263
Hillside quarry, possibly dating from the 16th century, which by the end of the 18th century, with the canal at Llanymynech available, was regularly turning out 1000 tons p.a.

From c1840 an incline replaced a combination of ropeway and perilous sledging down some 800' to the valley floor. Further galleries were opened, connected by tramways and inclines, and working taken underground.

Sometime after the railway came to Porth-y-waen in 1861, traction engine haulage was tried but abandoned due to damage to the roads. Output peaked at 2000 tons in 1878, but closure came in 1886.

The Tanat Valley Railway enabled a revival in the 1900s, with the incline being extended under the road to an exchange siding. Limited activity continued until WW2, manning increasing to 26 when West Llangynog closed. Latterly, an oil engine was used for generating electricity, and another drove one of the hitherto treadle operated dressing machines.

Remains The salient feature is the main incline, at the foot of which are traces of the old cartage wharf. The tunnel under the road is lost; behind the present cafe is a building and the site of the exchange sidings. The drum-house has a commodious hut alongside, possibly providing lodging for the brakeman. The drum gear is unusual in that the spiders were cast in two 2 halves. To the west, a track leads to a powder house. To the east, the tramway formation is benched out of the steep hillside to reach some dressing sheds and the foot of a short incline. At the head of this incline is a drum-house (remote type, as are most on site) with the remains of gear. Structures include the oil-engined generator house, and a stanchion for a floodlight. Chambers here are open and a hand winch, headframe, railtrack etc. inside, suggest that this was the location of the last working.

Further along the tramway is a further incline, with a level part way up with some evidence of early chambering. At the top is a working area with various buildings, including the drum-house with curious flat bar tie-rods, and a dressing shed with a neat aperture to allow trimmings to fall down the mountain side. At this level are the remains of a dressing machine, with a possible oil engine base adjacent.

There are the much degraded remains of another incline above this, and some rather confused workings and structures, possibly abandoned at an early date.

There are workings, that were clearly unconnected to any incline system, higher up and also some further east at a slightly lower level, which were possibly the very earliest workings.

Below is a path system which may have been the old sledgeway, and also structures that suggest a ropeway from the lowest working level to this path. It is believed that the existing exit incline replaced an earlier one; if so, its location has not been identified. (26)

CRAIG Y GRIBIN (Pengwern) SJ047262

A small hillside/underground working dating from the early 19th century. Closed in 1880s, but it was briefly re-opened in the 1930s. There was a short self-acting incline to the road.
Remains Dressing sheds, a great deal of stock (including flags) on ground. Chambers accessible at 2 points. Powder house lower down the hill. (21)

CWMMAENGWYNEDD SJ075326

A complex quarry, with ambitious infrastructure quite out of keeping with its minuscule output.

Operated in 3 phases: 1867 (or perhaps much earlier) -1871, 1876-86, 1899-1910, with a peak output in 1876 of 50 tons with 6 men. Apart from 1906/07 when there were up to 20 men employed on development, manning rarely exceeded 4.

Originally it worked an exposed outcrop on two levels with, probably in the second phase, some underground work and hand cranked saws. Later work on a lower level was entirely underground, served by a water powered mill. Most unusually, this later underground development had water-wheel powered ventilation.

There were at least two proposals for a railway up the valley but it was 1904 before their transport problems were eased by a traction engine towing a trailer to Llanrhaeadr-ym-Mochnant station.

Remains At the top of the site are the original open workings with an abortive tunnel. As well as roofing slate trimming waste, sawn ends show circular saw use, probably hand cranked with vestiges of a building that might have housed such a machine. Slightly lower down is a further working with one adit collapsed and another open; inside is a quantity of aluminium tubing; the remains of a crashed aeroplane (Wellington?). The tunnel which has bar rail directly tenoned into sleepers, divides to some limited chambering. Part-way along the tunnel is a side-cutting, now banked with off cuts and rubbish. The presence of sawn ends outside, and in the tunnel up to this point, together with the absence of any building strongly suggests that hand-powered circular sawing was done in this underground alcove. The shot holes are hand-drilled, and there is one large block and a number of slabs underground. The absence of trimming waste suggests that slab only was produced from this level. Adjacent is a building, an office and/or forge, with a shaft with gears that might be part of a saw-table drive. From this area a cart track leads out, off site.

Lower down is a run-in adit and nearby are traces of a building, either the forge or the office which were both near this adit. This was the site of the water-wheel which drove the ventilation fan, but no trace remains. Above is a depression with traces of walling, denoting the site of the tiny reservoir which fed the fan wheel, with a run-in ventilation shaft close by. A tramway formation leads to a drum-house with an uncommon, 4 spider drum by Turner of Newtown. One pillar carries the initials D.P.Ll. (D.P. Lloyd was manager 1906). The incline forms a forestry firebreak; at the foot are the pillars of a tramway bridge leading to a mills area, and traces of a Pelton wheel (possibly originally water-wheel) powered mill, which appears to have been open-sided. Possible other buildings and loading bank.

Uphill there is a fine granite dam and a powder house. Nearby is the ruin of a rake of four cottages, which may have been used as barracks.

At the edge of the forestry below the dam are two spoil runs, one to a run-in adit, the other to a 30' deep cutting that does not appear to have gone underground, both apparently abortive. (31)

CWM TYWYLL SJ052336
Early; 1706? Pit with possibly some underground work.
Remains Water-filled pit, dressing shed, wall with a curious alcove, rubbish runs, stock of slates. (10x16 & 8x14). Water on site but no evidence that it was used for power. (25)

DOLFEIRIG SH959343
Putative site, may not have been slate.
Remains Excavation. (10)

FFRIDD Y GLODDFA SH848362
Tiny open working.
Remains Excavation and ground disturbance. (1)

GELLI-GRIN SH946341
Tiny open working.
Remains Excavation only. (8)

GLANYRAFON SJ041271
Underground, dating from around 1860.
Remains Traces of dressing sheds; deep shafts; adit near road is open, but flooded. (18)

LLWYN-ONN SJ051289
1880s trial.
Remains Excavation. Traces of a building. (23)

MOEL CRYNDDYN SJ060278
Small underground working c1876.
Remains Flooded adit; rubbish run. (28)

NANT ALLTFORGAN SH969243
Hillside quarry on a steep site.
Remains Dressing sheds and rubbish runs. (12)

NANT FACH GYNAN SJ182311
Probably only a trial.
Remains Excavation. (34)

NANT-Y-SARN SH978315
Tiny digging, c1880.
Remains Excavation, now flooded; rubbish runs. Site cut by forestry road. (14)

POWYS (Pistyll Rhaeadr, Craig y Pistyll) SJ074294
A small hillside quarry, with possibly some underground working, opened 1834 closed 1873. Revived briefly in 1911 when 93 tons were produced. Block was lowered by an incline to a water powered mill. Cart transport.
Remains Quarry face; some traces of incline; mill site with the base of the oil engine used in the 1911 revival. A leat for a nearby lead mine cuts through the site. (30)

QUEENS SH995341
Small open working, with possibly some underground. Disused by 1904.
Remains Ruined buildings; wheel pit; flooded pit. Site much disturbed by forestry. (17)

RHIWAEDOG SH973353
Small open working.
Remains Small working face. Spoil in forestry. Drainage pipe under main road may be associated with a trial level. (13)

TŶ-GWYN SJ176303
Possibly only a trial.
Remains Excavation. (33)

TŶ MAWR (Glan-llyn, Tyddyn Llywarch) SH862291
Pit working, active 1880s/90s.
Remains Used as rubbish dump and landscaped. (2)

TY'N-Y-COED SH921371
Tiny pit.
Remains Almost nothing. (6)

WERN-FAWR SH915407
Tiny pit working.
Remains Almost nil. (5)

WEST LLANGYNOG SJ049259

Underground quarry with a series of adits up the hillside, opened in the 1860s. Material from the upper adits was brought down by incline to a small mill on the south side of the public road. After late 19th century closure, it was revived following the opening of the railway in 1904. Latterly only the road level adit was used. A 'home made' internal combustion loco hauled material from the 4 chamber working, with a producer gas engine, running off anthracite, powering a generator. Closed in 1938, when pillar robbing to meet an urgent order caused a serious collapse.

Remains Little in the quarry area apart from confused heaping of rubbish, but the incline is traceable. One building is in reuse, but only bases of other buildings remain. Just one adit remains unblocked. (22)

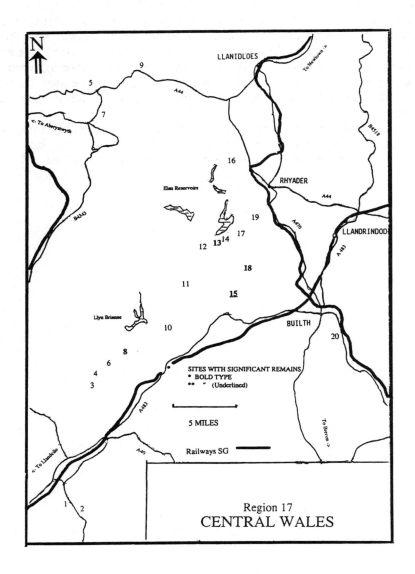

N

LLANIDLOES

To Newtown ->

9

A44

5

7

<- To Aberystwyth

16

Elan Reservoirs

RHYADER

A44

B4518

19

LLANDRINDOD

17

12 13 14

18

11

15

Llyn Brianne

10

BUILTH

20

8

6

SITES WITH SIGNIFICANT REMAINS
* BOLD TYPE
** " (Underlined)

4

3

5 MILES

A483

<- To Llandeilo

A40

Railways SG

1

2

Region 17
CENTRAL WALES

CENTRAL WALES
Region 17

General

There was no slate industry as such in this region, but dispersed throughout were many tiny workings of poor product from anomalous random occurrences. Several of these are extremely old, most of them producing solely for local use on an 'as required' basis.

Many old roofs are extant showing, in some remote and impoverished localities, buildings were slate roofed at a time when similar structures elsewhere had crude thatch.

Transport

Due to its vernacular nature, no transport needs arose. In fact the absence of transport created little local monopolies for the diggings.

The expansion of the 'Wells' towns, following the 1865/8 construction of the Central Wales railway, did spur some development. However the superior material which both that line and the mid-Wales railway of 1864 could bring in, made local quarrying uncompetitive.

1.   SN713256 Coed-Sion
2.   SN727247 Pontarllechau
3.   SN735417 Cwm Meirchion
4.   SN736421 Cwmgwenlais
5.   SN741808 Pentalwr
6.   SN752428 Craig Rhosan
7.   SN757799 Ty'n-y-ffordd
8.   SN787461 Chwarel Ystrad-ffin *
9.   SN802847 Eisteddfa Fach
10.   SN851500 Cwmirfon
11.   SN876565 Chwarel Ddu
12.   SN892608 Esgairgeiliog
13.   SN901614 Llannerch *
14.   SN902616 Craigymynach
15.   SN905536 Pengeulan **
16.   SN906715 Pontarelan

17. SN912617 Moelfryn
18. SN925567 Alltyddinas *
19. SN958637 Graig-ddu
20. SO067479 Hen-allt

ALLTYDDINAS SN925567

Small surface workings; some underground? A number of very shallow workings exploiting outcrops of shales, primitively worked. Probably operated on an 'as required' basis over many years, work ceasing well before the end of the 19th century. Material carted via Cwmdulais farm.

Remains At least 6 extraction points with associated dressing areas. Tips, but no buildings. Lowest working has an adit (open) which seems to have been investigative only.

One of the upper dressing floors has a large stock of much decayed product, mainly taper top moss-slates. The original cart track is traceable. (18)

CHWAREL DDU SN876565

Primitive operation on a scarp exposure.

Remains Virtually none apart from zig-zag access path. Early slates in the Elan valley have been identified with this source. (11)

CHWAREL YSTRAD-FFIN SN787461

A hillside quarry, deepened into a pit which was accessed by a tunnel. The 1870s expectation that the good quality of its slate could compensate for the cost of cartage to Llanymddyfri (Llandovery) proved to be in vain.

Remains Extensive rubbish runs; vestiges of several dressing sheds, but the tunnel has vanished under a massive slide. The access track, 2 Km long, is well engineered with nice retaining walling, and is spectacular. (8)

COED SION SN713256

Small pit working; shales?
Remains Possible excavation. (1)

CRAIG RHOSAN SN752428

A small working of shales bearing some cleavage material, in the grounds of Neuadd Fawr. It may date from the building of the house in 1784.

Remains Excavation, waste, working platform and access track. (6)

CRAIGYMYNACH SN902616
Tiny working by roadside.
Remains Traces of excavation. (14)

CWMGWENLAIS SN736421 737422 & 742423
The first two are tiny underground workings; the more easterly may have produced saleable product. The third is a slot working a band of shale-like rock about 1 metre wide, very much like a metal mine.
Remains The westerly adit is collapsed; the easterly is a cave like working with some possible trimming waste on the rubbish run. The slot working has the abutments of an access track bridge and a considerable volume of waste. (4)

CWMIRFON SN851500
Small pit working; an 1888 speculation apparently produced a surprising 100 tons p.a. by around 1890.
Remains In forestry, tips and some vestige of access road. (10)

CWM MERCHON SN735417
Small hillside working.
Remains Dressing shed. (3)

EISTEDDFA FACH SN802847
Very small.
Remains Slot working; trimming waste. (9)

ESGAIRGEILIOG SN892608
Several workings in a tiny rift valley, possibly part underground.
Remains Dressing sheds; some rail on ground; large quantity of waste. Unidentified building at valley mouth. (12)

GRAIG-DDU SN958637
Very small.
Remains Quarry face with interesting folding. (19)

HEN-ALLT SO067479
Open quarry, latterly (early 20th century) producing shale building block identifiable in nearby housing. May have yielded roofing material earlier.
Remains Excavation only. (20)

LLANNERCH SN901614
Very small working, possibly some underground.
Remains Dressing sheds on 2 levels. (13)

MOELFRYN SN912617
Small hillside working.
Remains Much degraded quarry face. Working area has been cleared. Access track. (17)

PENGEULAN SN905536
Open/underground. An old quarry developed c1870, with a notable attempt to chamber underground in the Meirionnydd manner. Material carted down valley. An 1883 attempt to float a company to exploit this quarry was unsuccessful.
Remains A series of working faces seemingly haphazardly developed in confusing rock conditions; dressing sheds – two sets in rakes of three. Adjacent to the upper adit are some buildings including a weigh-bridge. Trace of possibly uncompleted incline. The adit penetrates about 50 metres. Part way along, a start was made on a cross heading along the strike; opposite this is a strike tunnel from which there are two roofing shafts cut up the dip; ons is sound, the other collapsed. No extraction appears to have been made.

Lower down the site there were possibly two other levels with adits collapsed/tipped over. At the lowest level there is a further adit leading to 2 small chambers one of which opens up to the level above, which has been worked out to bank. (15)

PENTALWR (Cadno) SN741808
Hillside quarry, very shaley product. 1880s?
Remains Intense folding on working face exposure. Drum-house and incline formation which cut through disused Llanwernog lead mine leats. (5)

PONTARELAN SN906715
Shallow open quarry.
Remains Excavation; possible vestige of a building. (16)

PONTARLLECHAU SN727247
Hillside quarry of complex geology, later yielded roadstone.
Remains Interesting quarry face, bases of stone crushers. (2)

TY'N-Y-FFORDD SN757799
Hillside quarry. 1900s?
Remains Excavation only; intense local folding with some cleavable
material. (7)

To the north of the region, shales have been widely worked for building
stone and for coarse roof covering, but the tiny diggings at SN844932,
847931, 854875, 878858, 929868 & 951855, may have worked true
slate. There are undoubtedly other ephemeral sites which have not been
located.

Index

Cae'r-gors	SH599514	8	Clochnant	SJ043230	16
Cae Rhobin	SH775642	5	Cloddfa Cribau	SH701482	9
Caerhun	SH699634	5	Cloddfa Llechwedd D'G	SH786396	10
Caermeinciau	SH562601	2	Cloddfa Sion Prys	SH542398	7
Caethle	SN604994	12	Cloddfa Sion Llwyd	SH661439	9
Cambergi	SH765108	13	Cloddfa'r Coed	SH493532	3
Cambrian	SH566603	2	Cloddfa y Coed	SH617673	1
Cambrian	SJ189378	15	Clogau	SJ185463	15
Cambrian Railways	SH538397	7	Clogwyn Llwyd	SH701484	9
Carnedd y Ci	SJ051346	16	Clogwyn William	SH736596	5
Castell	SH632499	8	Clogwyn y Fuwch	SH759618	5
Castell Cidwm	SH552552	4	Clogwyngarw	SH732448	10
Castell y Bere	SH666084	12	Cnicht	SH643462	8
Cedryn	SH719635	5	Coed Cefn Maes M'R	SN724976	14
Cefn-clawdd	SH684336	10	Coed Cerrig Llwydion	SH897330	16
Cefn-coch	SH834637	5	Coed Ffriddarw	SH755175	11
Cefn-coed	SH493533	3	Coed Madog	SH490530	3
Cefn Cyfarwydd	SH767630	5	Coed-mawr	SH755727	5
Cefn-du	SH555604	2	Coed-mawr	SH700514	6
Cefn-gam	SH680256	11	Coed Pant-bach	SN763992	14
Cefn-glas	SH806376	10	Coed Sion	SN713256	17
Cefn Madoc	SH825654	5	Coed Tirllanerch	SJ130442	15
Cefn-y-braich	SH646448	8	Coed y Chwarel	SH538396	7
Ceinws Bach	SH762060	13	Coed y Chwarel	SH830095	14
Cerrig y Felin	SH676091	12	Coed-y-ffridd	SH747030	13
Ceunant Ddu	SH766099	13	Coedyllechau	SH590266	10
Chwarel Ddu	SH721521	6	Coetmor	SH619671	1
Chwarel Ddu	SJ057243	16	Colomendy	SJ085434	15
Chwarel Ddu	SN876565	17	Conglog	SH668467	9
Chwarel Fawr	SH552600	2	Conglog	SH763388	10
Chwarel Fawr	SH589616	2	Cook & Ddôl	SH560605	2
Chwarel Fedw	SH748525	6	Cornel	SH746602	5
Chwarel Gethin	SH687486	6	Cornwall	SH496531	3
Chwarel Glyn Lledr	SH779533	6	Corwen	SJ081434	15
Chwarel Goch	SH581617	2	Craig Glanhafon	SJ066274	16
Chwarel Isaf	SH579613	2	Craig-las	SJ193462	15
Chwarel Las	SH611696	1	Craig Rhiweirth	SJ053263	16
Chwarel Llew Twrog	SH730445	10	Craig Rhosan	SN752428	17
Chwarel Owen Parry	SH683520	6	Craig Wynnstay	SJ202473	15
Chwarel R. Jones	SH589645	1	Craig y Cribin	SJ047262	16
Chwarel Sion Jones	SH735526	6	Craig y Dduallt	SJ229399	15
Chwarel Twm Ffeltiwr	SH671446	9	Craigymynach	SN902616	17
Chwarel y Plas	SH525461	7	Craig yr Orin	SJ234362	15
Chwarel Ystrad-ffin	SN787461	17	Crawia	SH536643	2
Chwythlyn	SH838650	5	Crib-lwyd	SH637457	8
Cilgwyn	SH500540	3	Croesor	SH657457	8
Cilnant	SJ239364	15	Croesor Bach	SH639452	8
Clegir	SJ048478	15	Croes y Ddwy Afon	SH754424	10
Cletwr	SN666921	14	Crymlyn	SH645709	1
Cletwr	SH985348	16	Cwm Bach	SH564406	7
Clipiau	SH845102	14	Cwm Breichiau	SH708043	12

Cwm Bychan	SH683655	1	Dolgoed	SH781126	13
Cwmcaeth	SH605466	8	Dolydderwen	SH750029	13
Cwm Ceunant	SH626638	1	Donnen Las	SH555595	2
Cwm Cloch	SH579472	8	Dorothea	SH500532	3
Cwm Cŷd	SH581466	8	Drum	SH735431	10
Cwm Cynfal	SH735411	10	Dulyn	SH702663	5
Cwm Cynfal	SH614010	12	Dysyrnant	SN650998	12
Cwm Du	SH832125	14	Eglwyseg	SJ216472	15
Cwm Dwyfor	SH541505	7	Egryn	SH605205	11
Cwm Dylluan	SH732088	13	Eisteddfa Fach	SN802847	17
Cwm Ebol	SH689017	12	Era	SH760064	13
Cwm Eigiau	SH702635	5	Esgairangell	SH828107	14
Cwm Fynhadog	SH683479	6	Esgairgeiliog	SH759059	13
Cwm Glas	SH642697	1	Esgairgeiliog	SN892608	17
Cwm Gloddfa	SH766062	13	Faenol	SH578615	2
Cwmgwenlais	SN736421	17	Ffridd	SH633702	1
Cwmirfon	SN851500	17	Ffridd	SH770647	5
Cwm Llefrith	SH541469	7	Ffridd	SH709530	6
Cwm Leri	SN677885	14	Ffridd	SH573526	4
Cwm Machno	SN751470	6	Ffridd Bryn-moel	SH740539	6
Cwm Merchon	SN735417	17	Ffridd Cocyn	SH621040	12
Cwmmaengwynedd	SJ075326	16	Ffridd Ddwy Ffrwd	SH748723	5
Cwm Maesgwm	SH653437	8	Ffridd Isaf	SH702184	11
Cwm Mynach	SH678245	11	Ffridd Llwynhynydd	SH645038	12
Cwm Tywyll	SJ052336	16	Ffridd-lys	SH743733	5
Cwm Orthin	SH681459	9	Ffridd Olchfa	SH603191	11
Cwm Penamnen	SH732492	6	Ffridd Ucha	SH831651	5
Cwm Rhaeadr	SN755973	14	Ffridd-y-bwlch	SH693483	9
Cwm Teigl	SH736446	10	Ffridd y Gloddfa	SH848362	16
Cwm Tydi	SJ157453	15	Ffynnon Badarn	SH775114	13
Cwm Tywyll	SJ052336	16	Ffynnon y Gog	SJ208476	15
Cwm Ych	SH614073	12	Foel	SH717556	6
Cwm y Foel	SH658476	8	Foel	SH756464	6
Cwt y Bugail	SH734469	9	Foel	SJ210469	15
Cyfannedd	SH627124	11	Foel Clynnog	SH458506	3
Cymerau	SH779116	13	Foel Fawr	SH679055	12
Cymmo	SJ162448	15	Foel Gron	SH744428	10
Cynllwyd	SH751601	5	Foel Isaf	SH454407	7
Darren	SH721058	13	Foel Rudd	SH756452	6
Deeside	SJ138404	15	Foty	SH707468	9
Diffwys	SH712463	9	Foty y Waun	SH761128	13
Dinas Ddu	SH594453	8	Friog	SH621126	11
Dinorwig	SH595603	2	Fron	SH515548	4
Dolfeirig	SH959343	16	Fron-boeth	SH652448	8
Dolffanog	SH729104	13	Frondirion	SH584619	2
Dolfriog	SH611458	8	Fronfraith	SH757121	13
Dolgarth	SH538495	7	Fron-goch	SN664972	12
Dôl-goch	SH613677	1	Fronheulog	SH489517	3
Dôl-goch	SH653043	12	Fronheulog	SN600998	12
Dolpistill	SH636701	1	Fronhyfryd	SH579617	2
Dôl Wgan	SH516437	7	Fronolau	SH579409	8

Fron-serth	SH741175	11	Gyrn	SH646688	1
Fron Ucha	SJ195326	15	Hafod Arthen	SH758620	5
Gaewern	SH745086	13	Hafod-boeth	SH638418	8
Galltyfedw	SH499535	3	Hafod Dwryd	SH792498	6
Gallt-y-llan	SH601583	2	Hafod Fawr	SH729402	10
Gallt-y-mawn	SH648680	1	Hafod Gwynfe	SJ208378	15
Garreg Fawr	SH538582	4	Hafod Gwyrd	SH769464	6
Garreg Felen	SH534399	7	Hafod-las	SH489540	3
Garreg Uchaf	SH636446	8	Hafod Las	SH779562	6
Garreg Wen	SH555372	7	Hafod Uchaf	SH643434	8
Garth	SH566382	7	Hafod-y-llan	SH613524	8
Garth	SH777195	11	Hafod-y-wern	SH530571	4
Gartheiniog	SH822117	14	Hafoty	SH725064	13
Garth Fach	SH634070	12	Hafoty	SH632436	8
Gau Graig	SH745151	11	Hen-allt	SO067479	17
Gelli	SH637463	8	Henblas	SH827627	5
Gelli Bach	SH464513	3	Hen-ddôl	SH619122	11
Gelli Gain	SH728328	10	Hendre	SH698512	6
Gelli-grin	SH946341	16	Hendre Ddu	SH519444	7
Gernos	SH669094	12	Hendre Ddu	SH799125	14
Gerynt	SH631484	8	Hendreeirian	SH605206	11
Glandinorwig	SH572632	2	Hen-ffridd	SH826634	5
Glan Dulas	SH751038	13	Hen-gae	SH759115	13
Glandyfi	SN698961	14	Hen Gloddfa	SH765101	13
Glanrafon	SH581540	4	Dr Hughes	SH643672	1
Glan-y-don	SH697467	9	Hwylfa	SH819509	6
Glanyrafon	SJ041271	16	Hysfa	SH718467	9
Gloddfa Gwanas	SH798160	11	Idwal	SH648604	1
Glyn Aber	SH748472	6	Idris	SH738151	11
Glyn Iago	SH719072	13	Isallt	SH532448	7
Glynrhonwy Isaf	SH565607	2	Ladas	SH578610	2
Glynrhonwy Uchaf	SH560606	2	Lefel Fawr	SH562565	4
Goat	SH582468	8	Liberty	SH844642	5
Goedwig	SH752063	13	Llan	SH734523	6
Goedwig West	SH745066	13	Llaneilian	SH481925	1
Gofer	SH841727	5	Llanfair	SH580288	10
Golwern	SH621122	11	Llanfflewin	SH347892	1
Goodmans	SH572606	2	Llannerch	SN901614	17
Gorseddau	SH573453	7	Llechan Uchaf	SH756757	5
Graig Ddu	SH724454	9	Llechwedd	SH700470	9
Graig-ddu	SN958637	17	Llechwedd	SH670087	12
Graig Uchaf	SH649268	10	Llechwedd Gwyn	SJ209344	15
Graig yr Ogof	SH738002	14	Llechwedd Oernant	SH786482	6
Groeslon	SH470551	3	Llidiart yr Arian	SH633442	8
Groes-lwyd	SH749181	11	Lloc	SH582619	2
Gwastadfryn	SH678098	12	Llwyd-coed	SH470508	3
Gwern Bwys	SH829663	5	Llwyn-gwern	SH757045	13
Gwernlasdeg	SH584496	8	Llwyn-onn	SJ051289	16
Gwernor	SH501526	3	Llyfnant	SN717977	14
Gwydir	SH788610	5	Llyn Llagi	SH651485	8
Gyllellog	SH709019	12	Llyn y Gadair	SH564519	4

Lydan	SH851658	5	Nyth y Gigfran	SH689462	9
Machynlleth Station	SH746014	14	New Crown	SH513556	6
Maenofferen	SH715467	9	Oakeley	SH690466	9
Maesygamfa	SH818127	14	Ochrfwsoglog	SH683664	1
Maesypandy	SH700089	12	Oernant	SJ185469	15
Manod	SH742601	5	Old Braich	SH512549	4
Manod	SH725452	9	Olwyn	SH704473	9
Marchlyn	SH602628	2	Pandy	SH630029	12
Marine Terrace	SH497378	7	Pandy	SH760081	13
Matthews	SH768091	13	Pant Cra	SH756174	11
Meillionen	SH571485	8	Pantdreiniog	SH623671	1
Melynllyn	SH705654	5	Panteidal	SN652972	12
Minllyn	SH852139	14	Panteinion	SH620122	11
Moel Crynddan	SJ060278	16	Pant-glas	SJ215478	15
Moel Dyrnogydd	SH697497	6	Pant-gwyn	SH593252	11
Moel Faban	SH626679	1	Pant-mawr	SH658446	8
Moel Fferna	SJ125399	15	Pantperthog	SH748054	13
Moelfre	SH521451	7	Pantydarren	SH657698	1
Moelfryn	SN912617	17	Pantyrafon	SH697469	9
Moel Lefn	SH548483	7	Pantyronen	SH732152	11
Moel Llechwedd Gwyn	SH754416	10	Pant-yr-ynn	SH709454	9
Moel Tryfan	SH515559	4	Parc	SH626436	8
Moelwyn	SH661442	9	Parc (Slab)	SH632444	8
Moelycroesau	SH750384	10	Parc	SH755005	14
Moel-y-faen	SJ185477	15	Penarth	SJ107424	15
Moel-y-gest	SH559388	7	Penbryncaled	SH811652	5
Moel Pen-y-bryn	SH779499	6	Pencraig	SH519393	7
Moelygwartheg	SH681320	10	Pengeulan	SN905536	17
Morben	SN716993	14	Peniarth	SH626092	12
Morfa Lodge	SH567386	7	Pen-lan	SH760688	5
Mynedd Bychan	SJ160448	15	Penllyn	SH563622	2
Mynydd Ednyfed	SH507394	7	Penllyn	SH746522	6
Mynydd Ty'n y Ceunant	SH730082	13	Penmorfa	SH552408	7
Mynydd y Waun	SH763132	13	Pennant	SH817673	5
Nant Alltforgan	SH969243	16	Pennant	SH671097	12
Nant Canolbren	SH706709	5	Pennant Ucha	SH827666	5
Nant Dôl-hir	SH853157	14	Penrhiw	SH722540	6
Nant Fach Gynan	SJ182311	16	Penrhyn	SH620650	1
Nantglyn	SH978598	15	Penrhyn Gwyn	SH704149	11
Nant Heilyn	SH640706	1	Penrhyn Llwyd	SH559393	7
Nantlle Vale	SH497525	3	Pentalwr	SN741808	17
Nant Minllyn	SH849144	14	Pentre Dŵr	SJ201468	15
Nantyreira	SH685088	12	Pentrefelin	SJ218436	15
Nantyfron	SH486518	3	Pen-y-banc	SH562372	7
Nantymynach	SH643048	12	Penybedw	SH777476	6
Nant y Pandy	SJ148417	15	Pen-y-bryn	SH502536	3
Nantypistyll Gwyn	SH751433	10	Pen-y-bryn	SH706014	12
Nantyr	SJ165382	15	Pen-y-bryn	SJ215382	15
Nant-y-sarn	SH978315	16	Pen-y-graig	SH872134	14
Nant-y-wrach	SH840646	5	Pen-y-bont	SH783483	6
Nilig	SJ031546	15	Pen-y-ffridd	SH776612	5

Penygarreg	SH735099	13	Tal-y-llyn	SH757597	5
Penyrorsedd	SH510538	3	Talymieryn	SH825119	14
Perfeddnant	SH630055	12	Tal-y-sarn	SH496534	3
Plas-du	SH493524	3	Tan-y-bwlch	SH628683	1
Plas-y-nant	SH552562	4	Tanydarren	SH645145	11
Pontarelan	SN906715	17	Tan-y-foel	SJ199385	15
Pontarllechau	SN727247	17	Tanygader	SH718161	11
Pompren	SH726519	6	Tan-y-rhiw	SH758452	6
Pont-faen	SH763000	14	Tan-yr-allt	SH491523	3
Pont Rhyd-goch	SH394407	7	Tap-ddu	SH735092	13
Pontycarw	SH782618	5	Tap-twr	SH639141	11
Poth Llwyd	SH767672	5	Targwrmoel	SH855148	14
Porthreuddyn	SH573409	8	Tarran Cadian	SH733070	13
Porthreuddyn	SH578408	8	Tarren Hendre	SH684045	12
Powys	SJ074294	16	Trecastell	SH760745	5
Pretoria	SH515551	4	Treflan	SH539584	4
Prince Llywelyn	SH744528	6	Twll-coed	SH491522	3
Prince Llywelyn	SH518439	7	Twll Coch	SH561602	2
Prince of Wales	SH549498	7	Twll-llwyd	SH490518	3
Princess	SH553495	7	Tŷ Cerrig	SH550409	7
Queens	SH995341	16	Tŷ-coch	SH532565	4
Ratgoed	SH787119	13	Tyddyn Agnes	SH482517	3
Rhaeadr	SH682012	12	Tyddyn Llwyn	SH562386	7
Rhewl Mill	SJ177446	15	Tyddyn Mawr	SH506428	7
Rhiwaedog	SH973353	16	Tyddyn Sieffre	SH630135	11
Rhiw-bach	SH740462	9	Tyddyn Uchaf	SH881635	5
Rhiw-goch	SH749537	6	Tŷ-draw	SJ207375	15
Rhiw-goch	SJ169453	15	Tŷ-gwyn	SJ176303	16
Rhiw'r Gwreiddyn	SH760054	13	Tu Hwnt i'r Bwlch	SH561389	7
Rhiw Rhedyn Cochion	SH717171	11	Tŷ Mawr	SH603005	12
Rhos	SH729564	6	Tŷ Mawr	SH862291	16
Rhos Clogwyn	SH576530	4	Tŷ Mawr Green	SH497523	3
Rhos-goch	SH756466	6	Ty Mawr West	SH495524	3
Rhosydd	SH664461	8	Tŷ-nant	SH709198	11
Rhwngyddwyffordd	SH835624	5	Tŷ-nant	SJ163342	15
Rhyd-goch	SH862492	6	Ty'n-llwyn	SH479522	3
Rhydyronnen	SH625017	12	Ty'n-y-berth	SH738087	13
Rhyd-y-sarn	SH690421	9	Ty'n-y-bryn	SH742521	6
Rowlyn	SH759687	5	Ty'nyceunant	SH744088	13
Sarnhelen	SH731436	10	Ty'n-y-coed	SH652152	11
Sarffle	SJ141327	15	Ty'n-y-coed	SH921371	16
Serw	SH776414	10	Ty'n-y-fach	SH675095	12
Siglen	SH741643	5	Ty'n-y-fallen	SH752539	6
Singrug	SH490522	3	Ty'n-y-ffordd	SN757799	17
Spring Hill	SJ199351	15	Ty'n-y-ffridd	SH628677	1
Swch	SH755474	6	Ty'n-y-garth	SN692947	14
Taicynhaeaf	SH757304	10	Ty'n-y-graig	SJ161398	15
Tainewyddion	SH664062	12	Ty'n-y-llan	SH554406	7
Taldrwst	SH482526	3	Ty'nyllechwedd	SH738097	13
Talmignedd	SH535532	3	Ty'n-y-rhos	SJ074464	15
Tal-y-fan	SH738733	5	Ty'n-y-rhyd	SJ176342	15

Tynyweirglodd	SH495523	3
Vivian	SH586605	2
Waen Fedwen	SH759672	5
Wenlli	SH843657	5
Wern-ddu	SJ065481	15
Wern-fawr	SH915407	16
Wern Ifon	SH501535	3
West Llangynog	SJ049259	16
Westminster	SJ171478	15
Wynne	SJ199379	15
Wynnstay Castle	SH844031	14
Wrysgan	SH678456	9
Y Cefn	SH713421	10
Y Garnedd	SH739434	10
Y Garth	SH647667	1
Ymlych	SH508407	7
Ynys Cyngar	SH554365	7
Ynys Tywyn	SH572385	7
Ynys y Pandy	SH550433	7
Yr Ogof	SH648715	1
Yr Horon	SN600962	12
Ysgubor Gerrig	SH510427	7

Select Published Bibliography

Books

Anon, *Industrial & Independent Locomotives & Railways of North Wales*, (Birmingham Loco Club, 1968)

Baughan, P.E., *A Regional History of the Railways of G.B. Vols 11 & 12*, (David & Charles, 1980)

Bingley, W.A., *A Journal of a Tour through North Wales etc.*, (London, 1797)

Boyd, J.I.C., *Narrow Gauge Railways in Mid Wales*, (Oakwood, 1970)

Boyd, J.I.C., *Narrow Gauge Railways in South Caernarvonshire*, (Oakwood, 1972)

Boyd, J.I.C., *The Ffestiniog Railways Vols 1 & 2*, (1975)

Boyd, J.I.C., *Narrow Gauge Railways in North Caernarfonshire Vols 1, 2 & 3*, (Oakwood, 1981/6)

Boyd, J.I.C., *Tal-y-llyn Railway*, (Wild Swan, 1988)

Carrington, D.C., *Delving in Dinorwig*, (Gwasg Carreg Gwalch, 1994)

Christiansen, R., *The Forgotten Railways of North & Mid Wales*, (David & Charles, 1976)

Davies, D.C., *Slate & Slate Quarrying*, (Crosby, Lockwood, 1878)

Davies, D.L., *The Glyn Valley Tramway*, (Oakwood, 1962)

Dodd, A.H., *History of Caernarfonshire 1284-1900*, (Caerns. Hist. Soc., 1968)

Dodd, A.H., *The Industrial Revolution in North Wales*, (U of W Press, 1971)

Eames, Aled, *The Twilight of Welsh Sail*, (U of W Press, 1984)

Eames, Aled, *Shrouded Quays*, (Gwasg Carreg Gwalch, 1991)

Eames, Aled, *Heb Long Wrth y Cei*, (Gwasg Carreg Gwalch, 1991)

Edmonston, C., *Chwarel Wynne*, (Glyn Quarry, 1995)

Elis-Williams, M., *Bangor Port of Beaumaris*, (Gwynedd Arch. Serv., 1988)

Holmes, A., *Slates from Abergynolwyn*, (Gwynedd A.S., 1986)

Holmes & Thomas, *Quarry Tracks, Village Ways*, (Tal-y-llyn Rly Co., 1977)

Hughes & Hughes, *Chwarel y Penrhyn*, (Chwarel y Penrhyn, 1979)

Hughes & Eames, *Porthmadog Ships*, (Gwynedd Arch. Serv., 1975)

Isherwood, G., *Candles to Caplamps*, (Gloddfa Ganol, 1980)

Isherwood, G., *Cwmorthin Slate Quarry*, Merioneth F.S. Press, 1982)

Isherwood, G., *Slate*, (A.B. Publishing, 1988)

Jones, E., *Bargen Dinorwig*, (Tŷ ar y Graig, 1980)

Jones, G.R., *Chwarel Blaenycwm*, (Ff TyB, 1992)

Jones, G.R., *Hafodlas*, (G.R. Jones, 1998)

Jones, I.W., *Llechwedd Slate Caverns*, (Quarry Tours, 1976)

Jones, I.W., *Eagles Do Not Catch Flies*, (J.W. Greaves, 1986)

Jones, I.W. & G. Hetherill, *Llechwedd & other Ffestiniog Railways*, (Quarry Tours, 1977)

Jones, I.W., *Gold, Frankenstein & Manure*, (Llechwedd Pubs., 1997)

Jones, R.M., *The North Wales Quarrymen 1874-1922*, (Cardiff U of W, 1982)

Jones, R.J., *Felinheli*, (Bridge Books, 1992)

Lee, C., *The Welsh Highland Railway*, (Welsh Hld Rly., 1970)

Lee, C., *The Penrhyn Railway*, (Welsh Hld Rly., 1972)

Lewis, M.J.T., *Early Wooden Railways*, (R.K.P., 1970)

Lewis, M.J.T., *Llechi, Slates*, (Gwynedd A.S., 1976)

Lewis, M.J.T.(Ed), *The Slate Quarries of North Wales in 1873*, (S.N.P.S.C., 1987)

Lewis, M.J.T., *Sails on the Dwyryd*, (S.N.P.S.C., 1989)

Lewis & Denton, *Rhosydd Slate Quarry*, (Cottage Press, 1974)

Lewis & Williams, *Pioneers of Welsh Slate*, (S.N.P.S.C., 1987)

Lindsay, J., *The History of the North Wales Slate Industry*, (David & Charles, 1974)

Lindsay, J., *The Great Strike*, (David & Charles, 1987)

Lloyd, Lewis, *The Port of Caernarfon 1793-1900*, (Lloyd, 1989)

Lloyd, Lewis, *Pwllheli, The Port & Mart of Llŷn*, (Lloyd, 1991)

Lloyd, Lewis, *Wherever Freights May Offer*, (Lloyd, 1993)

Lloyd, Lewis, *De Winton's of Caernarfon*, (Lloyd, 1994)

Lloyd, Lewis, *A Real Little Seaport*, (Lloyd, 1996)

Mitchell & Eyres, *The Tal-y-llyn Railway*, (Past & Present Pubs., 1996)

North, F.J., *Slates of Wales*, (Nat. Mus. of Wales, 1925)

Owen, R., *Diwydiannau Coll*,

Parry, B.R. (Ed), *Chwareli a Chwarelwyr*, (Gwynedd A.S., 1974)

Rees, D.M., *The Industrial Archaeology of Wales*, (David & Charles, 1975)

Rhydderch, A., *Blaenau Ffestiniog*, (Gwynedd Arch. Serv., 1991)

Richards, A.J., *A Gazeteer of the Welsh Slate Industry*, (Gwasg Carreg Gwalch, 1991)

Richards, A.J., *Slate Quarrying at Corris*, (Gwasg Carreg Gwalch, 1994)

Richards, A.J., *Slate Quarrying in Wales*, (Gwasg Carreg Gwalch, 1995)

Richards, M., *Slate Quarrying and how to Make it Profitable*,

Tomos, D., *Llechi Lleu*, (Argraffdy Arfon, 1980)

Turner, S., *The Padarn & Penrhyn Rlys*, (David & Charles, 1975)

Williams, G.J., *Hanes Plwyf Ffestiniog*, (Hughes & Son, 1882)

Williams & Lewis, *Gwydir Slate Quarries*, (S.N.P.S.C., 1989)

Williams & Lewis, *Pioneers of Ffestiniog Slate*, (S.N.P.S.C., 1987)

Williams & Lewis, *Chwarelwyr Cyntaf Ffestiniog*, (S.N.P.S.C., 1987)

Wren, W.J., *The Tanat Valley*, (David & Charles, 1968)

S.N.P.S.C. = Snowdonia National Park Study Centre, Plas Tan-y-Bwlch

Journals:

The Mining Journal

The Quarry Manager' Journal

The Slate Trades Gazeteer

The Red Dragon

Glossary of Terms

Adit	The entrance to an underground working.
Back-filling	Practice of dumping rubbish from underground working in disused *chambers*.
Block	Crude or roughly trimmed slate from the quarrying face, suitable for reduction to product.
Blondin	A specialised form of *Chain Incline*, which allows loads to be picked up or set down at any point under a catena stretched across a pit. Requires a *Winder* with two coaxial drums.
Brake	For the control of a *balanced incline*, usually worked by a long arm. In the case of a *trwnc incline*, some form of pin-down arrangements were needed or else wheel-operated screw. Almost invariably a band-brake, occasionally externally-contracting shoes.
Caban	Mess-room. Traditionally a centre of debate and self-education, conducted with rigid protocol.
Chamber	The void usually 60' - 70' wide arising from the working of slate underground.
Channelling Machine	Device enabling a series of holes to be drilled to free a block from the face where jointing was sparse.
Crane	Usually a hand wound derrick; latterly a powered, possibly mobile, powered jib crane.
Crimp Sprag	A safety device at the head of an incline to prevent the premature descent of wagons.
Cupboarding	Pillar robbing by cutting alcoves in the wall supporting the roof of a chamber.
De Winton Locomotive	Early vertical-boilered loco, made by Caernarfon engineering firm formerly Union Foundry (1840-1892); responsible for much innovation in quarrying, marine and other machinery.
Dip	The angle from the horizontal at which a vein lies.
Dressing Machine	Mechanical device for trimming slates to size and squareness. Usually of the Greaves type; but for hard Cambrian slate the Francis, hinged blade, machine was used, commonly foot operated. Greaves machines were usually powered. The early Mathew's guillotines were driven by an eccentric in overhead shafting.
Dressing Shed	Open fronted shed for the splitting and trimming of roofing slate. (Welsh) Wal, Gwal.
Dixon Drill	A three-man hand cranked device for making shot holes of up to 3" diameter.
Drum-house	Normally two walls and a roof at the head of an incline through which trucks pass to descend under

the control of ropes wound round a drum, or occasionally a sheave located overhead. Occasionally the sheave or drum was located in a pit under the tracks.

Drum-house, Remote	A *drum-house* through which trucks do not pass.
Enamelling	A stoving process for applying decorative finishes to slab products.
Engine House	Building for a steam engine, or archaically, any building containing machinery.
Hones	Flat stones usually 8″ x 1½″ x 3/8″, used for sharpening edge tools.
Horse Whim	A vertical axis winding drum, powered by a horse walking in a circle.
Hudson track	Relatively modern temporary track with pressed steel sleepers.
Hughes rail	A patent system of temporary track consisting of round iron bars with turned down ends which fitted into cast iron sleepers. Frequently copied by the quarry's blacksmith!
Incline, Balanced	A ramp with two sets of rails, the weight of down-going loaded trucks on one track, serving to raise empty trucks on the other track. Also known as a Gravity or Self-acting incline.
Incline, Chain	An incline where loads travelled suspended from a rope or chain. Usually employed for up-hauling from a pit working, where a fixed ramp might interfere with future extraction.
Incline, Single Acting	A *Balanced Incline* with one operating track, empty trucks being raised by power or by a balancing truck (Mass Balanced Incline). Powered up-haulage inclines invariably single-acting.
Incline, Trwnc or Table	An incline where trucks do not run on their own rails but are conveyed on a carriage.
Incline, Water Balanced	An incline where a down-going load raises an empty cistern which, when filled, will up-haul empties.
Jointing	Natural cracks in rock which enable a block to be detached from a face.
Jwmpah	A long, weighted rod, used to drill holes for blasting by being repeatedly thrust into the hole.
Launder	Water trough supported clear of ground, usually on pillars.
Leat	Water channel cut into ground; can be in extensive networks.
Mill	A building for the mechanical sawing of slab.
Mill, Integrated	A mill which, besides sawing for slab product, also dealt with roofing slate and normally contains, besides

	saws, dressing machines.
Moss Slates	Small, crude, early slates, commonly sealed with moss.
Pelton Wheel	An enclosed system of buckets, on which water impinges radically to produce power. Calls for pipe feed and, though needing less flow than a turbine, requires a greater head.
Pillar	The wall of slate around 40' wide left between chambers to support the roof of an underground working.
Pillar Robbing	Obtaining slate by thinning pillars.
Planer	Machine with a moving table, having a wide flat blade for smoothing slab, or a contoured blade for shaping.
Plateway	L section rail for flangeless-wheeled trucks.
Polisher (Jenny Lind)	Traditionally a power driven mill-type stone fed with sand and water to polish slab. Modern machines use diamond impregnated heads.
Rock Cannon	A rock with a series of holes which, when filled with black powder, could be fired in succession to mark a celebration.
Roofing Shaft	The tunnel driven upwards at the top of vein in order to commence working a *chamber*.
Roofing Slate	Originally small and thick (½" or more) with tapered top, intended to be hung by one oak peg, and sold in random sizes. During late 18th century started to become standardised rectangles of up to 26" x 16" and more, and down to 1/8" thick.
Roofing Up	Driving a tunnel from below an existing working to enable rock to be more easily won.
Saw, Circular	Invariably Greaves pattern, with a moving table having square holes for wedges to secure the block, and with a circular toothed blade protruding from below. Table advances by double worm drive through a rack. Examples do survive of chain, hydraulic and of vavriable speed mechanisms. Some early versions were hand cranked. All of them leave curved saw marks.
Saw, Diamond	Modern machine, usually with a circular blade moving above a fixed table. Has advantages of speed, block does not need to be secured, and multiple cuts can be made with one set up. Requires electric power. Leaves fine curved saw marks.
Saw, Frame	Term can be applied to a hand-held or to a powered *sand saw*, or to a modern reciprocating diamond saw.
Saw, Gang	*Frame saw* having multiple blades.
Saw, Hunter	Had replaceable teeth on a circular blade, usually above a moving table. Slow rotation and coarse feed

	left wide indented curved saw marks.
Saw, Sand	A toothless reciprocating saw cutting blocks to size, by the action of wet sand. Can be hand or powered, if the former the cut does not go right through, the last few mm being broken off. All leave very fine, straight saw marks.
Saw, Wire	A modern machine with diamond impregnated segments on a cable, used for cutting block from a quarry face. Usually air-powered.
Slab	Generally defined as products more than ½″ thick. Could be:

a) Crude slab of declared thickness in random sizes.

b) Semi-finished items such as headstone or billiards table blanks.

c) Finished items such as cisterns, fireplaces, sills, pigsties etc.

Strike Tunnel	A tunnel driven at right angles to the dip of a vein, from which chambering may be commenced.
Take Note	Temporary permission to extract minerals.
Ton Slates	Small slates sold by weight.
Tramway	An imprecise term for a railed system, usually implying gravity, man or animal power.
Turbine	An enclosed array of blades to produce power from the, usually axial, passage of water. Since it is pressure-dependent, it has to be pipe fed.
Untopping	Reworking an underground quarry by opencasting.
Wagon	Apart from special purpose items, they were: flat wooden-bedded for block; iron open one end for rubbish; balustraded sided for finished slate. Commonly with double flanged wheels to cope with variations of gauge on rough track.
Water Wheel	An uncased wheel having buckets on its periphery. The weight of water in the buckets providing power. Fed by an open launder. Types:-

Overshot, water fed over top of wheel.

Backshot, water fed just short of top of wheel giving opposite rotation, slightly less efficient but pit self-scours.

Breastshot, as above but due to lack of head water had to be fed well below back of wheel, giving much lower efficiency.

Undershot, lower part of wheel immersed in a watercourse, calls for large flows, virtually unknown in Welsh slate working.

Winch	Basically a geared windlass, often used for lifting in conjunction with sheer legs, or underground via a

snatch block. Hand cranked or air, driven. In the former case old sailing ship units were sometimes used; in the latter either a dedicated item or an adapted marine donkey engine. Also could be steam or electric.

Winder	Permanently sited powered winch.
Windlass	A device whereby loads are raised by a rope being wound round a hand-cranked drum.
Writing Slates	Could be sawn rectangles or fully framed; generally with lines on one side, squares on the other.